AF564683

REPRODUCTIVE TECHNOLOGY AND HUMAN RIGHTS

REPRODUCTIVE TECHNOLOGY AND HUMAN RIGHTS

DR. SEEMA RATHI
LL.M. Ph.D.

DEEP & DEEP PUBLICATIONS PVT. LTD.
F-159, Rajouri Garden, New Delhi - 110 027

REPRODUCTIVE TECHNOLOGY
AND HUMAN RIGHTS

ISBN 978-81-8450-400-2

Typeset by RAHUL COMPOSERS
358, Pocket-B, Phase-2, Sector-16B, Dwarka, New Delhi - 110 075

Printed in India at MAYUR ENTERPRISES
WZ Plot No. 3, Gujjar Market, Tihar Village, New Delhi - 110 018

Published by DEEP & DEEP PUBLICATIONS PVT. LTD.
F-159, Rajouri Garden, New Delhi - 110 027 • Phone : 25435369, 25440916
E-mail : ddpubs@gmail.com • ddpubs@yahoo.com
Showroom :
2/13, Ansari Road, Daryaganj, New Delhi - 110 002 • Telefax : 23245122

Contents

Preface

Science in broader sense is a systematic study in any field. It includes developed and developing branches of various studies and the Medical Science is one of such branches. Techno-medical development is a gift of medical scientists to the humanity. This gift provides benevolent knowledge to human society to treat, heal, sustain, protect and prolong the very existence of human society.

The development of Medical Science had put a great effect on the Human Rights Jurisprudence. In fact, the Medical Science inventions or development of new medicines or machine or techniques of surgery have played a great role in making the human life more convenient and comfortable. It has made a positive and constructive impact on Human Rights Jurisprudence. The Reproductive Technology is one of the greatest achievements of the progress of medical science, but at the same it has posed some problems relating to human rights.

Therefore, it is realized that—law must keep balance between the advancement of medical science and maintenance of human rights and human dignity. Although legislative effort has been made at national level and international level, but no fruitful result came out because the law-breakers search out new devices to evade the provisions of law, this way or that way.

This work mainly confines to those aspects of Medical Science, Law and Human Rights, which have attracted and have become topics of heated discussions due to the legal and ethical issues involved in it, especially relating to Reproductive Technology.

The Reproductive Technology is one of the thrust areas in the field of Medical Science. The overall benefits of the Reproductive Technology has attracted the attention of legislatures, judges, jurists, etc. and put a great challenge before them to find out the solution to the existing moral, social and ethical problems.

In order to find out solution of all these problems and to devise a future guideline, I have chosen to conduct present work on the subject pertaining to impact of science and technology. The objective of proposed study is to examine the present legal provisions relating to medical science, especially reproductive technology, and to point out flaws in them. I have not only examined the problem in national and international perspectives but also tried to point out the weaknesses of existing laws and probable consequences of latest developments of globalization and privatization.

Collection of legal facts and comparison of laws of different countries has also become a part of present work. I have thoroughly examined the subject to find out truth of hypothesis made at the time of undertaking the study of this work.

This study would be helpful in understanding the problems pertaining to the impact of science and technology on human rights and in finding out probable solutions of problems arising out of it.

The study on this topic would certainly contribute in present legal literature. The study would be proved useful not only for students and teachers but also to every one who have some interest in the subject.

DR. SEEMA RATHI

Acknowledgements

No academics work whatever its scope or worth, can conceivably be completed without the able guidance of a mentor. I was fortunate enough to be benefited by the scholarly guidance of my Supervisor, Revered Professor S.S. Sharma, Former Dean and Head, Faculty of Law, JNV University, Jodhpur.

I wish to express my deepest and profound gratitude to him, who despite his preoccupation, took unfailing interest, gave encouragement, wise and sound consultation both at the stage of planning and arrangement of the scheme of this work as well as at the stage of its final presentation.

I would also like to express my deep respect to Professor R.N. Sharma, Dean and Head, Faculty of Law, JNV University, Jodhpur, who has provided his guidance and constant encouragement in conducting my present work.

I am also thankful to all members of the Faculty of Law, especially Professor M.K. Vyas, Professor M.K. Bhandari, Associate Professor Vijaya Sharma, Associate Professor R.K. Sinha, Associate Professor Chandan Bala for extending their constant guidance and encouragement in accomplishing this work.

I have taken the benefit of the services of the staff and officials of the library, Faculty of Law. I am thankful to them for their valuable services and assistance.

I thank Shri Nirmal Tak, who has taken in hand the task of typing this work and executed it with indefatigable spirit.

Finally and most importantly, I am grateful to my parents Executive Engineer I.P.S. Rathi and S. Lata Rathi (M.A.), brother and bhabhi Ashwaṇi Rathi (M.B.A.) and Anita Rathi (M.A. Economics), twin sister Dr. Sapna Rathi (LL.M., Ph.D.) and younger sister Er. Sonika (B.Tech., LL.B., M.B.A.) without whose cooperation, it would have been difficult.

DR. SEEMA RATHI

Introduction

The life is precious; therefore, the progressive development in human life with dignity is the guiding principle of all human activities. Since last few decades, due to development in the field of Science and Technology, there is a revolutionary transformation in the human life. These developments have offered many beneficial services to human communities but at the same time it has posed various challenges in the field of science, technology and law.

Science in broader sense is a systematic study in any field. It includes developed and developing branches of various studies and the Medical science is one of such branches. The word 'Medical Science' denotes a systematic study in medical field, which is related to human life and human body. Techno-medical development is a gift of medical scientists to the humanity. This gift provides benevolent knowledge to human society to treat, heal, sustain, protect and prolong the very existence human society.

The development of Medical Science had put a great effect on the human rights jurisprudence. In fact, the Medical Science inventions or development of new medicines or machines or techniques of surgery have played a great role in making the human life more convenient and comfortable. It has made a positive and constructive impact on Human Rights Jurisprudence. The Reproductive Technology is one of the greatest achievements of the progress of medical science.

The advancement of medical science changed the modern human life and modifies the quality of life. Therefore, it is realized that law must keep balance between the advancement of medical science while maintaining human dignity.

The Right to development through scientific progress is the first right of human beings. But we are enjoying this right at the cost of "Right to Health". A doctor or a researcher in medical science should know all the probable 'risk factors' before experimenting upon other human body and the patient should also know about his legal and other rights.

Now the people realizing that proper legislative measures are needed to protect the human rights of the recipient of the progress of medical science. The legislative measures, which are taking place, should also keep pace with the advancement of medical science. Further, there is a need to see that the Indian legislative efforts are at par with the standard setout at International level for protection of Human Rights or not.

Although legislative effort has been made at national level and international level, but no fruitful result came out because the law-breakers search out new devices to evade the provisions of law, this way or that way.

Indian judiciary has also made efforts for the protection of public health guaranteed under Article 21 of the Constitution of India. It was held by the Supreme Court in *Paschim Bang Khet Mazdoor Samiti* v. *State of West Bengal*[1] that Article 21 imposes obligation on the State to provide medical assistance to injured and protect public health. Preservation of human life is of paramount importance. Right to life cannot be a mere animal existence. Thus, better standard of life, hygienic conditions and healthy environment are must for good health.

Public Health is not only the aspect, which is being effected by the development of medical science but moral, social and ethical arena has also become a topic of debate through out the world. Indeed, the law is main instrument, which plays an important role in the social progress. The progress of Medical Science and other related technological advancement created new challenges, legal, ethical, social, etc. and made the human rights at stake.

These aspects of Medical Science, Law and Human Rights, which have attracted and have become topics of heated discussions due to the legal and ethical issues involved in it, especially relating to Reproductive Technology.

The medical progress promoted the welfare of present humanity and future generation. *"Declaration of Helsinki" and the "Nuremberg Code"* are main International efforts for minimizing the risk and harm to human subjects by medico-technology developments. Medical Science is one of the developing areas, which has attracted the attention of legislatures, medical men, judges, lawyers and other intellectuals and puzzled them in finding solutions of various legal problems, especially, pertaining to Reproductive Technology.

The Reproductive Technology is one of the thrust areas in the field of Medical Science. The overall benefits of the Reproductive Technology has attracted the attention of legislatures, judges, jurists, etc. and put a great challenge before them to find out the solution to the existing moral, social and ethical problems.

Assisted reproductive technologies (ART) have enabled millions of people in the world to have biological children who otherwise would not have been able to do so. According to the European Society for Human Reproduction and Embryology, more than three million babies have been born using ART worldwide in the last 30 years, enabling infertile women and men; single women and men; and lesbian, gay, and transgender couples to form genetically-related families. These new technologies have transformed the way we view reproduction.

While they have created new hopeful possibilities, they also require that we pay attention to issues of health, ethics, law, and policy. Key concerns include: lack of access; health effects on women and children; potential for devaluation of the lives of people with disabilities; limitations on use by lesbian, gay, bisexual, transgender, questioning, and inter sex individuals and couples; dangers of selecting characteristics of children; the commercial environment surrounding ART; and the nature of regulation in the US and other countries.

The Gender, Justice, and Human Genetics Program of the Center for Genetics and Society has written this document to provide basic background information on ART and offer our allies a perspective on ART using a reproductive justice framework. It is concerned with the health and rights of all communities; this document is primarily intended for use within the reproductive health, rights, and justice movements and therefore focuses largely on women. We hope that this document will contribute to building a foundation from which to promote ART policies that reflect social justice and human rights values and principles.

Legally, we are faced with the reality that there are no laws nation wide to regulate the fertility clinics, or to provide criminal penalties for those professionals who do cross the line. The need in the field of reproductive medicine is not only ethics and morality, but laws. Certainly morality and ethics cannot be legislated. However, this area of medicine and high tech fertility procedures has outpaced the laws, which reflect only traditional ways of "making babies".

There is a need for re-defining "mother" and "father" to include the variety of options available to patients at fertility clinics. Patients who do go through these procedures should take care to protect themselves by hiring an attorney who is an expert in the field of reproductive medicine.

By providing for contingencies, and transferring parental rights through such legal counsel, couples will avoid many of the heartaches later. Unfortunately, nothing can prevent the heartache of leaning that your embryos, which were to be in safe keeping, were sold off to the highest bidder.

The medical science is a neutral object, and we cannot blame it. The establishment of the relationship between medical science and human rights is depending on the Human. Hence, it is a man who uses the medical science for the purpose of saving the human values. Hence, with positive attitude and creativity the progress of science and technology can prove a mile stoning object in the field of Human Rights, whereas the negative attitude blended with authoritarian attitude can prove a mass destructive weapon for the humanity.

We know that the right to life is a fundamental right which recognized in all International instruments like—Universal Declaration and both the Covenant. Similarly, the right is also recognized in the regional as well as the national document like constitution. The right to life means the right with all amenities and commodities which make the right of life meaningful which can be enjoyed with the positive implication of medical science.

Furthermore, freedom of science and research which evolved in the context of freedom of expression and which is enshrined in a number of domestic bills of rights provides some protection against undue state interference with the further development of research in the fields of biology, medicine, biochemistry, etc.

It should be noted here that the traditional Western European concept of a nuclear family, that is to say husband, wife, and their possible offspring, has become a major point of discussion during the last decade. There is increasing opposition to reserving a number of privileges, such as access to artificial methods of procreation, only to married couples. Although family law as such is rather rigid, in many Western European countries the legislator has to some extent changed over to recognizing unmarried couples as families, including in some countries couples of the same sex, thereby conferring the same rights and duties upon them.

The first right which is usually relied upon as argument against the dangers involved in modern reproductive techniques is the inviolability of human dignity. Article 1 of the German Basic Law of 1949 is, for example, regularly invoked by German courts, lawyers, and scholars in this respect. Although respect for human dignity seems to be the foundation of human rights in general, international law does not provide an explicit right to the inviolability of human dignity.

The right to found a family is independent of the right to marry and includes the right of married or unmarried couples as well as single persons to have children by procreation or adoption. The scientific progress achieved in this field undoubtedly demands a dynamic interpretation which includes not only natural, but artificial procreation as well.

The protection of privacy and family life includes the rights to individual autonomy, communication (in particular in the emotional sphere), intimacy, and sexuality. One may assume, therefore, that artificial means of procreation fall under the scope of privacy. Any interference with one's privacy is, however, prohibited under international law.

With respect to modern reproductive techniques, the protection of health or morals, the prevention of crime, or the protection of rights and freedoms of others (in particular the child) might be legitimate objectives for states to restrict the right to privacy. Those restrictions must, however, be provided for by law and be necessary in a democratic society, i.e. proportional to the objective aimed at and acceptable in an open, free, tolerant, and pluralistic society. Although the right to privacy seems to afford less protection than the right to found a family, broad restrictions of artificial insemination and IVF could probably not be justified on the grounds of protecting morals or the rights of others.

From present practice it is obvious that there is an urgent need to define under which circumstances access to a form of artificial procreation can justifiably be refused, or when the woman/couple is entitled to such treatment.

According to the traditional Western concept of human rights, it is the primary function of civil and political rights to protect the individual against undue state interference. Only in exceptional circumstances do these rights oblige states to protect individuals by positive legislative or other action against interferences by private individuals or entities. Since modern reproductive techniques are normally not carried out by public authorities (apart from doctors or researchers employed in state clinics), human rights provide guidelines for legislative measures rather than strict obligations under international law.

This is, however, a very controversial issue among international lawyers. In general, the Strasbourg organs (the European Commission and Court of Human Rights) are more reluctant than, for example, the Human Rights Committee of the United Nations to recognize binding legal obligations to positive state action. Furthermore, such obligations also depend on the rights concerned.

Since artificial methods of procreation in principle aim at creating life it would be difficult to deduce prohibitive state measures from the obligation to protect the right to life. Such measures would only be required if certain reproductive techniques constituted an imminent danger to the life of the woman concerned. Under present medical conditions this is, however not the case.

If certain reproductive techniques would have proven harmful effects on the mental or physical well-being of children after birth the question of a positive state duty may arise. The fact that the drafters of the Convention on the Rights of the Child adopted by the United Nations General Assembly on 20 November 1989 did not include any specific provision on artificial procreation shows that such negative effects have not been suspected.

Progress in medical sciences and advanced treatment methods involves new challenges to humanity and the traditional regulation of societies. With the biomedical development, new opportunities and life perspectives have been created for those with previously intractable complications or health problems. Not only have the boundaries of life and handicaps been removed but, at the same time, new forms of procreation have been developed which have an enormous impact on our definitions of parenthood, family, descent, heredity, titles, and other concepts.

In the Preamble to the Universal Declaration of Human Rights, the United Nations recognized that "disregard and contempt for human rights have resulted in barbarous acts which have outraged the conscience of mankind" and that human rights are "the foundation of freedom, justice and peace in the world."

The right to health care is one of the rights that became internationally recognized as a fundamental human right after the Second World War. In this respect, both for physicians and patients, rights and duties were formulated, towards each other and towards third parties. It is important to note that, although sometimes erroneously referred to as such, there never has been formulated a right to health. A "right to health" can never be obtained, as it implies a right to a given good which cannot be formulated objectively and which thus cannot be protected.

The right to health care can be defined as the right to share the benefits of health care and health services available in society. The right to health care is primarily an obligation imposed on states to provide sufficient means to guarantee its citizens a certain standard of health, as well as equal access to health services.

As a general proposition it should be stated that the provision of health care must never be a means to curtail patients' rights, but should be aimed at the promotion of the autonomy and well-being of all persons. The rights of patients are based on two fundamental human rights—the right to health care and the right to privacy.

The right to privacy, as guaranteed in Article 17 ICCPR, Article 8 European Convention for the Protection of Human Rights and Fundamental Freedoms and Article 11 American Convention on Human Rights ACHR, reflects the old liberal idea that the individual should be protected against any undue interference with his or her private space and autonomy. In addition to the protection of one's family life, home, and correspondence, the right to privacy also protects the individual's particular identity, integrity, intimacy, autonomy, private communication and sexuality.

Autonomy means that an individual is completely free to arrange his/her private life in accordance with his/her own ideas and is responsible for his/her own life, as long as he/she does not interfere with the rights and freedoms of others. There is no consensus concerning the question of to what extent autonomy is fully covered by the right to privacy, or if this right has its own legal basis. Particularly in health law literature, autonomy, sometimes called "individual self-determination," is often referred to as a separate and inalienable right of individuals.

The right to individual autonomy is not explicitly enshrined in any of the major international human rights instruments but can, at least partially, be derived from the right to privacy. Some scholars consider this right as one of the pillars of the internationally recognized human rights law. In the absence of any legitimate restriction of the right to privacy, medical treatment, examination, and experimentation may only be performed with the voluntarily given and informed consent of the person concerned.

The human rights and the medical science both are the two sides of the same coin. On, one hand the Human Right jurisprudence encouraged the Medical Science for new inventions in the field of medicine, techniques, tests, experiments, etc., so that the valuable life of human being can be protected, as well as the standard of life can also be upgraded, but on the other hand, medical science encouraged human rights movement by emerging new rights.

But, the development of medical science also posed a great threat and damage to the Human rights. But, for the above reason we cannot held responsible to the medical science, since medical.

Science is an object in the hands of the man. These are human hands which use the development of the medical science for service of humanity or for destruction of humanity.

Undoubtedly, the developments made in above aspects of medical science have set a new milestone in the progressive development of humanity. General Public Health has improved because a large number of patients have been benefited and many precious human lives have been saved yet legislation remains silent or many technical aspects of like reproductive technology.

Since life is a gift of God to us; therefore, new inventions affecting human life raised many questions, which are to be answered by the human society. Does any one have a right and choice to experiment on another body by reproductive technology? Aren't we crossing our limits while extending our knowledge to unnatural experiments?

Today, civilized human society is facing new challenges of the development to moral, ethical, social and legal issues. How can we allow new experiments on human body by compromising ethical, social, moral and legal values, which we have developed from 'jungle life' to 'civilized life'?

Are such experimentation and discoveries always beneficial to us? Every coin has two faces. The other face of the coin has pain, permanent disability, injury or own death of human subjects. Is there violation of Human Rights in the name of scientific progress? All such questions are leading towards heated discussions in the field of law as well as of science and that are to be answered by the human society.

The ethical underpinnings of medical science will be enhanced by raising the visibility of human rights principles as part of the practice of science, in the broadest sense, including but not limited to scientific research. Explicit linking of international human rights principles to science ethics enhances recognition that medical science has both direct and indirect implications for humans and the world in which we live.

Doing so also will serve to promote a common respect for those involved in, or affected by scientific research, regardless of institutional context. If ethics codes guide the work of medical professional and help them identify with a profession, more firmly linking these to human rights principles will serve to bridge scientists across professions and geographical boundaries. These efforts will help to emphasize that medical science is not an exception in the application of human rights principles.

Hence, we can anticipate some of the grave problems that advances in technology will pose for the disciplines of law and human rights. In fact, it already appears to lawyers who are now taking an increasing interest in this area, that while science and technology are racing ahead, law and human rights are looking on helplessly from the sidelines because there is very little that they can do to match the speed of technology.

Law moves very slowly, while technology moves with lightning rapidity. The result is that technology is racing out of legal control. In consequence, there can be grave damage to human rights as well. It is possible to look at developed medical science in a kind of panoramic survey and see that almost every aspect of our lives is influenced.

This suggests that it would be valuable to build ongoing communication between the scientific and human rights communities to determine where and how quantitative and qualitative approaches and scientific tools and technologies can be useful to human rights work, and then assist in making these accessible to human rights practitioners.

Medical Science and Human Rights

(A) IMPACT OF MEDICAL SCIENCE ON HUMAN RIGHTS

Medical Science has profoundly influenced the course of human civilization. It has provided us remarkable insights into the world we live in. The scientific revolutions of the 21st century have led to many technologies, which promise to herald wholly new eras in human life and health. As we stand today at the beginning of a new century, we have to ensure fullest use of these developments for the well-being of our people.

The science technology has become of critical importance in understanding a host of public issue like health, environment, and medicine, education at national and global level. The concept of development is attached with the progressive evolution of Human Beings, since man is the only living creature who thinks and plan about the future. Therefore, the development of man in the field of science and technology is deeply concerned with the concept of his/her rights.

There is a dramatic change in human life since last few decades due to development in field of science and technology. The results on one hand have been beneficial and have proved to be a boon to human society, on the other hand these development have been fatal and posed new problems to human body and dignity. These developments have offered many beneficial services to human communities but at the same time it has posed various challenges in the field of law.

The word medical science includes developments and technology in the medical field which are related to human body. Science is derived from the Latin word *'scientia'*, which means knowledge. It is a system of acquiring knowledge based on the scientific method, as well as the organized body of knowledge gained through such research.

Medical science has helped to develop healthcare. Health care is the prevention, treatment, and management of illness and the preservation of mental and physical well-being through the services offered by the medical, nursing, and allied health professions.

Medical Science has been an integral part of Indian civilization and culture over the past several millennia. Few are aware that India was the fountainhead of important foundational medical science developments and approaches. These cover many great scientific discoveries and technological achievements in mathematics, astronomy, architecture, chemistry, metallurgy, medicine, natural philosophy and other areas.

Since Independence, India has taken the task of promoting the spread of medical science. The key role of medical science as an important element of national development is also well recognized. The Scientific Policy Resolution of 1958 and the Technology Policy Statement of 1983 enunciated the principles on which the growth of science and technology in India has been based over the past several decades. These policies have emphasized self-reliance, as also sustainable and equitable development. They embody a vision and strategy that are applicable today, and would continue to inspire us in our endeavors.

The Medical Science is a dual-edged sword, and can influence in both way, i.e. positively and negatively on the rights of individual and society. The path toward progress and development lies in maximizing the positive impacts and eliminating the negative ones. Direction of medical science progress and changes need to be guided by appropriate public policies for the objective to maintain balance between the progress of man and rights of man and the goal of sustainable development.

In modern era, there are various technological changes, new technologies including biotechnology, information and communication technologies, the medical science play a crucial role in innovation for sustainability. The potential roles of this emergent medical science need to be carefully assessed to design appropriate policies to enhance innovation and progress in the field of medical science for sustainable development as the progress with human dignity is the guiding principle of all human acts.

According to the World Health Organization, health care embraces all the goods and services designed to promote health, including "preventive, curative and palliative interventions, whether directed to individuals or to population". There is a wide range of traditional areas of health care, which have helped develop public health. The most common areas are: medicine, pharmacy, clinical laboratory sciences and various forms of therapy to supplement the healing process and restore proper activity.

Major breakthroughs in medical science and technology affect everyone. The life span has been dramatically extended. The role of medical science is to compress morbidity—to push illness further and further to the end of the life span so that people will enjoy many more years in good health than ever before.[1] Although the impact of medical science is widely felt across the life span, those technologies that have changed the nature and process of reproduction may be of greatest consequence to women.

In 1976, the WMA drafted the Tokyo Declaration which dealt with the role of physicians in treating the prisoners and

1. Fries, Issue and Challenges of NPT, 1980.

victims of custodial violence. Also, the UN General Assembly in December 1989 endorsed the resolution 1989/65 adopted by the UN Economic and Social Council on the prevention of extrajudicial executions and adequate investigation of such executions. This manual is also known as the model Minnesota Protocol for legal investigation of extra-legal, arbitrary and summary executions and model autopsy protocol.

Health and human rights, when the World Health Organizations redefined heath as a state of complete physical, mental and social well-being[2] is not only expanded health far beyond medicine but also openly acknowledged the vast accumulated knowledge about the central role of societal determinants of population health.

The discipline of public health has generally ignored the societal roots of health in favour of medical interventions which operate further downstream. For example, public health efforts at preventing and controlling sexually transmitted diseases have focused on diagnosis and treatment, along with educational programme, rather than confronting societal inequality or other societal issues as 'essential conditions' underlying the spread of sexually transmitted diseases.

Medical Science and professionals are realizing that promoting and protecting human rights may be essential for promoting and protecting health. This insight will be helpful in the evolving approach to population and women's health, drug and alcohol abuse and in the work of social welfare of the society. Medical professionals increasingly recognize that they must deal directly with the underlying societal issues that determine, to the largest extent, who lives and who dies, when and of what.

There is realization both at national and inter national level that a proper legislative measures should be developed to pace with science technology and protect the rights of individual. 'Law' is not the only aspect, which is being effected. The effect of Medical Science on moral social and ethical area has become a topic of debate through out the world. Medical Science, law and Public Health have become topics of heated

2. (World Health Organization Constitution, in: Basic Documents, 36th Edition, Geneva, WHO, 1986).

discussion due to legal and ethical issues involved in especially related to human experimentation, organ transplantation, euthanasia, sex determination test, reproductive technology, etc.

Medical research involving human subjects is conducted only by scientifically qualified persons and under the supervision of clinically competent medical person. The responsibility of human subject should lie on medically qualified person and not on subject though the subject has given consent for it.

Birth of the first 'test-tube-baby' in 1978 became headlines all over the world. The entire world, with the exception of the Vatican City, welcomed this new development in human science. After all, man is the prime creation of God and it has created the universe for human beings. During the last few decades, man has taken great leaps in the field of medical science; especially in human reproduction.

The development of reproductive technology has also adversely affected the sex ratio in the human society. In India, according to the 2001 Census, there are 933 females per 100 males.[3] This gender imbalance resulted due to progress of the Medical Science, which is a violation of human rights.

The invention of new medical tools and technology has made complicated operations/surgery too much easy. Today, due to new medicines, the normal life—span of man has been increased and death ratio had been decreased. Therefore, science had contributed in human life to a great extent. The scientific development not only uplifted the human life, but made it so comfortable and easier that was beyond the human imagination. Hence, science has contributed vitally for us. The development in the field of medical science has brought a revolution and transformation in the life pattern of man, as well as in the field of Human Rights Jurisprudence.

The progress of medical science and technology upgraded the quality of life of the man beyond imagination. Hence, the various intellectuals related to the field of Human Rights opined that the progress of medical science strengthened the

3. All India Census Report, 2001.

human rights progress and movement.

But, on another hand the uncontrolled use and blind race of medical science also affected the human dignity and values adversely. It has become a major destructive tool for the human value and a major cause of violation of human rights.

In civilized societies, Fundamental Rights are put under the guarantee of law and therefore, their protection becomes a mandatory duty of those who are assigned with the task of their protection. The object of these rights is to make an individual an effective participant in the affairs of the society. Unless these rights are available, neither full development of the human personality can be achieved nor can true democracy be said to exist.

Unfortunately, protection of social, economic and cultural rights compared to protection of civil and political rights, at both national and international level has been poor and irregular. At the domestic level, while Economic, Social and Cultural rights are acknowledged in the provisions of national constitutions but they are usually stated to be non-justifiable. A major part of the world's population is still continuing to suffer from hunger, poverty and illiteracy; today there is an urgent need to seek means by which these rights can be enforced especially when states fail to comply with the obligations they have voluntarily undertaken.

While medical science is progressing in its technical potentiality, the law, which should be the guard for protecting the rights of the public, is often inadequate to meet this new challengeable responsibility. The legal systems are adaptable to changing situations but there are several of inherent weaknesses that must be pointed out. There are basically two forms of law, i.e. judge-made law and parliamentary law or the law made by State legislature. Judge-made law has some weaknesses which make it rather inadequate to the age of modern science, because a judge gives his ruling only after the event. Any event occurs, the damage follows, the matter therefore comes to court and the judge then tries to work out responsibility.

Now before discussing the impact of medical science on human rights, it shall be essential to know the meaning and concept of human rights in brief.

(B) CONCEPT OF HUMAN RIGHTS

It must be realized that there can be no dream about good governance, if human rights are flouted and overlooked. Failure to implement the protection of human rights is a serious drawback and poses constant problems to the functioning of democracy. Protection of Human Rights is a vital for the functioning of a healthy democracy. Securing economic and social justice is a moral imperative for any democracy, which respects real humanity. The inter-dependence of both sets of rights is essential for full development of human personality. But, the Governments at the Centre and the States, as statistics shows, never whole-heartedly pursued the implementation of laws for protection of human rights.

Not caring the protection and promotion of human right is a threat to democratic process, which is a continuing process of expanding the political space to ensure for everyone equal access to basic rights and liberties. Hence, the Human Rights are essential for the realization of dignity and worth inherent in the human beings. It is the right time to realize the human rights as *sine-quo-non* of democratic citizenry. A constitutional democracy can never ensure prosperity. Ensuring protection and promotion of human rights and maintaining balance between the progress of science and technology will enable the most vulnerable to exercise true democracy.

(C) ORIGIN AND DEVELOPMENT OF HUMAN RIGHTS

The development of human rights in history of the world can be traced out from the favorite Magna Carta (1215) and Petition of Rights (1688), U.S Declaration of Independence (1776), Bill of Rights (1791), French Declaration of "The Right of Man". Over a century and half later and with the horrors and impact of two world wars behind them, offending the conscience of man, the representatives of the assembled nations met at San Francisco on 26th June, 1945 and adopted the United Nations Charter which *inter alia* is declaration of faith "in fundamental human rights, in the dignity and worth of the human person, in the equal rights of men and women and of nations, large and small".[4] It would be worthwhile to examine the development of Human Rights right from Greek period.

1. Ancient Greeks

The history of the origin and development of human rights is very fascinating in western tradition. The origin of human rights is traced, by some scholars, back to the times of ancient Greeks. Ur-Nammu, the king of Ur created what was arguably the first legal code in 2050 BC. Several other sets of laws were created in Mesopotamia including the Code of Hammurabi (1780 BC), which is one of the best preserved examples of this type of document. It shows rules and punishments including women's rights, children's rights and slave rights, etc.

The fact that the human rights were recognized as natural rights of man is illustrated by a Greek play Antigone. In this play, Sophocles describes the Antigone's brother, while he was rebelling against the king, was killed and his burial was prohibited by the King Creon. In defense of the order Antigone buried here brother. When she was arrested for violating the order, she pleaded that she had acted in accordance with the *"immutable, unwritten laws of heaven" which even the king could not override*. The notion of natural rights of man was contributed by the Stoic philosopher in the philosophy.

Initially the natural law theory was developed by them and virtue of it they explained the nature of human rights, i.e. rights which every human being possess by virtue of being human. However, it may be noted that the citizens of the Greek City states enjoyed some basic rights even before the formulation of natural law theory by the Stoic philosophers. These were in particular:

- the right of freedom and speech (*Isogoria*)
- the right to equality before law (*Isonomia*)
- the right to equal respect for all (*Istimia*)

The Stoic philosophers formulated the theory of natural law after the break down of the Greek City States. The main

4. AIR 1992 Journal Section-11, p. 113.

notion of the Stoic philosophy was that the principles of natural law were universal in their nature. Their application was not limited to any class or persons of certain States; rather it applied to everybody everywhere in the world. It discovered by human reason and as such was superior to positive law.

The natural rights of man being its embodiment were not the particular privileges of citizens of certain State, but something to which every human being, everywhere, were entitled in virtue of the simple fact of being human and rational.[5] They set forth further that men could comprehend and obey this law of nature because of their common possession of reason and capacity to develop and attain virtue.

In this way, the Stoic philosophers were able to preach the idea of universal brotherhood of mankind and laid stress upon the equality and freedom for all. The Stoic formulation of natural law was best suited to the Roman temperament, for they, in principle, believed that man should improve himself both rationally and morally.

Writing about natural law, Cicero (105-43) B.C., like Stoic philosophers, laid emphasis upon the universal nature of it and said that natural law is of universal application, unchanging and everlasting. It is sin to try to alter this law, nor is it allowable to attempt to repeal any part of it, and it is impossible to abolish it entirely. We cannot be freed from its obligation by Senate or People . . . and there will not be different law at Rome and at Athens or different laws now and in the future, but one eternal and unchangeable law will be valid for all nations and for all times.[6]

2. Roman Period

Roman applied the Stoic conception of natural law in the formation of body of legal rules for the administration of justice. It was the most exceptional intellectual contribution of the Romans in the field of law. The above body of rules was developed by them on the basis of the custom as well as application of reason. Acting in this manner, they not only

5. Crabstibm, M., Human Rights Today, 1962, p. 9.
6. De Republic, III xxii, 33, quoted in d' Entreves, Natural Law, 1960, pp. 20-21.

modernized their old law, but also laid stress upon the incorporation of high ethical standards in legal procedure.

Roman Law was divided into two categories of rules : *'jus civile'*, or Roman Civil Law dealing with citizens, things and actions; and *'jus genitum'*, or the law of non-citizens, which describe the rights of those who were not the citizens of Rome and they referred to those rights to which men were entitled in general. It also referred to the rules of international law at the same time. Many principles of *'jus genitum'*, were adopted from *'jus naturale'* (natural law) which enabled them to humanize these rules in such a way that a man of common sense and good faith could approve them as just.[7]

3. Middle Age

In the Middle Ages, the most original thinkers of their times like the scholastic philosopher—Abelard (1079-1142) and Thomas Aquinas (1224-74), laid stress upon the concept of natural law as the higher principles of law to be derived from reasons. But they did not go in quest of making the human personality as the main concern of law and social life.

Thomas Aquinas, like Aristotle, justified the existence of the practice of slavery. Thus, the "man" was dispensed with a central notion of mediaeval philosophy of law. Much attention was focused on the development of the principle of the sovereignty of State rather than on the development of respects for human qualities. This principle of "Natural Rights" late on became one of the greatest obstacles to the international protection of human rights.

Again, a set-back was also caused during 16th century to the development of the concept of natural rights by Machiavelli's teachings. He opposed the concept of natural law and supported absolute monarchy. His philosophy was not based on any mystical thought such as that of natural law, rather, it was "here-and-now-philosophy" for him the human nature was bad and selfish which necessitated the

7. Swain, J.E., a History of World Civilization, 1947, pp. 172-73. It may be noted 'here with concern that in the Greco-roman system of thoughts, particularly in the teachings of Aristotle the slavery was recognized as valid practice—Aristotle; Politics, Book one.

establishment of State to curb and crush the anti-social elements existing in human mind.

Later on, there was influence of the social contract doctrine. This influence was more profound in scope as well as in its impact. Further, the concept of natural rights was closely linked with the doctrine of social contract theory because the basis upon which the natural law theories were formulated was the same for the social contract doctrine also. This doctrine popularized during 16th and 17th century through the political philosopher's writing such as of Thomas Hobbes (1558-1778), John Lock (1632-1704) and Jean Jacques (1719-78).

However, in 17th century one of the protagonists of social contract theory, Rousseau emphasized that the State was an artifact, and artificial creation of the individuals or the result of the social contract. Rousseau began with the state of nature, in which man was free and independent in all respect. From this state of nature according to him, there emerged a political society by the separate acts of individuals, whereby they undertook with one another to set-up government which would be responsible to promote their common interests the political society, so created would, by majority will, proceed to appoint governors who would govern in accordance with the terms of contract, or the instrument of trust or an act of delegation by which he was so empowered. The governor was to act on the behalf of the people thus protecting their general interests and respecting their natural rights. The violation of the terms of social contract on the part of the governor would justify not only its disobedience but also rebellion against it.

Kant provides a means for justifying human rights as the basis for self-determination grounded within the authority of human reason. Kant's moral philosophy is based upon an appeal to the formal principles of ethics, rather than an appeal to a concept of substantive human goods.

For Kant, the determination of any such goods can only proceed from a correct determination of the formal properties of human reason and thus do not provide the ultimate means for determining the correct ends, or object, of human reason. Kant's moral philosophy begins with an attempt to correctly identify those principles of reasoning that can be applied equally to all rational persons, irrespective of their own specific desires or partial interests. In this way, Kant attaches a condition of universality to the correct identification of moral principles. For him, the basis of moral reasoning must rest upon a condition that all rational individuals are bound to assent to.

Hence, Kant's formulation was of the categorical imperative. Kant's moral philosophy is notoriously abstract and resists easy comprehension. Though often overlooked in accounts of the historical development of human rights, his contribution to human rights has been profound. Kant provides a formulation of fundamental moral principles that, though exceedingly formal and abstract, are based upon the twin ideals of equality and moral autonomy. Human rights are rights we give to ourselves, so to speak, as autonomous and formally equal beings. For Kant, any such rights originate in the formal properties of human reason, and not the will of some super-human being.

The philosophical ideas defended by the likes of Locke and Kant have come to be associated with the general Enlightenment project initiated during the 17th and 18th Centuries; the effects of which were to extend across the globe and over ensuing centuries. Ideals such as natural rights, moral autonomy, human dignity and equality provided normative bedrock for attempts at re-constituting political systems, for overthrowing formerly despotic regimes and seeking to replace them with forms of political authority capable of protecting and promoting these new emancipatory ideals. These ideals effected significant, even revolutionary, political upheavals throughout the 18th Century, enshrined in such documents as the United States' Declaration of Independence and the French National Assembly's Declaration of the Rights of Man and Citizen.

(D) JUSTIFICATION OF HUMAN RIGHTS

For the purposes of clarity and relative simplicity we will focus upon the two, presently most prominent, philosophical attempts to justify human rights Interest Theory and Will Theory. Before we do that, it is necessary to address a prior question.

Many people tend to take the validity of human rights for granted. Certainly, for many non-philosophers human rights may all too obviously appear to rest upon self-evidently true and universally valid moral principles. In this respect, human rights may be perceived as empirical facts about the contemporary world. Human rights do exist and many people do act in accordance with the correlative duties and obligations respecting human rights entails. No supporter of human rights could possibly complain about such perceptions. If nothing else, the prevalence of such views is pragmatically valuable for the cause of human rights.

However, moral philosophers do not enjoy such license for epistemological complacency. Moral philosophers remain concerned by the question of the philosophical foundations of human rights. There is a good reason why we should all be concerned with such a question. What might be termed the 'philosophically naive' view of human rights effectively construes human rights as legal rights. The validity of human rights is closely tied to, and dependent upon, the legal codification of human rights.

One must not confuse the law with morality, *per se*. Nor consider the two to be simply co-extensional. Human rights originate as moral rights. Human rights claim validity everywhere and for everyone, irrespective of whether they have received comprehensive legal recognition, and even irrespective of whether everyone is agreement with the claims and principles of human rights. Thus, one cannot settle the question of the philosophical validity of human rights by appealing to purely empirical observations upon the world.

As a moral doctrine, human rights have to be demonstrated to be valid as norms and not facts. In order to achieve this, one has to turn to moral philosophy. Presently, two particular approaches to the question of the validity of human rights predominate: what might be loosely termed the 'interests theory approach' and the 'will theory approach'.

Advocates of the interest theory approach argue that the principal function of human rights is to protect and promote certain essential human interests. Securing human beings' essential interests is the principal ground upon which human rights may be morally justified. The interests approach is thus primarily concerned to identify the social and biological prerequisites for human beings leading a minimally good life. The universality of human rights is grounded in what are considered to be some basic, indispensable, attributes for human well-being, which all of us are deemed necessarily to share.

Take, for example, an interest each of us has in respect of our own personal security. This interest serves to ground our claim to the right. It may require the derivation of other rights as prerequisites to security, such as the satisfaction of basic nutritional needs and the need to be free from arbitrary detention or arrest, for example. The philosopher John Finnis provides a good representative of the interest theory approach. Finnis (1980) argues that human rights are justifiable on the grounds of their instrumental value for securing the necessary conditions of human well-being.

He identifies seven fundamental interests, or what he terms 'basic forms of human good', as providing the basis for human rights. These are: life and its capacity for development; the acquisition of knowledge, as an end in itself; play, as the capacity for recreation; aesthetic expression; sociability and friendship; practical reasonableness, the capacity for intelligent and reasonable thought processes; and finally, religion, or the capacity for spiritual experience. According to Finnis, these are the essential prerequisites for human well-being and, as such, serve to justify our claims to the corresponding rights, whether they are of the claim right or liberty right variety.

Other philosophers who have defended human rights from an interests-based approach have addressed the question of how an appeal to interests can provide a justification for respecting and, when necessary, even positively acting to promote the interests of others. Such questions have a long heritage in western moral and political philosophy and extend at least as far back as the 17th Century philosopher Thomas Hobbes.

In contrast to the interests approach, the will theory attempts to establish the philosophical validity of human rights upon a single human attribute: the capacity for freedom. Will theorists argue that what is distinctive about human agency is the capacity for freedom and that this ought to constitute the core of any account of rights. Ultimately, then, will theorists view human rights as originating in, or reducible to, a single, constitutive right, or alternatively, a highly limited set of purportedly fundamental attributes.

He states that a 'right is absolute when it cannot be overridden in any circumstances, so that it can never be justifiably infringed and it must be fulfilled without any exceptions. "Will theorists" then attempt to establish the validity of human rights upon the ideal of personal autonomy.

The interest theory approach and the will theory approach contain strengths and weaknesses. When consistently and separately applied to the doctrine of human rights, each approach appears to yield conclusions that may limit or undermine the full force of those rights. It may be that philosophical supporters of human rights need to begin to consider the potential philosophical benefits attainable through combining various themes and elements found within these (and other) philosophical approaches to justifying human rights. Thus, further attempts at justifying the basis and content of human rights may benefit from pursuing a more thematically pluralist approach than has typically been the case to date.

Philosophical supporters of human rights are necessarily committed to a form of moral universalism. As moral principles and as a moral doctrine, human rights are considered to be universally valid. However, moral universalism has long been subject to criticism by so-called moral relativists. Moral relativists argue that universally valid moral truths do not exist. For moral relativists, there is simply no such thing as a universally valid moral doctrine. Relativists view morality as a social and historical phenomenon. Moral beliefs and principles are therefore thought of as socially and historically contingent, valid only for those cultures and societies in which they originate and within which they are widely approved.

The upholders of the social contract theory considered human right as the natural rights for the reason those human rights are based upon the contract concluded by the people with the State. They explained that when men entered into contract to form political society they renounced some of their natural rights which had previously been enjoyed by them in their free state of nature but certain basic rights, such as, the right to life, freedom and equality were preserved by them.

These rights so preserved constituted their *"natural and inalienable rights"* which must be respected by the State or governor. Thus in effect one of the purposes of the social contract was to preserve the natural inalienable rights to men and at the same time, to prevent the state from interfering with the exercise of those rights by the people. In this way the concept of inalienable, natural and imprescriptibly nature of human rights was established. The teachings of the social contract writes had not only empowered and revitalized the concept of natural rights but provided it with dynamic contents. As such it exercised great influence upon the American and French Revolution.

1. American Revolution and Development of Human Rights

In 1663, the American Revolution began in the form of the colonial revolt. There were many factors which dominated towards the rise of this revolution, for example, the growing importance of the notion of natural rights, teaching of the writers of social contract theory, the British bill of right of 1689[8] and the coercive actions of George III (1760-1820) and his predecessors. The British Government was of the view that the colonies should also share in the expenses incurred in their administration. With this view, the British Government in the last half of the 18th Century started to take various regulatory measures under which it introduced certain new taxes. This resulted into militant opposition by the American people. They argued that since they did not have their representatives in the British parliament, it had no right to impose taxes upon them.

The Declaration of Independence on July 4, 1776 was the result of the American notion of independence and their determination to overthrow the authority of the imperial tyrannical government. This historical document was drafted

8. British Bills of Rights of 1689 established the idea of representative government formally and became a charter of liberty for England.

and framed by Thomas Jefferson. It attacked not only against the divine right of the king to rule, but also against a government which did not reflect the will of the people. The document describes:

> "We hold these truths to be self-evident, that all men are created equal, that they are endowed by their Creator with certain inalienable rights, that among these are life, liberty and pursuit of happiness. That to secure these rights Governments are instituted among men deriving their just powers from the consent of the governed; that whenever and form the Government becomes destructive these ends, it is that right of the people to alter or abolish it and institute new Government".[9] Thus, Americans made their claim for independence on the basis of inalienable rights of man, popular sovereignty, and the right of revolution, but at the time of drafting the Constitution in 1787 they did not include a bill of rights for them. They did in 1791 by adopting ten amendments to the Constitution.

The 13th Amendments prohibits slavery and involuntary servitude, the 14th Amendments widens the base of American citizenship by conferring citizenship on all persons born or naturalized in the United States. They became entitled to the citizenship of United State as well as of the State in which they reside. It is further provided that States shall neither make nor enforce any law which shall abridge the privileges and immunities of citizens of the united States, nor deprive any person of life, liberty or property without due process of law nor deny to any person within its jurisdiction the legal protection of the laws; the 15th Amendment lays down that the citizen's right to vote shall not be denied or abridged by the United States or any state on the grounds of race, colour or previous condition of servitude; the 19th Amendment was added in 1920 providing that this right shall not be abridged or denied on the ground of sex.

---

9. Friedrich and Mc Closkey, From the Declaration of Independence to the Constitution, 1954, p. 3.

2. French Revolution and Development of Human Rights

The French Revolution was based upon those principles which were set in motion by the English and American Revolution. It differed mainly in that it was basically the result of economic and social inequalities and injustices of the French ancient regime. These inequalities were conspicuous not only among the third Estate (lower classes) but also in the First Estate (clergy) and in the second Estate (nobility).

It had caused the greatest amount of concern among the writers,[10] who were apparently influenced by the teachings of Rousseau. They enthusiastically claimed that it marked the dawn of new age for the mankind in general and believed in the prospect of right reason and natural and imprescriptibly right to life, liberty and the pursuit of happiness. The government, in their option, must preserve and safeguard these rights and if it fails to do so it has no right to remain in existence.

The National Assembly thus established was, evidently, dependent on the consent of common people for its authority and not on the royal prerogatives. The members of the National Assembly although worked under strains and restrictions but their achievement was nonetheless of great significance. They completed their work almost by the end of spring of 1791. A list of inalienable rights of free citizens was prepared which was proclaimed as the "Declaration of the Rights of Man and of the Citizens". In it the philosophical teachings of Rousseau permeated to its full extent. This document was of the rank of the English Magna Charta and the Bill of Rights in the Constitution of United States of America.

The birth rights of the individual which they had lost were now restored. It proclaimed that men were born free and equal in their rights. The proclamation of the Declaration of the Right of Man and of the Citizens was annexed to the Constitution when it was adopted in 1791. According to Gaius Ezejiofor, this completed one of the most crucial epochs in the development of the concept of human rights. Before, the American and

10. Ferguson and Brun: A Survey of European Civilization, pp. 565-612; Martin, French Liberal thought in the 18th Century.

French Revolution it had what was for all practical purposes only a philosophical appeal but after the Declaration and the Constitutional Bill of Rights, the concept assumed a positive importance.

3. Nineteenth Century and Onward

Similarly, the concept of individual rights continued to resound throughout the 19th Century exemplified by Mary Wollstencraft's *Vindication of the Rights of Women* and other political movements to extend political suffrage to sections of society who had been denied the possession of political and civil rights.

The concept of rights had become a vehicle for effecting political change. Though one could argue that the conceptual prerequisites for the defense of human rights had long been in place, a full Declaration of the doctrine of human rights only finally occurred during the 20th Century and only in response to the most atrocious violations of human rights, exemplified by the Holocaust.

It was believed that no permanent peace could be established without securing international safeguards for human rights and fundamental freedoms. President Roosevelt took the lead in the matter and in his message to Congress on January 6, 1941; he referred to the four essential human freedoms to which he looked forward as the foundation of a future world. These are:

- Freedom of speech and expression.
- Freedom of every person to worship God in his own way.
- Freedom from want.
- Freedom from fear.

Although, the list of rights as here described is not very exhaustive but still it had exercised immense influence on the movement of human rights. Then the British Prime Minister, Mr. Churchill was equally concerned with the violation of human rights and racial persecution. He proclaimed that racial persecution would come to an end with the end of Second World War and human rights would be promoted.

The Prime Minister of Great Britain Mr. Winston S. Churchill and the President of the United States Mr. Franklin D. Roosevelt had met at the sea and issued a Joint Declaration on August 1941. It is known as the Atlantic Charter. Through this Declaration the two leaders deemed "it right to make known certain common principles in the national policies of their respective countries on which they base their hopes for a better future for the world".

It was agreed among other things that "they respect the right of all people to choose the form of government under which they will live: and they wish to see sovereign rights and self-government restored to those who have been forcibly deprived of them. After the final destruction of the Nazi Tyranny, "They hope to see established a peace which will afford to all nations the means of dwelling in safety within their own boundaries, and which will afford assurance that all the men in all the lands may live out their lives in freedom from fear and want.

The General Assembly has been assigned with the duty of initiating studies and making recommendations for the purpose of assisting in the realization of human rights and fundamental freedoms. The Economic and social Council is authorized to make recommendations to the General Assembly, to the members of the United Nations and to the concerned specialized agencies for the purpose of promoting respect for and observance of, human rights and fundamental freedoms for all. The Economic and social council is further empowered to prepare a draft conventions for submission to the General Assembly, and to set-up commission for promotion of human rights. The Economic and social council constituted the Human Rights' Commission in its first session with the responsibility, *inter alia,* to formulate an International Bill of Right.

Working in union, with the Economic and Social Council the Universal Declaration of Human Rights was adopted by the General Assembly on December 10, 1948, which formed the basis for the preparation of other documents on human rights. The most prominent among them are the International Covenant on economic, social and Cultural rights, and the international Covenant on civil and Political rights.

These three documents, the Universal Declaration of Human Rights, the International Covenant on civil and Political Rights, aiming at the Abolition of the Death Penalty and the international Covenant on Economic, Social and Cultural Rights, Constitute the International Bill of Human Rights. They are followed by over ninety other global human rights and humanitarian treaties. Hence, the concept of human rights reached in its present form after passing through the above described phases and movement which had dominated up to a great extent in development of the human rights

The Universal Declaration of Human Rights (UDHR) was adopted by the UN General Assembly on 10th December 1948 and was explicitly motivated to prevent the future occurrence of any similar atrocities. The Declaration itself goes far beyond any mere attempt to reassert all individuals' possession of the right to life as a fundamental and inalienable human right.

Indeed, many writers on human rights agree in the identification of three generations of human rights. First generation rights consist primarily of rights to security, property, and political participation. These are most typically associated with the French and US Declarations. Second generation rights are construed as socio-economic rights, rights to welfare, education, and leisure, for example. These rights largely originate within the UDHR. The final and third generations of rights are associated with such rights as a right to national self-determination, a clean environment, and the rights of indigenous minorities. This generation of rights really only takes hold during the last two decades of the 20th. Century but represents a significant development within the doctrine of human rights generally.

Human rights are rights that attach to human beings and function as moral guarantees in support of our claims towards the enjoyment of a minimally good life. In conceptual terms, human rights are themselves derivative of the concept of a right. This section focuses upon the philosophical analysis of the concept of a 'right' in order to clearly demonstrate the various constituent parts of the concept from which human rights emerges. In order to gain a full understanding of both the philosophical foundations of the doctrine of human rights and the different ways in which separate human rights function, a detailed analysis is required.

4. Concept of Human Rights in Indian Tradition

The Indian culture is one of the most developed and rich among the others. The concept of the term "Human Rights" is not new in the perspective of Indian culture and civilization. The human rights are the minimal rights which the every individual must had against the State or other public authorities by virtue of his being a member of the human family irrespective of any other consideration. We can take the example of any period in Indian Civilization regarding existence of the concept of Human Right; we shall find that these were in existence in one or in other form. It is a matter of necessity of the society, that the concept and meaning of the human Rights had been modified according to the requirement of the people.

The phase wise development of the Human Rights in India is discussed below in the next paragraphs. The Human Rights in India had been reached to the present position after developing through the following phases:

- First Phase of Human Rights in India (Vedic Era).
- Second Phase of Human Rights (Islamic Era).
- Third Phase of Human Rights (Modern Era).

(a) Development of Human Right in Vedic Era

The quest for truth, equality, harmony and knowledge inspired the ancient Indian minds more than their counterparts the Greeks and the Romans. About 5000 years ago, ancient Indian philosophers and thinker expounded a theory of higher moral law over and above positive law embodying certain values of universal validity like *Dharma, Artha, Kama and Moksha,* i.e. Righteousness, wealth, desires and salvation, with a view to develop and establish a harmonious social order by striking a balance between inner and outer, spiritual and material aspect of life.[11]

---

11. Dhyani, S.N., Fundamental of Jurisprudence—The Indian Approach, Central Law Agency, Allahabad, p. 79 (1992).

The ancient Indian legal philosopher were universalisms, humanists rationalists and above all moralists who evolved a system of legal theory which was based on higher values and ideals, i.e. on their conception of Dharma, which governed in an integrative manner all civil, religious and other actions of men in society be it king or his subjects. Every aspect of life was regulated by Dharma the supreme law in ancient India. The kings in India unlike the Tudor kings or French Louis XIV were subjected to the supremacy of the law of Dharma.[12] Law of Rita or Dharma in ancient India made a bold attempt of building an organized social life wherein each individual realized his goals within the parameters of social norms of morality. It is this Supreme Law which sustained individuals together in the society.

It is Dharma which has impelled men since Vedic ages to strive for "righteousness'". The Natural law so revealed in *Vedas, Puranas, Mahabharata, Bhagwad Gita,* etc. was extolled by the mystics, saints, poets and philosophers during the Vedic age. The philosophy expounded by the saints of Vedic time is nothing but a reinstatement of Natural law with religious fervor to enthuse people towards the path of Dharma, enlightenment and unity. It is this higher law of morality, justice and righteousness which has been continuously guiding and directing Hindu thought, spirit and action from times immemorial and would continue to mould for the realization of Dharma in a timeless fashion.

The Rights of man were embedded in highly developed ancient Indian civilization. The study of *Rigveda* reveals that there was a rich jurisprudence in ancient India which provided an adequate frame-work for the regulation of the behaviour of the ordinary persons as well as the Sovereign, the king. Two norms, viz., Dharma and Danda, which were necessarily influence by the theological tenets of the Vedic Aryans, contained several features of a regulatory mechanism for religious practices.

Referring to the social responsibility of the king, Manu states:

12. *Ibid.,* at p. 86.

> "To end lawlessness was crested the institution of the king whose supreme duty was to protect his subjects against disorder and anarchy".

Detailed rules were laid down for the guidance of the king. It was his duty to uphold the law, and he was as much subject to law as any other person. It was obligatory upon him to enforce not only the sacred law of the texts but also the customary laws (rights and claims) of the subjects. This was possibly the human rights enforcement system in its embryonic stage.[13]

The philosophers of Vedic age endeavored to define human rights as those rights which were inherent in our nature and without which we could not live as human beings. They supported vehemently the view point that human rights and fundamental freedoms allow us to fully develop and use our human qualities, our intelligence, our talents and our conscience and to satisfy our spiritual and other needs. They considered human rights as based on mankind's increasing demand for a life in which the inherent dignity and worth of each human-being will receive respect and protection. They had a strong conviction that human rights are universal and apply to all persons without discrimination.

They felt that respect for individual rights needs to be upheld at all times irrespective of circumstances or political systems. There are many references in Vedas which focus light on the existence of human rights. The Vedas proclaim Liberty of Body (Tan), dwelling house (skridhi) and Life (jibase). In 1367 B.C., Bahmani and Vijaynagar kings are stated to have entered into an agreement for the humane treatment of prisoners of war and the sparing of lives of the enemy's unarmed subjects.[14] It is also apparent that protection of the rights and the individual was the main object for which the stated existed.

The philosophy of Vedic age enlightens us of the fact that the human right enveloped within its fold the "constant

13. Jaswal, Dr. Paramjit S., Human Rights and the Law, APH Publishing Corporation, New Delhi, p. 97 (1995).
14. Jaswal, Dr. Paramjit, S. and Jaswal, Dr. Nishtha, *op. cit.*, p. 5.

perpetual desire of giving to every man what is due to him". It is established beyond doubt that Vedic India had a strong tradition of respect for Human Rights. We find many references in Ancient scriptures and epics to the effect that—let every one be happy, let everyone be free from all ills. The ideal human unit and of a world free from traces of conflicts and misery has always stirred the Indian hearts since times immemorial.

Human Rights have always occupied a place of prime importance in India's rich legacy and believed in the 'Welfare of all', i.e. "Vashudhaiva-kutumbakam".[15] Panini, the great Sanskrit grammarian of the 5th century B.C., interprets Dharma as an act of religious merit, custom and usage. Mahabharata describes it as being ordained for the advancement and growth of all creatures for restricting creatures from injuring one another and to uphold all creatures. Thus in India, the Dharma of the Vedic period provided for the protection of the rights of man.

Hindus no less than Greeks and Romans excelled in propounding philosophical ideals and constructing scientific concept and methods which deeply influence the law and life of people. In the words of Max Muller (six systems of Indian philosophy):

> "It is surely astounding that such a system as the Vedanta should have been slowly elaborated by the indefatigable and intrepid thinkers of India thousands of years ago, a system even now makes us feel giddy, as in mounting the last steps of swaying spire of an ancient Gothic cathedra..."[16]

(i) Natural Rights and Human Rights

As natural rights they are seen as belonging to men and women by their very nature. They may also be described as Common Right, for they are rights which all men and women in the world would share, just as the common law in England,

---

15. Dhyani, S.N., Fundamental of Jurisprudence—Indian Approach, Central Law Agency, Allahabad, p. 41 (1992).
16. *Ibid.*, at pp. 79-80.

for instance, was the body of rules and customs which unlike local customs, governed the whole country.[17]

Since the human rights are not created by any legislation, they resemble very much the natural rights. Any democratic and civilized country or body like the United Nations must recognize them. They cannot be subjected to the process of amendment even. The legal duty to protect human rights includes the legal duty to respect them. Members of the U.N. have committed themselves to promote respect for and observance of human rights and fundamental freedoms.

(ii) Moral, Legal and Human Rights

The distinction drawn between moral rights and legal rights as two separate categories of rights is of fundamental importance to understanding the basis and potential application of human rights. Legal rights refer to all those rights found within existing legal codes. A legal right is a right that enjoys the recognition and protection of the law. Questions as to its existence can be resolved by simply locating the relevant legal instrument or piece of legislation.

A legal right cannot be said to exist prior to its passing into law and the limits of its validity are set by the jurisdiction of the body which passed the relevant legislation. An example of a legal right would be my daughter's legal right to receive an adequate education, as enshrined within the United Kingdom's Education Act (1944).

Suffice it to say, that the exercise of this right is limited to the United Kingdom. My daughter has no legal right to receive an adequate education from a school board in Southern California. Legal positivists argue that the only rights that can be said to legitimately exist are legal rights, rights that originate within a legal system. On this view, moral rights are not rights in the strict sense, but are better thought of as moral claims, which may or may not eventually be assimilated within national or international law.

For a legal positivist, such as the 19th Century legal philosopher Jeremy Bentham, there can be no such thing as

17. Fawcett, J.E.S., the Law of Nations (Alien Lane, The Penguin Press, London, 1968), p. 151.

human rights existing prior to, or independently from legal codification. For a positivist determining the existence of rights is no more complicated than locating the relevant legal statute or precedent. In stark contrast, moral rights are rights that, it is claimed, exist prior to and independently from their legal counterparts. The existence and validity of a moral right is not deemed to be dependent upon the actions of jurists and legislators.

This particular line of opposition and protest could only be pursued because of a belief in the existence and validity of moral rights. A belief that fundamental rights which may or may not have received legal recognition elsewhere, remained utterly valid and morally compelling even, and perhaps especially, in those countries whose legal systems had not recognized these rights. No one could legitimately argue that the legal political rights of non-white South Africans were being violated under apartheid, since no such legal rights existed. The systematic denial of such rights did, however, constitute a gross violation of those peoples' fundamental moral rights.

It would be a mistake to exclusively identify human rights with moral rights. Human rights are better thought of as both moral rights and legal rights. Human rights originate as moral rights and their legitimacy is necessarily dependent upon the legitimacy of the concept of moral rights. A principal aim of advocates of human rights is for these rights to receive universal legal recognition. This was, after all, a fundamental goal of the opponents of apartheid. The legitimacy claims of human rights are tied to their status as moral rights.

The practical efficacy of human rights is, however, largely dependent upon their developing into legal rights. In those cases where specific human rights do not enjoy legal recognition, such as in the example of apartheid above, moral rights must be prioritized with the intention that defending the moral claims of such rights as a necessary prerequisite for the eventual legal recognition of the rights in question.

(iii) Claim Rights and Liberty Rights

To gain an understanding of the functional properties of human rights, it is necessary to consider the more specific distinction drawn between claim rights and liberty rights. It should be noted that it is something of a convention to begin such discussions by reference to W.N. Hohfield's (1919) more extended classification of rights. Hohfield identified four categories of rights: liberty rights, claim rights, power rights, and immunity rights. However, numerous scholars have subsequently tended to collapse the last two within the first two and hence to restrict attention to liberty rights and claim rights. The political philosopher Peter Jones (1994) provides one such example.

Jones restricts his focus to the distinction between claim rights and liberty rights. He conforms to a well-established trend in rights' analysis in viewing the former as being of primary importance. Jones defines a claim right as consisting of being owed a duty. A claim right is a right one holds against another person or persons who owe a corresponding duty to the right holder.

Jones defines liberty rights as rights which exist in the absence of any duties not to perform some desired activity and thus consist of those actions one is not prohibited from performing. In contrast to claim rights, liberty rights are primarily negative in character. For example, a person may be said to possess a liberty right to spend his vacations lying on a particularly beautiful beach in Greece. Unfortunately, no one has a duty to positively provide for this particular exercise of his liberty right.

The making of substantive distinctions between human rights can have controversial, but important, consequences. Human rights are typically understood to be of equal value, each right is conceived of as equally important as every other. On this view, there should not be any conflict between fundamental human rights. One is simply meant to attach equal moral weight to each and every human right. This prohibits arranging human rights in order of importance.

Human rights are said to be possessed equally, by everyone. A conventional corollary of this claim is that everyone has a duty to protect and promote the human rights of everyone else. However, in practice, the onus for securing human rights typically falls upon national governments and international, inter-governmental bodies. Philosophers such as

Thomas Pogge (1995) argue that the moral burden for securing human rights should fall disproportionately upon such institutions precisely because they are best placed and most able to effectively perform the task.

(iv) Need for the Protection of Human Rights

In the first instance, national governments are typically held to be primarily responsible for the adequate provision of their own citizens' human rights. The object of human rights is to secure 'minimal levels of decent and respectful treatment.' It is important to note, however, that the duty ensure the provision of even minimal levels of decent and respectful treatment cannot be strictly limited by national boundaries.

The adequate protection and promotion of everyone's human rights does require, for example, the more affluent and powerful nation-states providing sufficient assistance to those countries currently incapable of adequately ensuring the protection of their own citizens' basic human rights.

National and international institutions bear the primary responsibility of securing human rights and the test for successfully fulfilling this responsibility is the creation of opportunities for all individuals to lead a minimally good life. The realization of human rights requires establishing the conditions for all human beings to lead minimally good lives and thus should not be confused as an attempt to create a morally perfect society. The impression that many have of human rights as being unduly utopian testifies less to the inherent demands of human rights and more to the extent to which even fairly modest aspirations are so far from being realized in the world today.

We have established that human rights originate as moral rights but that the successful passage of many human rights into international and national law enables one to think of human rights as, in many cases, both moral rights and legal rights. Furthermore, human rights may be either claim rights or liberty rights, and have a negative or a positive complexion in respect of the obligations imposed by others in securing the right. Human rights may be divided into five different categories and the principal object of securing human rights is the creation of the conditions for all individuals to have the opportunity to lead a minimally good life.

In this age of science and technology the task for the protection of human rights has become more arduous. We can reap the fruits of benefits of the development of science and technology while maintaining the norms of human rights. The globalization has further posed some new challenges to human rights, which are to be met.

(b) Development of Human Right in Islamic Era

The concept of human rights got lost on its way in the dark and narrow alley of the second phase. In the Islamic period the philosophical and ideal speculation were replaced by new ideal of chivalry, war and other heroic traditions which led to confusion and uncertainty. With the invasion of India by Muslims created new situation wherein the Muslim rulers or Sultans followed a policy of discrimination against the Hindus. So the significance of Muslim rule in India was counter-productive to harmony, justice and equality.

(c) Development of Human Right in Modern Era

(i) Constitution of India

With the commencement of the new Constitution on January 26th, 1950, the Natural law rights have been incorporated in the Preamble, in Chapters III and IV concerning Fundamental Rights and Directive Principles of State Policy.

Under Part III, Fundamental Rights are included which are right of equality, right to six freedoms, right to life and personal liberty, right to freedom of religion, right to property, Cultural and educational right, right against exploitation and right to Constitutional remedies.

Under Part IV Directive Principles of State Policy are included which are right to adequate means of livelihood, right against exploitation, right to both sexes to equal pay for equal work, right to work, to education and public assistance in cases of unemployment, old age, sickness, right to equal justice and free legal aid, right to living wage, right to worker's participation in management of Industries, etc.

Reproductive Technologies

I. ARTIFICIAL INSEMINATION

(A) Concept of Artificial Insemination

(a) History

Apart from the natural means of procuring children in the olden days and even today there have been via media. Medical Science has added to it one, i.e. Artificial Insemination (AI). This practice in animals is not new; it started in 1707 and in view of its real advantage in improving the breed of the animals, it has been used at large scale in animal husbandry.

Among humans some successful experimentations were done in the later nineteenth century, but due to public indignation it could not be carried forward. It was in 1909 onwards, when, in spite of public resentment, artificial insemination could be adopted by a few couples for procuring children. Presently, it has been accepted by a few European countries and America as an alternative means for procuring children, and it is being used there at large scale. Although the exact figure, due to secrecy reason, is not known, the estimated number runs into millions.[1]

In India, resort to artificial insemination is scanty. It has been practiced in the cities having cosmopolitical culture, e.g. Bombay. In Bombay, some Sperm Banks are present. It suffered from social non-acceptance, yet gradually it is gaining popularity.

People resort to artificial insemination when there is inability or unwillingness to have a child by to natural means. Inability implies sterility, impotency or physical defects preventing pregnancy. In case of impotency, on part of either husband or wife, the husband's sperm is utilized provided both are fertile, but since it is a adopted in case of only impotency, it is relatively insignificant and has been only moderately successful.

When the husband is sterile, any third person's sperm is utilized for Insemination. There can be unwillingness to have a child by natural means, when medical history of any of the spouses has a hereditary disease, or when R.H. factor of the spouses are incompatible, or where there is history of insanity in any of the spouses. In all these cases also third person's sperms are utilized. But generally male's sterility is the most prevalent condition resulting in the inability to have children which prompts artificial insemination with the third person's sperm. Approximately ninety percent of the inseminations are done due to the husband's sterility.

Procreation is a natural aspiration of every human being. The advancement in science and technology has not only enabled mankind to restrict and control birth rate by the use of contraceptives but has also enabled childless couples to become parents through the device of artificial insemination, i.e., transmission of male seeds into the female body artificially through a syringe.

The history of artificial insemination can be traced back to 1322 when mares were successfully breeded by the Arabs. The superior mares of the enemies were artificially impregnated by the sperm of inferior horses to weaken them. From this time

1. There are Sperm Banks and Recognized Centers and Doctors are there to perform the Insemination.

onward, until the middle of the sixteenth century, successful experiments were made on fish and other animals.

There was a lady who was the wife of a merchant and infertility patient of Dr. William Pancoast. She was a woman whose name was never recorded. Dr. Pancoast, a professor at Jefferson medical college in Philadelphia, had already examined and tested her numerous times. Finally, he discovered that she was fertile and that the problem was her husband's; there were no sperm. Pancoast (or may be it was one of his students) had an idea. He called her in. He just wanted to examine her once more, he told her.

The woman lay on the table as she had been told to do. Pancoast's six medical student—all young men—stood around her body. Pancoast anesthetized the woman with chloroform. He took the receptacle into which one of his students had masturbated. With a hard rubber syringe, he inserted the student's semen into her uterus. He them plugged her cervix with gauze.

When she awoke; he did not tell her what he had done. He never told her. Nine months later, she bore a son in the year 1884. This was the first reported human artificial insemination with donor semen. It was a rape.

The first successful artificial insemination of a human being is credited to Dr. John Hunter, an English physician, who used this device upon a married woman using her husband's semen, in the late eighteenth century. In 1890, Dr. Robert L. Dickinson established the practice of artificial insemination using a donor's semen. However, it was not until the twentieth century that recourse was had to artificial insemination for the purpose of procreation.[2]

Today, artificial insemination is practiced in clinics or in the woman's home. It is done with some success on a do-it-yourself basis, and the chances of conception are reasonable with several cycles of insemination. For better or worse, semen is freely available for purchase in many cities.

---

2. Hager, John W., "Artificial Insemination: Some Practical Considerations for Effective Counseling, 39, *North Carolina Law Review,* 217 at pp. 219-20 (1960-61).

Many people think of artificial insemination as a modern technology but it has a long history. Thus, apparently artificial insemination was attempted on Juana, wife of King Henry IV of Castile. In 1677 the Dutch scientist Anton van Leeuwenhoek saw spermatozoa through the newly invented microscope. Efforts to develop practical methods for artificial insemination were started in Russia in 1899. Papers on artificial insemination in horses had been published by 1922.

By the mid 1940's artificial insemination had become an established industry. In 1949 improved methods of freezing and thawing sperm were developed. The idea for adding antibiotics to the sperm solution came in 1950 from Cornell. Improved methods of sperm collection were developed in the 1970's and 1980's. Research to improve methods of artificial insemination continues and is usually studied under animal science curriculums.

In the past, couples who were unable to have children had to accept their childless state or adopt a child. Since adoption did not always satisfy the desire of parents to have their own child medical science for centuries has aimed at identifying the causes of infertility and at providing remedies.

(b) Meaning and Definition of Artificial Insemination

- Artificial Insemination is a relatively simple medical procedure by which semen obtained by masturbation is deposited by means of a syringe in or near the cervix of the woman's uterus. It is an introduction of semen into the vagina or cervix of a female by any method other than sexual intercourse. The procedure has become widely used in animal breeding and for the impregnation of women whose husbands are sterile or impotent.
- Artificial Insemination is a technique to impregnate women. Who are physically capable to conceiving and bearing a child but who cannot do so through sexual intercourse, usually because their husband is sterile or impotent? Fresh semen is obtained from the husband (if he is impotent) or forms some other male donor (if the husband is sterile) and is introduced by

a syringe into the woman's vagina or cervix during the middle of her menstrual cycle.

- Artificial Insemination is solution where the reason for the child lessness is the man's infertility or his inability to deposit semen into the vagina. Artificial insemination (AI) may be defined as the deposition of semen in the vagina the cervical canal, or the uterus by instruments to bring about pregnancy which is not attained or is unattainable by sexual intercourse.

(c) Kinds of Artificial Insemination

Artificial insemination can be practiced in three ways.

First is the artificial insemination homologous or husband (AIH), where the semen injected into the female body is that of her husband. This is resorted to when some weakness due to physical or psychological reasons prevents copulation or when the husband or wife is impotent (not sterile).

In the second type, semen is that of the third party donor and is known as artificial insemination donor (AID). This is resorted to normally, when the husband is sterile or suffering from some hereditary disease, etc. The third kind of artificial insemination, which is not very popular, is one in which the seed of the husband and that of a third party is co-mingled. This is known as confused or combination artificial insemination (CAI).

1. Artificial Insemination by Husband (AIH)

Artificial insemination by husband is used when the husband can produce semen, but his semen is not quite adequate to achieve fertilization. The inadequacy of semen can be attributed to low number of active sperms or the inability of sperms to swim fast enough towards the ovum. Artificial insemination by husband can also be used when the husband is suffering from premature, etc.

In artificial insemination by husband, the sperm is obtained from the husband by his masturbation and is then concentrated and 'improved' in the laboratory. This semen is then introduced into the wife's cervix at the best fertile days. The semen is introduced by an injection. Depending on the regulations of each institute, the injection can be carried out by a doctor or a nurse, or by the couple themselves.

As far as the law is concerned, there is no problem in the Artificial Insemination by Husband as it is done between lawfully wedded couples. Masturbation is forbidden, then how can the husband's semen be obtained for artificial insemination by husband? It is true that masturbation is forbidden in religion, but that masturbation by one's spouse is permissible. Therefore, in case of artificial insemination by husband, the wife can masturbate the husband in order to obtain the semen. It will be interesting to know how the Roman Catholics intend to solve this problem. The Roman Catholic Church does permit artificial insemination if the husband's semen is used and is the product of intercourse with his wife, not masturbation, but this usually involves intercourse in a doctor's office and is 'hardly romantic,' Father Wolak said.[3]

An artificial insemination by husband child raises no question of surrogate parenthood being a product of its own parent's seeds. It can be regarded as legitimate, and process of impregnation both justifiable and unobjectionable. In the case of artificial insemination by donor, fertilization takes place inside the woman's body with two possible variations. An artificial insemination by donor, child is, thus, genetically linked to a parent outside its own family.

Earlier, a popular form of artificial insemination was, artificial insemination combined, in which the sperm of the husband and a donor were mixed. The advantage of this procedure was that it could not be conclusively stated that the husband was not the father of the child. This was important in an age where artificial insemination was considered to be immoral and tantamount to adultery, with the resulting child being considered as illegitimate and having no inheritance rights. With the acceptance of artificial insemination in society, the popularity of AIC diminished.

2. *Artificial Insemination by Donor (AID)*

Because of the difficulty in treating many forms of male infertility and the limited success with artificial insemination

3. *The Vancouver Sun* (March 11, 1987), p. A7.

by husband, the majority of infertile couples with a significant and non-responsive male factor must eventually consider artificial couples with a significant and non-responsive male factor must eventually consider artificial do not insemination as an option. The involvement of a do not creates another dimension in the fertility pictures and some couples are not able to make this leap. Even though the donor will always be anonymous, these couples are not being able to accept the intrusion of an extramarital element into their marriage.

There may be social and religious considerations that prevent Artificial Insemination by Donor. There are always questions about the legal implications of Artificial Insemination by Donor legitimacy, adoption, and birth certificate. Whether or not a couple decides to proceed with Artificial Insemination by Donor there must be ample time available to counsel and support the couple faced with absolute male factor infertility. Their anxiety must be minimized and their confidence maximized if donor insemination is to achieve a successful conclusion.

Artificial Insemination by Donor is very similar to artificial insemination by husband. However, Artificial Insemination by Donor is used in cases where the husband's semen is definitely inadequate in quantity or quality. In the Western society, some single women who wish to remain unmarried but have a child also use this method to become pregnant. In England, two to four thousand births in a year are attributed to Artificial Insemination by Donor. As far as Islam is concerned, Artificial Insemination by Donor is absolutely forbidden because it is by a donor and not by the woman's husband.

The Quran clearly says, "Say to the believing women that they . . . should guard their private parts". (24:30) The divine command to guard the private parts is unqualified; it does not say that guard only from illicit sexual intercourse; it says that guard from everything except from your spouse. Allah describes the believers as "those who protect their private parts except from their spouses. . . . Therefore, whosoever seeks more beyond that, and then they are the transgressors". (23:5) Therefore, even injecting the sperm of another man would constitute a transgression and a violation of the command of Allah.

Let us examine the status of a child conceived by Artificial Insemination by Donor from religious point of view with specific reference to Islam. If, God forbid, a woman conceives a child through Artificial Insemination by Donor, then the child will not be considered an illegitimate child because he was not conceived through illicit sexual relations. Child-mother relationship is clear in such cases; as for the child-father relationship, most of our present *'ulama* clearly state that he will be considered the child of the donor the child will inherit him, be a *mahram* to his wife and children.

This decision of the mujtahids is based on a hadith which provides an example very similar to the case of a child conceived by Artificial Insemination by Donor. This hadith has been narrated by various sources from Imam Hasan, Imam Muhammad al-Baqir and Imam Ja'far as-Sadiq (peace be upon them all).

A question was put to the Imams that if a woman had intercourse with her husband, and then immediately she goes to her slave-girl and has lesbian relations with her in which semen of the husband flows from the woman into the vagina of the slave-girl and makes her pregnant. What happens in this case? The Imams, after explaining the punishment which has to be imposed upon the two women, say that the child born from the slave-girl will be related to, and given in the custody of, the owner of the semen.

(d) Success Rate of Artificial Insemination

Success raters depend on woman and her partner's fertility problem and your age. Most couples who turn to U have a 5 to 25 percent chance of becoming pregnant with each cycle. Your chances will be closer to 25 percent as you take family drugs in conjunction with the procedure.

(e) Purpose of Artificial Insemination

- Right to men and women of marriageable age to marry and to found a family.

- The right of respect for one's privacy and family life.
- Afford explicit protection by society and the state to the family, which is conceived as the "natural and fundamental group unit of society".
- Carvel, inhuman or degrading treatment is prohibited.
- Surrogacy arrangements to a slavery like practice as prohibited.

(f) Procedure of Artificial Insemination

To improve odds of becoming pregnant a doctor will probably administer a fertility drug while undergoing artificial insemination. Taking the drug near the beginning of menstrual cycle to stimulate oversees to develop several mature eggs for fertilization, because normally a woman releases only one egg a month.

The woman may use an ovulation detection kit or doctor may perform an ultrasound to detect ovulation and time insemination. Once ovulation, partner will produce a sperm sample, which will then be "washed" a process that concentrates the hardiest sperm into a small amount of fluid. Using a catheter, a doctor will put the concentrated sperm directly into uterus and then there can be a pregnancy test about two weeks later.

(B) Challenges Regarding Artificial Insemination

In India there is no legislation regarding reproductive technology except organ transplantation. But the doctor has to follow general principal of law. For instance a child born as a result of artificial insemination is considered as legitimate, provided the child was born during lawful wedlock. Conception of the wife by AI does not amount to consummation of marriage; if there was no successful sexual act due to the impotence of the husband. The marriage can be declared null and void and in that case the child will illegitimate. "AI" does not amount to adultery, even if it was done without the consent of the husband. For adultery to be committed both the parties should be physically present and engage in sexual act and sexual union should take place. AI is not equivalent to sexual intercourse.[4] AI does not contravene ethical principles of medical practice.

An AI child is practically divorced from the spiritual, mental emotional and physical lives of the adoptive parents thus, besides the question of morality and human values involved in it, AI could give rise to the socio-legal issues listed below:

(a) Before or After Delivery

Does AI amount to consummation of marriage or adultery? Can the non-consenting spouse claim divorce, on the ground of adultery or non-consummation of marriage? Can the stranger donor of the male or female seed, claim to be the spouse of the accepting donee?

(b) Post-Delivery

Is the child of AI, a legitimate child? If so, to whom is the paternity or maternity of the child to be attributed? Is the woman's non-consenting husband liable to maintain such a child as its father? What are the custodial or visitation rights of a surrogate father or mother? What would be the nature of relation of the AI child with a natural or adopted child of the same family? Would the rule of prohibited degrees be operative on a child of AI? If so when, how and with whom? How and from whom the child of AI would be entitled to inherit? Can it also be subject to rules of inheritance *vis-a-vis* consenting or not consenting relatives?

Artificial insemination is the oldest artificial technique, whilst AIH involves the traditional three dimensional process of reproduction. AID introduces an external made agent in the role of a donor. It raises questions as to determination of paternity, matrimonial rights, and the choice making capacity of the woman, psychological and moral issues.

So long as the process of AID involves the consent of the husband and non-assertion of parental right by the donor, the artificially inseminated woman can blissfully enjoy her motherhood. Absence of husband's consent raises questions

---

4. AIR 373-1984.

such as whether the woman is guilty of adultery or in the alternative matrimonial cruelty.

A conference or two with the couple contemplating AID should be a prerequisite any donor insemination program.[5] It takes time to explain the details of the process, the medical-legal considerations, the problems, and the potential for success. There is always concern about the selection of the donor, the confidentiality of the process, and the status of the AID child.

At the conclusion of the interview, a consent form must be signed by physician, husband, and wife. The document allows the physician to perform the procedure, absolves the physician and/or hospital from responsibility for any resultant congenital deformity, and requires the husband to recognize any child conceived by AID as his own, with full inheritance and support rights.

In addition to being concerned with the donor selection process, the couple considering AID may wonder about such things as the birth certificate, legitimacy, and the advisability of adoption in an AID pregnancy.[6] There are understandably no legal problems associated with AIH because it is accomplished with the consent of both husband and wife and involves no extramarital factor. Donor insemination is a different story because the social father may not be the biological father. This fact raises a question that often couples a great deal of anxiety.

1. Adultery

It is both ethically and legally wrong to brand the compelling urge of a woman to be a mother as amounting to adultery more so because AI does not involve actual sexual intercourse. Thus, by no stretch of imagination could a women's individual choice of reproduction be considered as an act of adultery. However, in the matrimonial context, the rights of the spouses are not individualistic in their nature. So, owing to the psychological impact and the matrimonial expectations

5. Beck, W.W., A Critical Look at the Legal, Ethical and Technical aspects of Artificial Insemination. *Fertile Sterile*, 27:1, 1976.
6. Rosenberg, A.H., Legal Aspects of Artificial Insemination, *N. Engl. J. Med.*, 278:552, 1968.

of the husband whose wife is artificially inseminated without his consent, the act of Al can be treated as amounting to matrimonial cruelty. However, law has to make a distinction between withholding of consent and withdrawal of consent. The former may be made a ground for matrimonial relief. If there is withdrawal of consent subsequent to Al, the husband should be stopped from pleading his lack of choice as a ground of matrimonial relief.

The word adultery has been derived from the Latin term adulterate which according to Harper's Latin dictionary means, 'to defile' to counterfeit 'to adulterate'. Introduction of something spurious is adulteration. Since AID has the potentiality of introducing into the husband's family a 'spurious' child, it has been argued by some that it (AID) amounts to adultery. The question that arises is, what constitutes adultery? Is sexual intercourse a necessary ingredient of adultery? What constitutes sexual intercourse? Is penetration a necessary ingredient? And so on.

The ancient Indian law-givers recognized three degrees of adultery. A man meeting a woman in a lonely place at an improper time taking to her, casting amorous glances, smiling at her, are examples of adultery of the first degree. Sending messages to a woman, touching her ornament or clothes also constitute adultery of the first degree according to Vyasa. Sending perfumes, garlands, fruits, wines, food or clothes and conversing with her in secrecy is adultery of the second degree.

Sitting on the same bed, dallying, kissing and embracing, this is adultery of the highest degree.[7] These, however, are outmoded concepts and modern definitions require sexual intercourse between two persons of the opposite sex, at least one of whom is married, as a necessary ingredient of adultery.

(a) Indian Penal Code

The Indian Penal Code defines the adultery as whoever has sexual intercourse with a person who is and whom he knows or has reason to believe to be the wife of another man, with-out the consent or connivance of that man, such sexual

7. Jha, Ganganath, 1, Hindu Law and its Sources, Chapter XVIII.

intercourse not amounting to the offence of rape, is guilty of the offence of adultery. . .[8]

Thus, the essential ingredients of adultery are:

- The accused must have sexual intercourse with a woman.
- That woman must be the wife of another person.
- The accused must have known or should have reason to believe that the other party was the wife of another person.
- The sexual intercourse should not amount to rape.
- The act must have been performed without the consent or connivance of the husband.[9]

Sexual intercourse thus is a necessary ingredient of the offence of adultery. Even under the Hindu Marriage Act, 1955, in the absence of any special definition, "adultery means consensual sexual intercourse between married person and another person of the opposite sex during the subsistence of the marriage".[10]

What constitutes sexual intercourse is another question. Under the explanation to section 375 of the Indian Penal Code, which defines rape, mere penetration is sufficient to constitute the sexual intercourse necessary to the offence of rape. The same test may be applied in the case of adultery as well. There have been, however, cases under the English law where, even in the absence of an act of sexual intercourse, a verdict of adultery was given.

In *Rutherford* v. *Richardson*[11] and *Russell* v. *Russell*[12] adultery was said to have been committed even though there was no penetration but "some lesser act of sexual gratification". In *Sapsford* v. *Sapsford and Furtado*[13] the court recognized that

8. S. 497 of The Indian Penal Code, 1860.
9. *Ibid*.
10. Gitabai *v.* Fattoo, A.I.R. 1966 M.P. 130.
11. (1923) A.C. 1.
12. [1924] A.C. 687.
13. [1954] 2 All E.R. 373.

voluntary submission to or participation in intimate physical contact may be inconsistent with the duties of a wife towards her husband. Karminiski, J.,[14] stated:

> "I have no doubt that, if whole penetration was not achieved, some lesser act of sexual intercourse was performed", and granted a divorce on proof of such act. Though these cases had nothing to do with artificial insemination, yet the effect is the demolition of the concept of sexual intercourse with penetration as an ingredient of adultery".

The Indian position, however, continues unchanged and penetration whatever the extent, irrespective of ejaculation is a necessary ingredient. In *W.J. Phillips* v. *Emperor*[15] the court held that "sexual intercourse is a necessary ingredient of the offence under S. 497, I.P.C. Nothing short of it would justify a conviction under that section".[16] Similarly, *In re* Anthony[17] where a boy of fifteen years, the court held that "while there must be penetration in the technical sense, the slightest penetration would be sufficient, and a completed act of sexual intercourse is not at all necessary".[18]

The issue whether artificial insemination amounts to adultery was raised for the first time in a Canadian court in *Orford* v. *Orford*.[19] The marriage was not consummated because of some physical affliction of the wife. The wife, however, gave birth to a child.

The husband accused the wife of adultery, while he stayed in Canada and she was in England. According to the wife, she had resorted to artificial insemination as the doctors had advised her that the only way she could be cured of the affliction was by bearing a child and that it might be done artificially. The court disbelieved the story and came to the

14. *Id*. at page 375.
15. A.I.R. 1939 Oudh 506.
16. *Id*. at p. 509.
17. A.I.R. 1960 Mad. 308.
18. *Id*. at p. 311, per Anantanarayanan, J.
19. 58 D.L.R. 251 (1921); 49 Ontario L.R. 15.

finding that the wife had sexual intercourse in the ordinary way. It, however, dealt with the aspect of artificial insemination also and observed:

> That no authority can be found declaring, directly or indirectly, that "artificial insemination" would constitute adultery is not be a wondered at. This is probably the first time in history that such a suggestion has been put forward in a Court of justice. But can anyone read the Mosaic law against those sins, which, whether of adultery or otherwise, in any way effect the sanctity of the reproductive functions of the people of Israel, without being convinced that, had such a thing as "artificial insemination" entered the mind of the lawgiver, it would have been regarded with the utmost horror and detestation as an invasion of the most sacred of the marital rights of husband and wife, and have been the subject of severest penalties?[20]

The essence of the offence of adultery consists, not in the moral turpitude of the act of sexual intercourse, but in the voluntary surrender to another person of the reproductive powers or faculties of the guilty person; and any submission of these powers to the service or enjoyment of any person other than the husband or the wife comes within the definition of "adultery". . . . So long as nothing takes place which can by any possibility affect that function, there can be no adultery; so that, unless and until there is actual sexual intercourse, there can be no adultery.

But to argue, from that, that adultery necessarily begins and ends are utterly fallacious. Sexual intercourse is adulterous because in the case of the woman it involves the possibility of introducing into the family of the husband a false strain of blood. Any act on the part of the wife which does that would, therefore, be adulterous. That such a thing could be accomplished in any other than the natural manner probably

20. *Id.* at pp. 257-58.

never entered the heads of those who considered the question before.[21]

The question whether AID amounted to adultery or not was discussed at length in the House of Lords during its debates in March 1949.[22] "Adultery", according to the Lord Archbishop of Canterbury.

Is the surrender outside the bonds of wedlock, and in violation of it, either of the sexual organs alone . . . or of the reproductive organs alone by A.I.D. or, of course, of both, as in normal intercourse. If that be so, A.I.D. is adultery.

Lord Merriman,[23] however, was of the view that penetration of the female sexual organ was an essential element to constitute adultery. According to him Lord Dunedin in his dictum in *Russell* v. *Russell*[24] used the phrase fecundation ab extra which had nothing to do with artificial insemination. Besides, according to Lord Merriman, AI does not involve the act of sexual intercourse at all and hence no adultery. A penetrating study was made by Tallin who, in an article,[25] argued that AID is adultery.

Sexual intercourse without risk of pregnancy, and risk of pregnancy without sexual intercourse, may be equally destructive of a happy marriage relationship, and it may therefore be that either would constitute adultery. . . .[26] Refuting Tallin's contention that AI constitutes adultery, Hubbard, in his article,[27] points out that the act of sexual intercourse requires the mutual co-operation of a man and a woman acting together at the same time. Their mutual activity constitutes a single act of intercourse. An act must be localized in time. . . . When can the act of "sexual intercourse" be said to have occurred in artificial insemination?[28]

21. *Id*. at p. 258.
22. Parliamentary Debates (Lords) 404 (1948-49).
23. *Id*. at p. 412.
24. [1924] A.C. 687.
25. Tallin, G.P.R., Artificial Insemination, 34, *The Canadian Bar Review* (1956).
26. *Id*. at p. 22.
27. Hubbard, H.A., "Artificial Insemination: A Reply to Dean Tallin", 34, *The Canadian Bar Review*, 425 (1956).
28. *Ibid*.

The act . . . cannot rationally be said to have commenced with the ejaculation of the semen and subsisted qua act until the insemination took place. This would not be one act but two separate acts. The donor and the ultimate recipient of his seed cannot be said to have acted together at the same time in their act . . . if the activity is discontinued the act ceases.

In artificial insemination the act of obtaining the seed is quite distinct from the act of artificial insemination. If a man manufactures a bullet knowing that it will be fired into something, he cannot be said to have pulled the trigger of the weapon and fired the bullet home simply because but for him there would be no bullet.[29]

In the practical affairs of life with which courts have to deal it may only be necessary to say that an act began not later than a certain moment and ended not later than another certain moment. An act of murder may be held to have begun not later than the purchase by the murderer of the poison and ended not later than the moment the victim was pronounced dead by the doctor.

It is not necessary, in order to find that murder or an act of murder has been committed, to say that it took place when the poison was put in the victim's coffee or when he drank it, or when he died. . . . Each had a beginning, duration and ending which might defy definition.[30] According to Tallin, it would be equally impossible to determine the time of sexual intercourse because of the various processes involved in it.

The question came up for consideration comparatively recently in the Scottish Court of Session at Edinburgh in *Maclennan* v. *Maclennan*.[31] The husband field a petition for divorce on the ground of his wife's adultery.

The wife alleged that the child she gave birth to was conceived by artificial insemination. The husband contended that AID was adultery in the eye of law and also that he did not consent to his wife's impregnation. The court, however, conceded that a married contract by submitting to artificial

29. *Id*. at p. 433.
30. *Id*. at p. 629.
31. Klayman, E.I., (1958) Sess. Cas 105, Therapeutic Impregnation, 39, *Cincinnati Law Review*, 291 at 310 (1970).

insemination without her husband's consent, nevertheless, this, according to the court, was a matter in respect of which the legislature should determine an appropriate remedy.

It was considered to be quite irrelevant to the issue before the court. In a preliminary judgment, the court held that AID would not constitute adultery in law but adjourned the case for verification of AID by the wife. The wife declined to provide the necessary information and the court held that she had committed adultery. After considering a few English cases,[32] the court derived the following propositions, viz:

- For adultery to be committed there must be two parties physically present and engaging in the sexual act at the same time.
- To constitute the sexual act there must be an act of union involving some degree of penetration of the female organ by the male organ.
- It is not a necessary concomitant of adultery that male seed should be deposited in the female's ovum.
- The placing of the male seed in the female ovum need not necessarily result from the sexual act, and if it does not, but is placed there by another means, there is no sexual intercourse.

The court also considered that if AID were deemed to be adultery, the question would arise whether the donor whose seed has been used is also guilty of adultery. If that be so, at what point of time adultery is committed?

If adultery is deemed to take place at the time of the parting of the seed then, suppose the seed is never used? If the crucial time is the time when the seed is injected into the woman's body, then suppose, this is done after the donor's death?

The decision of Lord Wheatly in the above case was the subject of debate in the House of Lords in February 1958[33] as a

32. Russell *v.* Russell, [1924] A.C. 687; Rutherford *v.* Richardson (1923) AC 1; Sapsford *v.* Sapsford, [1954] 2 All E.R. 373.; Dennis *v.* Dennis, (1955) probate Division 153; R.E.L. *v.* L., (1949) Probate Division 211; Clarke *v.* Clarke, (1943) 2 ALL E.R. 540.
33. 207 parliamentary Debates (Lords) 926-1016 (1957-58).

result of which a department committee was appointed in September to enquire whether, and if so, what changes in the law were necessary, in view of this practice. The committee expressed the view that a clear distinction be drawn between artificial insemination and adultery. It endorsed the view of the Royal commission on Marriage and Divorce 1951-55 that artificial insemination of the wife without the consent of her husband be made a new and separate ground of divorce or judicial separation. It may be pointed out here that from a physician's point of view also the two, viz., adultery and artificial insemination are different.

The object of an adulterous act is carnal pleasure and emotional and physical satisfaction. These are missing in artificial insemination which is resorted to for the purpose of begetting offspring. In fact, they are antithesis of each other. Whereas in artificial insemination the only purpose is procreation, i.e., it is not a sexual but a professional and therapeutic act, in adultery it is sensual pleasure alone and if pregnancy results, it is normally unsolicited.

The reason why adultery has been made an offence or a ground for divorce appears to be the risk of pregnancy involved in the act. Besides, it disturbs marital peace and is an invasion for the right of a souse to have exclusive sexual pleasure from the other. The Indian law, as stated above, when it talks of merely penetration (without ejaculation) does not confine adultery to a situation which might lead to conception. However, in the present context, suffice it is to note that carnal knowledge with the risk of pregnancy will certainly constitute adultery, though risk of pregnancy alone cannot be the basis of adultery.

In the present day scientific development when resort to contraceptive devices and sterilizations are increasingly common and popular, the risk of pregnancy is greatly diminished or eliminated even in a complete normal sexual act. In artificial insemination the basic question is whether lack of carnal knowledge in the actuality of conception or introduction of a foreign element with a view to conception would amount to adultery or not. It seems that in the absence of this element, the answer should be in the negative.

One argument that is often given in support of AID is that by the use of this method, the marriage bond is violated voluntarily, for a good reason, by the consent and wish of the husband and wife concerned. A childless marriage often causes severe psychological disturbances bringing in its wake, strain, stress and rupture. Artificial insemination if successful comes to the rescue of the couple. Its opponents, however, argue that instead of solving the difficulties, AID might create more problems.

Husband often has a great longing to have children, and sometimes his longing is frustrated by the sterility of his wife. No one has yet suggested that he should relieve his frustrations by introducing into his family a child whom he as fathered by A.I.D. or otherwise by another woman. He has to bear his frustration, and so can a wife.[34]

If difficulties and jealousies arise in their married life these will surely be complicated and aggravated by the father's knowledge that the child of the marriage is not his at all. It is not to be supposed that every marriage will be delivered from all frictions from the fact that A.I.D. has been employed and the intruded child may easily become a source of recrimination.

It is the fundamental principal of Christian belief that God is Love and our common Father, from which belief springs the dignity of human personality. This requires its correlative principle that children should be born of love of their parents. In A.I.D. the purely material and mechanical element in procreation is separated, and not temporarily but absolutely separated, from the organic and personal lives of the two persons involved. . .

2. *Legitimacy and Custody of the Child*

Another controversial issue that an AID child poses is whether such a child is the legitimate child of the father and as to the father's right and duties *vis-a-vis* the child. So for as the legitimacy of the child is concerned, modern courts in many countries consider Al children as legitimate. Equity demands that the AI child whose right to birth is not determined by his

34. Parliamentary Debates (Lords) at pp. 406-07 (1948-49).

own individual choice should never be considered as illegitimate.

To avoid unwanted complications, it is quite desirable that the donor should be not more than a donor simpliciter without awarding any parental rights or obligations to him. In view of the possible psychological impact of AID on infertile couple, the donor and the child, it is highly essential that the law should not even grant visitation rights.

The legitimacy issue in AID has sporadically found its way into the courts because of divorce proceedings that involve child support and/or inheritance. Happily, this is rare thanks to the solidarity of AID couples. With the national divorce rate approaching 40 percent, less than 1 percent of AID couples experience irreconcilable marital problems. On occasion, however, a husband has left and rejected responsibility for the AID child, claiming that it was not his child. Court rulings in the United States have generally supported the AID child.

The highest ruling was made by the Supreme Court in California in 1968 and stated that there is no question about the legitimacy of an AID child providing that there has been voluntary involvement and an informed written consent on the part of both husband and wife. Since that time, a number of states have passed statutes that legalize the insemination process and assure the legitimacy of the child conceived by AID.

In *Strnad* v. *Strnad*,[35] the question of custody of AID child was considered by the New York Supreme Court. It was held that the husband had a right of visitation although the child was not his offspring biologically. The court observed:

> The child has been potentially adopted or semi-adopted by the defendant. In any event in so far as this defendant is concerned, and with particular reference to visitation, he is entitled to the same rights as those acquired by a foster parent who has formally adopted a child, if not the same rights as those to which a natural parent under the

35. 78 N.Y.S. 2d 390 (1948); The case has been referred to in 21, *Modern Law Review*, 236 at 240 (1958).

circumstances would be entitled. . . . In the opinion of this court the child was an illegitimate child.[36]

In *Doornbas* v. *Doornbas*,[37] however, the court took a different view. It held that AID was adultery and contrary to public policy and that the child born through this process was illegitimate. It further ruled that although the husband had consented to artificial donor insemination of his wife, yet he had no visitation rights to the child. The court said:

Heterologous artificial insemination (when the specimen of semen used is obtained from a third party or donor), with or without the consent of the husband, is contrary to public policy and good morals, and constitute adultery on the part of the mother. A child so conceived is not a child born in wedlock and therefore illegitimate. And as such it is the child of the mother and the father (sic) has no right or interest in said child.[38]

In a later case, *Gursky* v. *Gursky*[39] again, the New York Supreme Court found that a child born through AID is not a legitimate child of the husband. In this case, the wife, defendant in her husband's unsuccessful action for annulment, counterclaimed for an annulment of the marriage for impotency of her husband and for custody of and support for a child born through artificial insemination with semen from a third party donor. The husband had given his written consent for the insemination, nevertheless, the court granting annulment refused to recognise the child as husband's legitimate child.

The effect of the written agreement by the husband, however, was that he was bound to support the child. Similarly in *Anonymous* v. *Anonymous*[40] a husband had consented to his

---

36. Bartholomew, G.W, "Legal Implications of Artificial Insemination", 21, *Modern Law Review,* 236 at 240 (1958).
37. *Time,* December 27, 1954, p. 41, the case has been reviewed in 41, A.B.AJ. 263 (1955); see also 23 U.S.L.W. 2308.
38. 41 A.B.A.J. 263 (1955).
39. 39 Misc. 2d 1083; 242 N.Y.S. 2d 406 (Sup. Ct. 1963). See also, 39, *Cincinnati Law Review,* 291 at p. 311 (1970).
40. 41 Misc. 2d 886; 246 N. Y.S. 2d 835 (Sup.Ct. 1964), referred to in 39, *Cincinnati Law Review,* 291 at p. 316. (1970).

wife's therapeutic impregnation .in a claim by the wife for alimony the husband asserted that such a child was illegitimate. The court refused to accept this argument and awarding alimony held "that the written consent carried an implied promise to furnish support for the resulting progeny

In *People* v. *Sorensen*[41] a divorced woman sued her former husband for non-support of their AID son. In this case, the defendant had consented, after fifteen years of marriage and a medical determination of his sterility, to allow his wife to be artificially inseminated. AID was administered and a child was born. For about four years prior to their separation the defendant represented that he was the child's father. The California Supreme Court held that the defendant was the lawful father of the child born to his former wife, that the child was conceived by artificial insemination to which the defendant had consented, and that his conduct carried with it an obligation to support.

Thus, we find that there is no unanimity on the point and there are conflicting and contradictory decisions. The author, however, feels that innocent children should no be made to suffer the stigma of illegitimacy. A father who consents to the wife being so impregnated or holds such a child as his own should be treated as the real father of the child and the Sorensen decision lends support to this point of view. In case of insemination without consent, the father should not be burdened with the liability to maintain the child. It is necessary that formal written consent should be made obligatory in order to avoid a controversial situation.

3. *Consumation*

Another legal issue that stems from the practice of AID is whether AID is tantamount to consummation of marriage, in a case when a wife resorts to AID (whether it is successful or not is a separate issue) and later seeks to avoid the marriage on the ground of non-consummation or impotency of the husband? According to Lord Archbishop of Canterbury, "in marriage, mutual surrender either of the sexual organs without

41. 68 Cal. 2d 280; cited by B.J. Davies, Family Law Recent cases, 23, Buffalo Law Review, 548 at 550 (1973-74).

procreation or of the reproductive organs by means of A.I.H. is to be regarded, in my view, as consummation".

In one of the cases, a wife whose husband was unable to consummate the marriage because of psychological infirmity was artificially inseminated with her husband's seed. This process spread over a period of twelve months. A few weeks after an insemination, the wife, unaware that she was pregnant, left the husband. The child was subsequently born. The wife filed a suit for nullity of the marriage.

The court held that the conduct of the wife in allowing herself to be artificially inseminated with her husband's seed and the conception of the child did not necessarily amount to an approbation of the marriage; nor was the court prevented on any ground of public policy from pronouncing a decree even though the result of that decree would be to bastardize the child. The court observed: "If the child should be made illegitimate it is most regrettable, but the stigma of birth are of less effect that they were, and sons are not judged by the errors of their parents".

The author, however, is unable to reconcile with this point of view. When both the parties had agreed to the insemination and especially when the seed is that of the husband there is no reason why the parties should not have been stopped to plea non-consummation. Besides, it is very unfair that a child who is in every manner legitimate being the biological offspring of both the parties and born within wedlock—should be labeled illegitimate by annulling such marriage on ground of non-consummation.

The issue whether artificial insemination amounted to consummation or not was raised against in *Slater* v. *Slater*.[42] In this case AID was resorted to but was unsuccessful and ultimately, a child was adopted. It was held that the attempted insemination could not constitute consummation and that the doctrine of approbation could not be applied to defeat the wife's claim despite the insemination and adoption.

However, it all depends on the circumstances of each case and nothing can be said categorically as to whether that act of artificial insemination—whether AID or AIH—would or would

42. (1953) Probate Division 235.

not amount to approbation of the marriage. By the very nature of the process of the device, in the absence of organic intercourse, it would be hard to believe that such a marriage is physically consummated, nevertheless, if such a marriage is easily liable to be annulled on the ground of non-consummation, then the very purpose and object of the insemination would be defeated, viz., the purpose of relieving the parties of the frustration of not bearing a child and removing a principle cause of disharmony in the family.

In a case where the husband consents and a child is born by this device, it is reasonable and logical to assume that the marriage has been consummated and neither the husband nor the wife should be allowed to plea non-consummation and get out of the wedlock. Difficulty, however, is bound to arise in cases where a wife gets inseminated without the consent of the husband. It appears that in such cases the wife's resort to AID should not deprive the husband of the plea of non-consummation of the marriage.

4. *Adoption*

The subject of adoption is a matter that most couples have not considered.[43] The advice by some to adopt an AID conceived child comes from the well-intended desire to prevent the child comes from having any inheritance or support problems in the future.

However the adoption procedure makes that AID pregnancy a matter of public record while the parents' main concern is confidentiality and anonymity. In light of the current legal thinking and the fact that almost one-third of the states have enacted statutes concerning AID, it does not appear that the status of an AID child is vulnerable; therefore, it would seem inappropriate at this time to recommend adoption and add the fear of disclosure to the couple's anxieties.

5. *Birth Certificate*

Almost every couple has a question concerning the birth certificate. They want to know whose name goes on the father's

43. Snowden, R. and Mitchell, G.D.: The Artificial Family, Allen and Unwin, Boston, 1981.

line. It has been suggested that physicians are perjuring themselves when they knowingly insert the husband's name on the certificate of a child conceived following AID. Because of this, the recommendation has been made that a woman pregnant by AID be sent to a new obstetrician who has no idea of the means of conception.

However, I know of no physician who has difficulty with the birth certificate in an AID pregnancy. Very few men are azoospermic; consequently, we often mix the donor's and husband's sperm. Even though it is highly unlikely, the pregnancy could, theoretically, be the husband's, it has happened with us a dozen times over the last 6 years. The bottom line is that the birth certificate is no problem. The husband's name is inserted as the name of the father. In fact, the purpose of birth certificates in some states is not to establish paternity, but rather to establish citizenship.

6. *Unmarried Couples and Lesbians*

AID makes the sexual intercourse separate from reproduction. This leads to the possibility of the use of AI techniques by nontraditional parties such as unmarried couple and lesbians giving scope for further complicated legal questions. Though in India such situations are rare, a legal specification allowing only the hetero-sexual couple to resort to AID would help as preventive measures in disallowing such deviant practices. Though such legal specification may be attacked on the ground of being violative of right to equality (Art. 14), such a measure can be justified on the ground that motherhood is not so much of a biological urge as a social response and hence falls under the purview of reasonable restrictions clause.

7. *Sperm Banks*

Another by-product of the new technology is the so-called sperm bank where sperms and fertilized ovum are preserved in frozen state.

The practice of AID has given rise to sperm banks in Western Countries with an unashamed commercialism, assuring an acceptable level of stable personality, intelligence and character, e.g. The repository for germinal choice uses insemination of sperm from Nobel Prize Winners to create exceptional babies (Zimmerman, 'Alternatives in Human Reproduction for involuntary children couples' (Family relations, 31 (April 1982) 234-36). Such blatant commercialism leads to undesirable results such as elimination of an unwanted race, risk of inbreeding within restricted pool and the loss of a great human value as manifested in the coping up capacity. Unhygienic and unscreened storage of sperm banks might also lead to health complications for the women resorting to AI.

8. *Frozen Embryos*

There are four questions which must be answered here. *Firstly*: Is man allowed to preserve his sperms in frozen state? Similarly, are married couples allowed to preserve their fertilized ova fo: future use? It is no different from the act in which a person banks or donates his blood. *Secondly:* Is it permissible to sell the sperms or the fertilized ova? One cannot sell his sperms to be injected into the uterus of another woman; he may only sell it to a scientific institution for medical research.

Similarly, a couple cannot sell their fertilized ova to be implanted into the womb of another woman. *Thirdly:* Can a woman use the preserved fertilized ovum or sperms of her husband after the latter has died? Apparently, there is nothing to prevent her from doing so. The frozen ovum (fertilized by her husband's sperm) is her property and therefore she can use it. The child will, of course, be legitimate.

However, this would be allowed only if the woman does not marry another person after her husband's death. Since most of the civilized societies do not allow a woman to have more than one husband at a time, the second husband will take the place of the first in the verse which says; protect their private parts except from their spouses.

Fourthly: Can a woman use the fertilized ovum after she has been divorced from her husband?

This is allowed only if she has not married another person. As soon as she marries another person, she cannot use the ovum fertilized with the sperm of her previous husband. The basis of this view is the same as mentioned above.

(c) Destroying the Extra Fertilized Ova

In most cases of artificial insemination, three ova are removed from the woman's body and all three are fertilized by the husband's sperms. But only one is used for reimplantation into the woman's womb. And if it fails in the first attempt, then the other fertilized ova are used. The question which has created much controversy is about the extra and unwanted fertilized ovum. What should be done with the extra fertilized ovum? Must it be used? Can it be destroyed?

It will not constitute abortion because, *firstly*, abortion only takes place after the implantation of the fertilized ovum in the womb and, *secondly*, abortion takes place in a woman's body not in a test-tube or a laboratory dish!

(d) How does A.I. Affect Men?

With regard to A.I., men participate most prominently by donating sperm. Men who provide the semen for donor insemination have been called donors by most authors, although other terms, such as vendor (for men who sell their semen) and consignor (for a man who hands over his semen as the rights to it) have been proposed. The majority of men who provide semen do so for monetary compensation, rather than out of altruism.

Sperm clinics compensate men for their services either by reimbursing them for travel expenses and the like. Sperm collectors find it beneficial to pay providers because the pecuniary incentive attracts a large number of younger men, increasing the variety and number of samples available to patrons. In general, sperm providers argue that payment is necessary to compensate for the physical and psychological strain provision.

Moreover society stigmatizes sperm donors, and men express the need for a monetary reward to comfort them in their period of psychological turmoil. This especially occurs with infertile married men who accompany their wives to fertility clinics. Most are consumed that he and the child will not share physical traits.

(e) Psychological and Social Considerations of AI

AID offers certain potential psychological benefits over the alternative adoption. Both husband and wife can be involved in the pregnancy from conception onward sharing the experience of delivery and the early days of the baby's life. There is a greater chance that the child's physical appearance will at least match that of the mother, and if there are several children they are more likely to resemble one another. There need be no sub-conscious fear of the sudden appearance of the natural mother, as there may be in adoption. And, of course the desire on the part of the mother to carry a child is satisfied as it cannot be in adoption.

However, AID also poses psychological dangers to the wife, the husband, and the child. In the more usual situation of procreation by husband and wife, the child can be understood to be the joint issue of both parents. Both husband and wife fulfil for the other the opportunity to become father and mother. Their love for one another can be strengthened and deepened as a consequence of this mutually shared experience.

(f) Psychological Danger to Husband

The husband, likewise, faces certain psychological danger. He may feel himself to be a stranger to the new life developing in his wife's womb. His masculinity may be threatened, not only by his infertility, but the sense of inadequacy in comparison to donor who made possible his wife's pregnancy. "AID thus threatens to evoke very deep seated feelings of helpless dependence in relationship to women and also feelings of inadequacy in relation to other man. The husband may psychologically withdraw from the home, investing his energy in his work or other forms of self-achievement by which he may hope to regain his sense of masculinity.

These psychological dangers for husband and wife also threatened the psychological development of the child. The child may become subtly aware of a family secret involving his or her father. If the psychological dangers for husband and wife materialize the child may find him or herself alienated from the father, creating another set of psychological difficulties for the child.

Closely aligned to this psychological danger is the matter of dealing with the child's genealogy. Like adoption in an earlier age, AID is usually maintained as a secret amount the parties involved. The doctor, the husband and wife, and the donor conspire together to deceive the child and society regarding the child's genetic identity:

> Several arguments can be offered in favor of disclosing his or her true 1 genealogy to the child. In the first place, the risk of accidental disclosure or 1 suspicion may cause parents to decide that forthrightly telling the child at an I appropriate age would contribute to a healthier relationship. This is similar to an argument for disclosure of adoption. It recognizes the fundamental importance of truth for basic human relationships.

(g) *Psychological Danger to Wife*

In the case of AID however, the situation can be very different. The wife may have a feeling of having being "cheated" by the discovery of the husband's infertility. The desire to procreate despite this discovery may become, in part, an act of revenge or hostility towards the sterile husband. If AID is successful, the wife may sense that the new life she bears within her has no relation to the love she has for her husband. She may, in fact may secretly years to meet the man who "helped" her when the husband could not.

(h) *Psychological Danger to Child*

An argument can also be made on the basis of the child's right to know his or her genealogical heritage. Experience with adopted children in recent years has shown the significance of this knowledge of genealogical heritage for child identity as child matures.

A final argument in favor of disclosure, and the kind of record-keeping that would make disclosure meaningful, is that knowledge of one's genealogical heritage may be crucial if the child suffers any genetic illness or needs a reliable family medical history. Moreover, genetic counseling at some point in the child's life—an increasingly useful tool in preventive medicine—can be critically skewed if the child does not know his or her parental genealogy or, what is more likely.

There are, of course, a number of arguments against disclosing either the fact of AID or the identity of the donor.

Some of these arguments pertain to the desire of maintaining healthy family relationships with the stigma of AID might disrupt. Disclosure might have a particularly devastating impact upon the acting father's sense of fatherhood.

Other arguments against disclosure are more concerned about protecting the anonymity of the donor. The case for donor anonymity is sometimes argued to protect the donor from legal involvement in legitimacy and inheritance rights and to encourage donors to participate.

It should be noted that a middle way exists, whereby records containing pertinent genetic information could be kept are made available to the child at an appropriate time and under appropriate circumstances, while not disclosing the identity of the donor. Such a procedure of course, would meet only some of the objections of those who argue the need for disclosure of the child's genealogical heritage.

Another social consideration closely related to the concern for genealogical or genetic heritage has to do with the possibly of unwitting incest between half-siblings. The concern is that AID children of some donor may fall in love and marry, considering the fact that semen from the same donor is used with women who live in the same geographic community and who may represent a rather homogeneous ethnic or social group, the possibility of incest, though small, is not farfetched.

Another issue of social significance in considering the practice of AID concerns the small but apparently growing numbers of unmarried women who I are seeking artificial insemination as a way of becoming mothers. One study indicated that at least 9.5 percent of the doctors responding had used AID for single women. The acceptance of "bachelor mother" appears to be a growing trend in our society. The issue becomes even more complex. Of course, when AID is used by lesbian couples and the resulting child grows up to discover that both his and her parents are female. Such developments clearly deal a serious blow to the child and to our accepted understanding of the family as the basic unit of our society.

Eugenic considerations—the attempt to influence the genetic quality of the human species by carefully selecting donors—pose other question beyond the scope of this paper.

(C) Artificial Insemination and Law in India

Though no popular as yet in India, the practice of artificial insemination is bound to attract the attention of medical practitioners and childless couples, and give rise to legal problems. So far the artificial insemination by husband (AIH) is concerned, legal problems are not significant. Legal issues are mostly related to artificial insemination by donor (AID). In every case of AID five persons are there: wife, husband, doctor, donor and the child. Rights and liabilities, if any are related to them only.

(a) Right to Artificial Insemination

If the spouses are agreed for Artificial Insemination, they can claim it as a matter of right. To ascertain the agreement of both of them, there should be sufficient procedural safeguards, e.g., both the spouses must apply to the doctor of the authorized centers showing their intention and agreement for AIH with sufficient proof that they are legally wedded couple and the marriage still subsists. The doctor must meet them, so as to ascertain their keenness to AIH and he should perform insemination on only after three months from the date of the application. In absence of such safeguards there can be chances of break-down of the marriage and detriment to the child.

If wife's solitary right for AIH is recognized, she can proceed without taking consent of the husband, or some time even against the wishes of the husband. No husband in such circumstances will like to continue any more with his wife. He may desert the wife or may search any reason for divorce, which will lead to proliferation of cases of either restitution of conjugal rights or maintenance or divorce.

The ultimate result will be divorce. Since none of the spouses can be forced to live as husband or wife, the AIH without the consent of the husband will have to be made a ground for divorce. To avoid all such complexities the Western Countries have provided facility of AIH only to married couples and on consent of both the spouses.

In United States, all the State Statutes (29 states have statutory law) sanction the use of AIH by married woman. Several of the statutes expressly limit it to the married women. Four of the states provide for situations in which AIH is such a way that they can be interpreted as disapproving it for unmarried women or leaving the question open.[44]

In U.K., the Warnock Committee 1984[45] and the Law Commission[46] recommend for prohibiting of AIH for unmarred or divorced or widow women. The socialist countries have statutory prohibition for it.[47]

The reason which can be appended for restricting the AIH only to married women may be: marriage institution, in the present set-up of the law and the society anywhere in the world is more important than right of a woman to have a child by any of the means. The child of an unmarried woman in all circumstances will be an illegitimate child.

By law legitimacy can be provided to him, but will be least social acceptance of it and the child will be deemed as illegitimate child and he will have to bear rigors of the society, because all the religions consider such a child as an illegitimate one. When both husband and wife are present, the child will not have psychological set-back, as he will have a father too. It will be easy to them (husband and wife) for rearing the child.

Moreover, in absence of the male partner, the woman alone will have to bear the expenses of the child; it will be uncalled for burden upon the donor of the sperm (genetic father).

We can, therefore, conclude, on the basis of the above discussion, that there is a growing trend to become unmarried mother, but there is no special acceptance of this phenomenon. The ID can be claimed as a matter of right even in absence of any special legislation, if we stretch the constitutional right of personal liberty to that extent. But the AID child of an unmarried mother will be illegitimate. Even, if legitimating is provided to him, he will have to suffer the social rigors.

---

44. Vetri Dominiah, "Reproductive Technologies and United States Law," (1988) 37, *International and Comparative Law Quarterly,* 512.
45. J.P. Alec Samuels, "Warnock Committee (Human Fertilization and Embryology)" (1984), *Medico-Legal Journal,* 174.
46. Working Paper, 74.
47. Haderka, J., "Artificial Reproduction in Czechoslovak Law with Special Reference to other European Socialist Countries," (1987), *Int. Journal of Law & the Family,* 74.

There is no statutory law in India for A.I. Legal problems may arise on the allied aspects of the procedure adopted for the purpose. To avoid possible problems certain procedural precautions are recommended which are:

- The donor should not have any physical, mental or hereditary disease which may be transmitted to the child.
- Consent of both husband and wife is necessary.
- Consent of the donor and his wife is also necessary.
- The donor should have his own child.
- The donor must not be a relative of either spouse.
- There should be parity of race, religion and as much as possible, the morphological appearance between the donor and the husband of the recipient woman.
- The identity of the donor must remain secret and the donor should not know to whom the semen is donated and the result of insemination.
- The donor should give in writing denying the parenthood claim for any child on the ground of donation of semen.
- A female attendance (witness) must be present during the process of insemination.
- Maintenance of strict confidentiality of all the records is a must.
- compatibility between the recipient and the donor should be tested.
- Though the procedural precaution is there to avoid undesirable circumstances, the legal problems can arise after the child's birth by A.I. The legal aspects are discussed below:

(b) Adultery and Artificial Insemination

The donor and recipient cannot be held guilty of adultery in India as Section 497 I.P.C. require sexual intercourse is necessary as part of adultery. This is also the concept of I.C.M.R. In a Canadian case of 1921, *Oxford* v. *Oxford*,[48] a woman was alleged in committing adultery because she

48. 49 Ontario Law report, 15.

constituted A.I. England when her husband was in Canada, the Court stated that such woman commits adultery but definite answer was not given to that. The Court described Adultery as "The Voluntary surrender to another person of the reproductive power of faculties of the guilty person".

In India one may not seek, divorce in the same case on the ground of adultery. But claim divorce on the ground AIH without consent of Husband, according I.C.M.R. Code.

In *Maclmnan* v. *Maclmnan*, where divorce was filed by the husband on the ground of adultery, Wife denied the same and said that the child was result of A.I.D. Here it was held that AIH did not constitute Adultery, because of absence of sexual act. The Court considered this to be self adultery and said that it was a concept not yet known to law.

Now a crucial question arises, Might rape be alleged if the procedure is performed by force of fraud upon on unwilling patient or person? Here one may argue because there is no ground of rape is present it cannot be rape. Here sexual act is absent but A.I. may cause pregnancy. Undersigned pregnancy is a personal as well as social problem; Society will not accept the same. Hence, definition of rape must be changed to accommodate such type of situation and the punishment for rape must be applied in such cases.

(c) Legitimacy of the AIH Child

The AIH child is legitimate, because although impotency is a ground for nullity but marriage subsists till it is repudiated. Also there is consent of the husband. Even in the eye of religion, the AIH child is a natural child of the spouses.[49]

Question of legitimacy is important in case of AID. The AID child is procreated with the use of the semen of a third person, therefore, the donor presumably will be the real father of the child, and he will thus be deemed a bastard child.

The Western Jurisprudence, by the suitable legislations or by the case law, has accorded the AIH child legitimacy. In United States, every state, who has legislation for A.I. has

49. In India, marriages of the minors are not valid. But the Courts have granted them validity on the basis of the equitable principle of Factum Valet.

provided legitimacy to AIH child. The jurists also agree to it. The legislatures have made such provision because there is consent of the husband.

The early case law suggested that the donor was the natural father based on the biological connection and to make the husband the legal father, it would be necessary for the husband to adopt the child. But the adoption theory had been rejected by the legislatures.

Somewhere, even in the absence of a statute, the case law supports the legitimacy of the child when the husband expressly or impliedly had consented for insemination.[50] Certain evidentiary protections have also been accorded to the child; child born in a lawful wedlock is presumed legitimate.[51] Thus the Supreme Court of lowa has stated that "every reasonable presumption will be admitted in favour of legitimacy and the burden of proof is upon the person alleging the contrary".

Every child born in lawful wedlock is presumed to be legitimate on a rule founded upon decency, morality, public policy, sacredness and peace and harmony of the family relationship.[52] The reason for this presumption is to protect the child from the stigma of bastardy. But this presumption has been made rebuttable, with sterility, impotency, or non-access. The U.S. legislatures had to make law due to existence of this exception appended to the presumption of legitimacy.

English law has presumption about the consent and parentage. The law Commission in its report[53] suggested that where there is consent of the husband for insemination, the child should not be deemed of the donor. The recommendations of the Law Commission was partly adopted in the Family Law Reform Act, 1987.[54] Section 27 (1) of the Act brings a deeming provision, whereby for the AIH child, it will be deemed that there is consent of the father and the child, it

50. 13 Fam. Law Reporter 1244 (S.C.) 23 Feb., 1987.
51. Wigmare, J., Evidence, 2527 (3rd Ed. 1940).
52. Bowers *v.* Baily, 237 Iowa, 237.
53. Report No. 157 (1986).
54. The Family Law Reform Act, 1987 came into force on 4th April, 1988.

will be deemed of the spouses. But this presumption is rebuttable through the Court of Law.

The Commission had recommended for proper recording of the consent of the husband, but this was not translated into Law. To avoid any conflict in future between the donor and the spouses or the spouses inter se, it is necessary to permit the insemination only on the written consent of the husband, and duly recorded.

In *Doornbos* v. *Doornbos*,[55] the Court held that "where the practice issue of legitimacy has been squarely presented for determination, it has been held that heterlogue artificial insemination by third party donor with or without the consent of the husband, constituted adultery on the part of the mother and that a child so conceived is not a child born in wedlock and is therefore illegitimate.

But in *Strand v. Stand*[56] the New York Court considered a situation where a woman artificially inseminated by a third party donor (A.I.D.) with the consent of her husband. The Court held that the husband was entitled to visitation right rejecting the wife's petition on the plea of child was born by A.I.D. for altering the Court's authorization to husband for week end custody. The Court also held that the child had been potentially or semi adopted by defendant. The husband was entitled to the same right at that required by a foster parent who has formally adopted a child, if not the same rights as those to which a natural parent under the circumstances would be entitled. Here child will not be illegitimate because husband has given consent.

In India, neither there is statutory law nor case law to determine the legitimacy and the parentage of the AIH children except the presumption that the children during the subsistence of the marriage will be deemed of the legally wedded souses. Muslim Hanafi Law, thus, says that child taking birth months of the solemnization of marriage and after two years of the repudiation of the marriage or death of the husband will not be of the husband. There is strong presumption about the parentage of the child. There is also provision for

55. No. 54, S. 1495 (Superior Court Cook Co. December 13, 1954).
56. 190 Misc. 786, 78; Y.Y.S. 2nd 390 Sup. ct. 1948.

acknowledgement by the father about the legitimacy of the child.

But the law does not have provision for legitimation. When the children are roved to be illegitimate, law does not provide legitimacy to them. Therefore, the law provides that the above mentioned presumption is rebuttable. The grounds for rebuttal can be impotence, sterility and non-access.

In case of AIH, there cannot be any presumption; as it would be evident from the facts that the natural father of the child is the donor. Therefore, the AIH child will be illegitimate. However, about the legitimacy of the AID child (with or without consent of the husband) when marriage subsists, the fatawas given by Imarat-e-shariy, Bihar Sharif, Nadwatul Ulema, Lucknow, Aljamiatul Islamia, Deoband and Riazul Uloom, Jaonpur maintain that the child will have legal rights to inherit their properties.

Section 112 of The Indian Evidence Act, 1872 also provides for similar presumption. According to it, the child born during the continuance of a valid marriage or within 280 days after the dissolution of the marriage, the mother remain unmarried, shall be conclusive proof that the child is of the husband. This presumption is also reputable on the ground of access.

But by advanced A.R.T. it is possible for woman to conceive much after this period. Hence law on legitimacy of child needs a change. We are of the opinion that here also, for the above reasons, the AIH child will not be deemed legitimate. In Hindu law also there is no provision for legitimation.

In the light of the existing law, however, if the facts of AIH are not known due to extreme secrecy, the child would get the protection of the above provisions. But in absence of such secrecy the child will be illegitimate.

Therefore, the legitimacy can be granted to such children only by legislation. Legislation can be any of the two types: *First,* to make all the children born by way of AIH to be legitimate children of the legally wedded spouses during the subsistence of the marriage: *second,* to grant legitimacy only when there is consent of the husband for AIH. So far the AIH is concerned; there is no doubt about the legitimacy of the AIH children.

(d) *Artificial Insemination and Adoption*

In case of adoption 74 Misc. 2d99 345 N.Y.S. 2d 430 (sup Ct 1973) husband has given consent for AI. He was the father on birth certificate. Later couple was divorced. The separation agreement referred to the child as the "*daughter*" or child of the couple. Support and visitation were awarded. Husband performed the same faithfully. When the wife remarried, her second husband wanted to adopt the child. The second husband argued that consent of the first husband should not be required as he was not the 'parent of the child'.

The Court held that a child born by A.I.D. during a valid marriage is a legitimate child entitled to the rights and privileges of naturally conceive child of the same marriage. The Court made a statement that the first husband's consent was required for the adoption.

(e) *Artificial Insemination and Maintenance*

In *People* v. *Sorenson,*[57] a sterile husband and his wife consented to her A.I.D. After a 4 years normal life they were divorced. The former husband did not support the child. He was convicted of criminal non-support and ordered to make necessary support payments for the child.

Court held that child is the result of active participation and consent of husband. The person who consents to the use of sperm, not his own be responsible for fathering the child. Court said husband is the lawful father. Hence, he cannot deny supporting the child. On this regard we may spy that Section 125, Cr. P.C. of India should be applied to the child born by A.I.

(f) *Artificial Insemination and Nullity of Marriage*

In 1963 *Gursky* v. *Gursky,*[58] on the consent of husband, wife went on A.I.D. The husband paid all expenses of A.I.D. and taken all the risk involved in the procedural treatment. A child was born by A.I.D. The birth certificate mentioned the wife as mother and husband as father. Thereafter an annulment was granted by the trial court because the husband was unable to consummate the marriage.

---

57. (62 Cal. Rep. 462 1967).
58. 39 Misc., 2d 1983, 242 N.S.S., 2d 406 (sup Ct. 1963).

In a similar case husband was important. The wife wanted divorce on this ground after A.I.D. In the report of Royal Commission on marriage and divorce 1956 it was recommended that when parties had resorted to artificial insemination of wife, these should therefore be not permitted to declare their marriage void on grounds of importance of either of them. This has not been acted by legislature.

Here the problem is that proof of impotence of father would bastardize the child and this will hamper the status of the child. Hence practitioners recommending A.I.D. in cases where one of the spouses is impotent should bear the possible result and effect on the child, if the marriage is nullified. (*Brit. Med. Jour.*, June 18, 1960, p. 1900)

(g) *Artificial Insemination in Unmarried Couple*

In *C.M.* v. *CC*[59] the couple are unmarried (C.C.) conceived a child by semen of C.M.C.C. is denying the visitation right to C.M. just like a natural father. But the Court found C.M. is the natural father and allowed the visitation right.

According to I.C.M.R. code there is no legal bar on an unmarried woman going for A.I.D. But the child will be illegitimate. But I.C.M.R. code says: "A child born to a woman with the sperm of her deceased husband should be considered a legitimate despite the existing law".

(h) *Provisions for Licensing*

In absence of sufficient governmental control and supervision, there are chances that the individual doctor of the institution may not take enough precautions. If this state of affairs prevails then it will be detrimental to the family and the AID child. It is, therefore, advisable that the institutions or the doctors must get license for performing insemination from the appropriate governmental body. It will be feasible if the Central Government constitutes a body to this effect comprising at least three senior doctors of the area. On receiving application for running the insemination centre, the body should investigate and ascertain the fitness of the proposed centre, and the

59. 337 A, 2d 821 (N.J. Super 1977).

certification of recognition be granted only when the member s of the body are satisfied.

In absence of such mandatory provision for licensing, the act of insemination can be performed by a doctor with less precaution or even a non-doctor may perform the act. If this is done socio-legal complex problem may arise. In California (U.S.), a nurse inseminated one donor's sperm into an unmarried woman which resulted in litigation.

Thus, in *Jhordan* v. *Mary*[60] while deciding on the question of the legal father of the AID child, the Court cautioned not to go beyond the Statute. We are of the opinion, therefore, that the law should prescribe penalties to all connected to such insemination. Law should declare the donor or legal father of the AID child.

The licensing policy in the Western countries is being made stricker. In England Warnock Committee has recommended for having a governmental licensing body in place of the private body. This suggestion has been welcomed by the jurists and the doctors, of course with some modifications, e.g., the licensing body should not be dominated by the non-physician members.[61]

(i) Doctor's Responsibility/Liability

The doctor concerned must be satisfied before performing insemination about the consent of the husband and that the person who has given consent is the husband. By the tests, if any required, he must also he satisfied about the suitability (compatibility) of the donor for the recipient. For suitability he must also ascertain about the religion and the blood relationship of the wife, the husband and the donor, as there is religious injunction against the inter-religious marriage and marriage within the prohibited degree.

There should be responsibility of the doctor to maintain records, so that, if need be the genetic origin of the child could be known. At the same time, he has to maintain confidentiality and to release the records to which the law permits access. If

60. 224 Cal. Reporter 530 (1986).
61. Priest Jacqueline A., "Assisted Reproduction—Developments in England, (1988), 37 I.C.L.O., 536.

the doctor fails to do his duty mentioned above, then he should be held liable, and penalty should be prescribed for it.

(j) Age of the Donor and Recipient

It will be against the public policy and also against the law to permit the A.I to a minor wife. In India, marriages of the minors are not valid. But the Courts have granted them validity on the basis of the equitable principle of Factum Valet.

Minor husband can also not give a valid consent. In some cases, the responsibility to maintain the child can also be fixed upon the donor, e.g., the donor represents before the doctor to be the husband and asks for AIH; the donor and the recipient can get insemination done by a non-recognized physician.

For all these reasons, one can doubtlessly say that AIH and AID should not be allowed when the wife, the husband or the donor as the case may be are minor under the law to which they are subject. Appropriately, the donor's and the husband's age can be fixed as 21 years and the wife's age as 18 years. Some of the countries have fixed maximum age limit. Also, we are of the opinion that to fix-up the maximum age is not advisable.

To the minimum age for AI there can be a counter-argument of Islam. Islam permits for sexual relations to the spouses when they have attained the puberty. According to Indian Criminal Law, the husband can be guilty of rape when the wife is less than 15 years old. This law is also based on the puberty principle. But we would like to distinguish the age of A I with that of sexual relations between the husband and wife, because in case of AI, the doctor and the donor are also involved.

(k) Artificial Insemination and the Donor

As pointed out above, the donor should be major, from beyond the prohibited degree of the spouses and from the same religion to which the spouses belong. Of these, the age criteria should be mandatory. The rest two can be left at the option of the spouses.

When marked under the special Marriage Act, we have also mentioned above, that there must be medical compatibility of the donor and the recipient. Also the donor must be healthy, without demonstrable genetic defect. It is suggested that it would be better to enumerate the requirements that are set out in the Hungarian provision as to donor's health, viz., favourable outcome of the genetic and psychological examination, the ascertainment of blood groups and the administration of tests for syphilis, gonorrhea and trichmoniasis and screening of sperm quality.

A test of AIDS virus should also be done. We have pointed out above about the responsibility of the doctor concerned about such tests. But if the donor knows about any such disease, then he should also mention it to the doctor, failing which he could be held liable.

We have pointed out above the AID should be permissible only to the married couple with consent of the husband and to be conducted by a recognized institution or the doctor. The single woman should not be allowed to avail the facility of AID. If the donor falsely represents to be the husband of the woman (when she is Spinster, widower or divorcee, or when she is married somebody else is her husband) and gets the woman inseminated with his sperm, then he should be held liable along with the woman. He should face the punishment (as prescribed) in that case. He should also be made liable to maintain the child. It is necessary to mention here that punishment should not be in terms of fine alone.

So as to deter a man from being professional sperm donor, one should not be allowed to donate sperm more than thrice in whole of his life. For violating this, punishment should be prescribed. For ensuring this and above mentioned requirement about the knowledge of the disease, a declaration from should be prescribed to be filled and signed by the donor.

We have favoured above the tight frame work of law for AID. Still, if any case occurs wherein the AID had been done without consent of the husband, the husband should have right to divorce, or get the marriage dissolved by the Court.

(l) Right of the AIH Child to Know about his Genetic Origin

In India, the AID child would like to know about his genetic origin for his matrimonial relations. This right has been recommended by the Warnock Committee in England also. But this right of AID child should be available to him only when he becomes 18 years old. For this, provision should be made for making application to the authorized centre confidentially. The authorized centers may be empowered to release such information's, but in confidentiality.

(m) Status of Child Born by AI to that of Natural Born Child

Law should keep it in view that child born by AI should get equal status if any child born naturally after it. According to some natural born child will carry its legitimacy status and the child born by AI will be illegitimate if not adopted.

It has been estimated that the single donor, donating two specimens weekly could produce some 400 children weekly and some 20,000 annually. A single found donor in an area could thus lead to consanguineous marriage in the future which is a relationship in marriage.

Keeping in view various possible problems I.C.M.R., Code has been drafted by the Central Ethical Committee on human Research of I.C.M.R. under the Chairmanship of Former Supreme Court Chief Justice M.N. Venkatachalaia which says following points regarding surrogate mother:

- Surrogate motherhood should be legal only when it is coupled with authorized adoption.
- It should be *"rebuttably presumed"* that a woman who carries the child and gives birth to it, is its mother.
- The intending parents should have preferential right to adopt the child subject to six weeks *post-partum* delay for necessary maternal consent.
- Surrogate motherhood should be legal only if it is medically certified as the only solution to infertility or any other medical bar on pregnancy by the intending mother.
- Abortion under the law (M.T.P. Act) on medical ground should be an inviolate right of surrogate mother and the adopting parents have no claim over the amounts already paid in the contract of surrogacy.

- Here the only remedy for the genetic father then would the claim for custody on the grounds of the best interest of the child.

In the matter of Baby M. [537A.2d.1227 (N.J. 1988)] Court held surrogacy contract is invalid and the surrogate mother is the legal mother. Still problems persist. The contracting couple divorced after the start of pregnancy may pressurize the surrogate mother to abort in some cases. If the medical ground will not allow aborting, then what will be status of the children? Sometimes surrogate mother may try to abort or harm the child after getting the proper payment. These are problem still to be solved.

(n) Sperm Banks

To avoid delay in searching the suitable donor, Sperm Banks are there. In India also, this practice has been adopted. In the Western Countries, to have a close vigil on the Banks, Licenses are granted and they are required to maintain records and to maintain confidentiality. The Warnock Committee, thus, opined:

> "Sperm Banks should be unlawful unless licensed by the Secretary of State. They should be subject to medical supervision, contain no more sperm than is reasonably good reason and their charges should be approved".

The precautionary measures suggested by the Committee have in principle been adopted by the legislature. We are of the opinion that the license for the Sperm Bank should be given to the centers only to whom the license for AI have given. Other provisions can be the same.

(D) Global Endeavours for Controlling the Vices of Artificial Insemination

A number of massive global endeavours have been taken at different platforms and various countries have taken care to legislate pertaining to artificial insemination.

(a) Anonymity and Non-Anonymity of Gamete Donor

One of the most problematic human rights aspects relating to AIH is concerned with the anonymity of gamete donor. At the international level, the vast majority of countries endorse anonymous gamete donation and some countries such as France, Denmark and Norway do not allow offspring any information. In *England, the Human Fertilization and Embryology Act, 1990* stipulates that gamete donation should be anonymous; the identity of the donor cannot be given to either the donor offspring or the couple receiving the gametes. There are, however, in recent years discernible trends towards allowing children access to identifying information about their gamete donor.

The first country to remove the anonymity of gamete donor was *Sweden,* allowing the child, when sufficiently mature, to find out the identity of sperm donor. *Austria* also allows the child to gain identifying information. In the *US,* there is no legislation, at either federal or state level, that either prohibits or enforces anonymous gamete donation. The matter is regulated by non-legally binding professional guidelines, which recommend the anonymity of gamete donors.[62]

(b) Child's Right to know vis-à-vis Parent's Right not to Disclose Genetic Origin

Many societies in the present time have begun to place greater emphasis on the right of child. Articles 7 of the UN Convention on the Rights of the Child, 1989 can be seen as being of fundamental importance as it provides for the right to know one's parents. In the context of donor anonymity it has been expressed as the child's right to know the identity of gamete donor. In our contemporary culture young people have strong moral claims to know the genetic identities. It has been contended by some that now it is time for these moral claims to convert to legal rights. Such a right-based argument has been used by various legislators to justify policies of non-anonymous gamete donation.

62. Frith Lucy, "Gamete Donation and Anonymity", 16, *Human Reproduction,* 819 (2001).

There are some people who argue that in case of gamete donation there are compelling reasons for not telling the child. It has been contended that it is not in the best interest of child to tell about the gamete donation because there is a fear that telling a child how they were conceived would cause serve social and psychological problems. A further reason for not telling the child is that parents should have a right to privacy and if they keep such information confidential that is their prerogative.

(E) Ethical and Legal Issues of Artificial Insemination and Judicial Response

(a) *Artificial Insemination—Religions View Point*

As mentioned above, in India the practice of artificial insemination is scanty, and in future also, as compared to the Western Countries, it will not be readily acceptable. It is due to the strong grip of religions on the Indian Society.

For a Hindu, son is not less important than marriage. Son is, for them means for salvation, he delivers father from hell;[63] through a son one conquers the world; through a grand-son one obtains the immortality, and through a great-grandson on ascends to the highest heaven.[64] This, along with the social reasons, has prompted to have a son, by natural means (own son) or by secondary means. Thus, in Vedic literature, we find references to Khetraja (Soil born), Putrikaputra, Kanina (men AIH born) and Dattaka (adopted).

There are thirteen types of sons, but Manu recognizes only twelve of them and put them into two categories:[65]

1. *I Category*

- Aurasa, body born;
- Kshetraja, soil born;
- Dattaka, adopted;

---

63. Manu, V, 138.
64. Manu, IX, 137-38.
65. Diwan, Paras, Modern Hindu Law, Allahabad Law Agency, p. 208 (1988).

- Kritrima, appointed;
- Gudhotpanna, secretly born, and;
- Apavindha, cast-off.

2. *II Category*

- Kanina, men AIH born;
- Sahodha, along with the bride;
- Krita, receiving bought;
- Paunnarabhava, self be gotten on remarried woman;
- Swayamdatta, self given; and
- Shaudra, son of a Brahman by a Sudra wife.

Manu has not mentioned putrikaputra, but this was also one of the kinds. Except Aurasa, Putrikaputra and Dattaka rest became obsolete in the post Smriti period. Even before these were disapproved by the Hindu Law. In Rig Veda, we find: (1) "Agni, no son is he who springs from other". At another place it again says: "A son begotten of other though worth of regard is not to be contemplated even in mind as fit for acceptance. . . ." Although Manu has mentioned about them but he very categorically disapproves them.

These eleven, the soil born and the rest, the wise one calls substitutes of a son taken with a view to the failure of the religious duty".[66] He further comments: "The one who tries to cross the hell with the help of a sieve".[67] It seems that such sons existed under some customs and probably their existence could not be ignored, and the devotion of sages to systemization was so great that they placed them in the classification of sons.

One thing is clear that all sages have in Unmistakable terms condemned them.[68]

Presently only Aurasa and Dattaka are in practice and recognized by the law. Niyoga has also been a process, whereby, the wife was asked to cohabit with another man (fixed for that) till she become pregnant. This practice was not commonly accepted and was resorted to only in case of sterility

66. Manu, IX, 180.
67. Manu, IX, 16.
68. *Ibid.*

and impotency part of the husband. Niyoga was also not recognized by the sages.[69] This has been in practice in Punjab even before the independence of India in a changed form. As a matter of custom the wife of the elder brother was compelled to cohabit with younger brothers also. But now, even there, it is an obsolete phenomenon.

Niyoga, although different in practice, is in effect similar to artificial, insemination donor (hereinafter referred as AIH). AIH, therefore, is approved neither by the Hindu religion nor by the modern Hindu Law. But since the case of Artificial Insemination Husband (hereinafter referred as AIH) is entirely different and no third person is involved, there cannot be religious injunction against it.

Before the advent of Islam, adoption was in practice in the same manner, as the Roman law and the Hindu Law. It remained in practice for quite some time during the life time of Prophet (S.A.W.). He had also adopted one male child named ZAIH. But the practice of adoption was abandoned, when Quran prohibited it with retrospective effect.[70] Islam, thus, approves only natural child.

It does not even validates the adoption. AIH, therefore, is prohibited in Islam. Since there is no express mention about artificial insemination in the basic Islamic Literature, we sent a questionnaire to the eminent Muftis of the Sunni School. They unanimously say that AHI is permissible, whereas the AIH is a haram act.

Catholic Church is also against the artificial means of reproduction including the AIH. In 1956 Pope Pious XII, in a discourse to those taking part in the II Naples World congress on Fertility and Human Sterility, stated that:

> "It is never permitted to separate those different aspects to such a degree that as positively to conclude either the procreative intentions or this conjugal relations".[71]

69. *Ibid.*
70. Quran 33:4, 33:40.
71. Rapinet Michael, "The Religions and moral Dilemmas posed by Scientific Developments in the Field of Genetics: A Catholic View," (1988) 28:3, Medicine Science and Law, 258.

In the opinion of the Church, therefore, conception can only be brought about as a result of parental love and cannot be perceived as product of an intervention of medical and biological techniques, which would be equivalent to reducing the embryo to an object of scientific technology. This argument is added with argument that the conjugal act ceases to be a conjugal act leading to procreation and becomes instead a technological mass-oriented and controlled act.

In the year 1993 in Italy a married couple got a son on the basis of AIH, but later on the husband disowned the son. The Supreme Court of Italy upheld this act of the husband on the basis of the Catholic belief.

3. *AIH and Adoption*

Adoption is a strong variable to the AIH, Methodology of the two is different, but in effect they are same. In both of them there is interception in the family, in case of adoption somebody else's child is utilized. However, they differ in the sense that AIH fulfils the maternal urge of the woman. If in AIH confidentiality is maintained, then the child and the father can be detracted from an alien feeling. Also, unless the law is made to legitimize AIH child, AIH increases illegitimacy.

The AIH increases the fertility rate. In the Western Countries, people are keen to adopt children, but they are steering-off from it because children for adoption are not readily available and they have to pass through a lengthy procedural requirement. Moreover, when a child is adopted, in most of the cases, there is problem of adjustment.

Therefore, in case of adoption there is a transit period, in which the parents and the child pass through a changed psychological state, and to cope with this they employ child reformist and psychologist. So, for them the process of adoption is time consuming.

In India, circumstances are different. Adoption for a Hindu is a sanctimonious religions performance, as the ancient Hindu law prescribes religion rites to it. Although, the Hindu Adoption and Maintenance Act, 1956 have changed characteristics of adoption from religions to secular, the rites attached to it are still performed in most of the cases of adoption. In India due to high fertility rate and increasing trend of poverty, the availability of children are in plenty, except when guardian is giving away the child. Therefore, the procedure is very simple.

4. *AIH and Psychology*

Some inherent psychological problems are there is in case of AIH. The husband, who has sterility or impotency, will always be reminded of this deficiency by the child. He will have to develop sense of owners for the child from within; he may fail to do so. If relations of the spouses are strained, then there are chances of disclosure of the fact to the child causing ill-feelings and sense of insecurity in him. The husband may blame to the wife for bad genetic qualities of the child, or wife may take credit of such good qualities. On the other hand, AIH fulfils the urge of the spouses to have a child. AIH child gives them new status in the society. Thus, child can save them from separating for quest of a child.

Although none of the above conflicting views have factually been proved, they can summarily not e denied. It is therefore, necessary to adopt some precautionary measures. *First,* the doctor concerned should wait, watch and should advice to only those couples who are very keen for AIH; *second;* he should maintain anonymity between the couples and the donor.

It will be better, if secrecy is maintained so that on one, except the doctor, the couple, and the donor could know about the genetic origin of the child. There is a reason for them to know about the child, because there cannot be a marriage with in the prohibited degree.

This principle will be applicable for the couple and the donor, i.e., none of them should be from the prohibited degree, and also for the AIH child as regards his marriage. The disclosure of the facts to this extent is also essential for religious congruity between the donor and the recipient.

(b) Artificial Insemination—Legal View Point

Artificial Insemination has been used in cases where procreation is impossible by natural means. The practice is widely used by the medical community as a method of treatment for infertility. It would seem that artificial insemination with the semen of the husband (AIH) can be regards as a justifiable and unobjectionable procedure. However, the birth of a child in wedlock as a consequence of such insemination does not constitute evidence of proper consummation of marriage.

Still, there are many unresolved problems relating to the use of artificial insemination for procreation. When for any reason AIH is not possible and artificial insemination is done with the semen of an unknown donor (AIH) the position is radically different from the above. The legal issues arising there form are as follows:

- There is certainly danger of litigation against the doctor following the birth of a defective child.
- The husband and is clearly not the father of the child and therefore the child illegitimate. Any attempt of conceal this fact by registering the husband as the father actually amounts to perjury.
- The illegitimate child is not the rightful successor to the father's property.
- The maintenance and custody of the child in the event of divorce would raise complex issues.
- There is risk of incestuous relationship between the offspring and children of the donor.
- The process of AIH can certainly be regarded as an adulterous act not only by the woman concerned but also by the donor if he himself was a married man. If the husband was unaware of the matter, he will almost certainly be entitled to sue his wife for divorce and the practitioner for damages.

Artificial insemination except in animals is not yet popular in India the law in India is therefore not clear on the various legal issues arising form AIH. However, the consensus of opinion is as follows:

- For all practical purposes, the husband is accepted as the father of the child. The child is therefore treated as legitimate and entitled to inherit parent's property.
- The recipient is not guilty of adultery because there is

no physical union in the form of coitus. For the same reason, the donor is not guilty of adultery.

- Since the 'act' is performed with the consent of both spouses, it cannot be a ground for divorce.

While the practice of artificial insemination by a donor must be strongly discouraged, married couples who want a child under such circumstances should be urged to adopt one.

Traditional concepts like adultery and non-consummation of marriage create problems in this field. For example, the questions whether artificial insemination amounts to adultery and can non-consummation of marriage be claimed by the wife when resorting to artificial insemination by donor (AIH) has been raised. Similarly, issues like right of the, (i) child, (ii) donor and duties of the inseminating physician may also arise.

Whether artificial insemination by wife is a ground for nullifying marriage on account of non-consummation has been settled now. The generally accepted opinion is that this does not amount to non-consummation of marriage leading to nullity of marriage.

1. *Adultery in Artificial Insemination*

The question whether AIH by the wife in the absence of her husband's consent amounts to adultery[72] was raised before the Canadian Supreme Court in *Oxford* v. *Orford*.[73] The court held that recourse to AIH in the absence of the consent of the husband amounted to adultery:[74]

> Under the English legal system, however, traditionally AIH has been thought of as not amounting to adultery. At present this issue has been almost settled and artificial

---

72. Ivor, L.M. Richardson, "Artificial Insemination", 30, Aust. L.J., 125 at 127 (1956-57); K. Rudlow, "Legal aspects of artificial insemination", 28, Aust. L.J., 490 (1954-55).
73. [1921] 49 Ontario LR 15 as referred to in G.W. Bartholomew, "Legal implications of artificial insemination", 21, *Mod L Rev,* 236 at 238-39 (1958).
74. *Ibid.*

insemination is no more held to amount to adultery and does not become a matrimonial offence under any legal system.

The question of adultery, as a result of AIH, in India does not arise because section 497 of the Indian Penal Code reads as follows, "Whoever has sexual intercourse with a person who is and whom he knows or has reason to believe to be the wife of another man, without the consent or connivance of that man such sexual intercourse not amounting to the offence of rape, is guilty of the offence of adultery, and shall be punished with imprisonment of either description for a term which may extend to five years, or with fine, or with both.[75] In such case the wife shall not be punishable as an abettor".

So sexual intercourse must be present.[76] Since penetration is a necessary element for a successful completion of sexual intercourse, which is an essential element for adultery.[77] AIH does not amount to adultery.

2. *Legitimacy of Child in Artificial Insemination*

The purpose and object of the new reproductive techniques being the child, his interests have to be taken care of many problematic issues emerge regarding rights and interest of the child in artificial insemination.

For legal purposes, paternity is a question based on the genetic factor. Use of the husband's sperm for inseminating the wife either *in-vitro* or *in-utero* does not pose any problem to the question of paternity of the offspring.

However, the use of donated sperm in AIH inevitably creates conflict with social reality and genetic truth. In the absence of statutory intervention, the child is illegitimate,[78] his

75. *Ibid.*, at p. 240.
76. Franklin, C.A. (ed.), Modi's Textbook of Medical Jurisprudence and Toxicology, 350-52 (21st ed. 1988).
77. Khan, Ateeque, "Artificial insemination and surrogate parenthood: An Indian socio-legal perspective", 31, JILI, 394 at 401 (1989).
78. Ansari, A.H., "Artificial Insemination : Indian Perspective", (1995) ISCJ (Jn.) 11 at 19: Kusum, "Artificial Insemination and the Law", 19, JILI, 283 at 292-93 (1977).

rights being those enforceable against his genetic father, i.e. the anonymous donor, and his social father is a legal stranger to him. This state of affairs creates problems in his inheritance rights.[79]

This problem has been solved to same extent by the English system by enacting the Human Fertilization and Embryology Act 1990.[80] This Act provides for the presumption of paternity. By S. 28(2), Human Fertilization and Embryology Act, 1990, if a child is born as a result of artificial insemination or embryo transfer to a woman who was at the time of artificial insemination or transfer of embryo, married, then her husband will be treated as the father of the child.

If the woman is unmarried, but avails of treatment together with a man whose sperm is not used for artificial insemination, he is to be treated as the father of the child.[81] The S.28(6) provides that the donor of the sperm to be used for artificial insemination is not to be treated as the father or the child. If the sperm of a man or an embryo created by that man's sperm has been stored and is used after his death; he will not be treated as the father of the child.

A perusal of these provisions points out that all situations which arise as a result of artificial insemination have not been met with under this Act. If an unmarried woman avails of treatment, then, the child born will be without any father, as social parentage cannot be assumed.

The Act does not expressly prohibit treatment of single and unmarried persons. But it states that while treatment is being provided, the well-being of the child including the presence of a father has to be taken into account by the inseminating physician. It is doubtful whether the physicians have the right to take such cases and whether in such circumstances, the child would be illegitimate. This does not solve the problem of legitimacy of the child.

---

79. Sackville Ronald and Annemaree Lanteri, "The Disabilities of Illegitimate Children in Australia: A Preliminary Analysis", 44, Aust., L.J. 5 (1970): Bedwa, "Problems of illegitimate children under various personal laws in India", 11, *Ind Bar Rev,* 337 (1984).
80. *Ibid.*
81. Section 28(3) of Human Fertilization and Embryology Act, 1990.

In India, legitimacy of children is governed by the personal laws. There is no provision for legitimating under the Indian legal system. Section 16 of The Hindu Marriage Act 1955 provides that any child born out of a marriage which is null and void or is voidable under S. 11 and 12 respectively of this Act to be considered legitimate to inherit property of the parents only.

And Special Marriage Act, 1954[82] confer legitimacy on children of void marriages enumerated under those Acts alone and deny legitimacy to children of other void marriages which fall outside the purview of these Acts. An AIH child will not come under the provisions enumerated under any of the Acts mentioned above. Hence they will be illegitimate in the absence of any legislation legitimizing the AIH children.

The same is the condition under the existing Muslim law, where parentage is established only on biological parents and the child is born out of wedlock. Legitimacy cannot be conferred on an illegitimate child.

This situation necessitates legislative intervention in India. Hence, in the absence of statutory prohibition of single or unmarried persons from availing of this technique, the child born as a result of AIH will be a legal limbo. In such cases, the law should prohibit unmarried persons and women without a male partner, who can act as social parent, from availing AIH in the interests of the child.

3. *Right to Know*

Every child has a right to know about its origin. In artificial insemination by donor's sperm, the identity of the donor being kept secret, the biological father is kept out of the picture. If the donor's identity is revealed to the child, will it be contradictory to the secrecy attributed to the donation of gametes and be detrimental to the donor's interests?

In certain countries and adopted child is granted the right to know his parentage. Section 51 deals with the disclosure of birth records of adopted children. On an application made to

82. Section 26 confers legitimacy on children born out of marriages declared void and voidable under S. 24 and 25 respectively and gives such children the right to inherit property of their parents.

the registrar general in the prescribed manner by an adopted person who has attained 18 years of age, and on payment of the prescribed fee, such information as is necessary to enable a person to obtain a certified copy of record of his birth is made available.[83] As a child born by AIH is not different from an adopted child, can that child be given a right to know of its origin?

If an AIH child is treated at par with the adopted child and granted the right to know, divulgence of the donor's identity might create a host of complex problems. The right to know may be necessary in certain cases like, when the child wants to marry and also in cases where there is a necessity to detect genetic diseases. So whether the right to know can be given to an AIH child and if given, under what circumstances, has to be determined by the legal system.

Under the existing legal system in Sweden, it is now possible for an AIH conceived child to trace its origin.[84] But in Switzerland, France and Canada, there is total anonymity and secrecy of the donor, which is done in the best interest of the child.[85]

The participants at the international colloquium on artificial procreation genetics, and the law after pointing out the lack of psychological data to prove which system is really better for the child, felt that an analogy between an AIH child and an adopted child should not be made in the matter of tracing parental origin and so donor secrecy has to be maintained.

On the other hand, it was felt that important date should always be maintained in case it is needed to deal with medical problems or to trace genetic diseases.[86] In UK, the Human Fertilization and Embryology Act, 1990 provides for access to knowledge as regards origin by a child conceived by artificial insemination from the authority. He is allowed to get

83. Adoption Act, 1976 (England), Sec. 6, *Halsbury's Statutes of England and Wales,* 483 (5th ed. 1985).
84. Baudouin Jean-Louis, "International colloquium on artificial procreation, genetics and the law", 37(2), IDHL, 404 at 406 (1986).
85. *Id.* at 406-7.
86. *Id.* at 407-9.

information as to whether the person whom he is going to marry is related.[87]

We have, under the Indian legal system, degrees of prohibited relationships[88] under which, a person who falls under that degree is not allowed[89] to marry another in the same degree. As the practice of AIH is now common in India, the need for getting information about the donor for medical and matrimonial reasons arises. Now this area is mainly governed by the ethical principle which is followed by the inseminating physician.

A legislation empowering a statutory body with the maintenance of records of the donors of sperms and the children conceived as a results of it is necessary. The authority should provide information on an application being made, either by the child or any person who is related to the child for medical and matrimonial reasons.

4. *Prenatal Sex Selection*

The legal issues arising out of the use of artificial insemination as selective fertilization techniques to effect sex selection are slightly more varied and complex than issues arising out of the use of the Shettles regime.

The legal issues and rules governing the doctor—patient relationship in regard to whether the physician is acting as a guarantor of the technique and whether the physician has abandoned the doctor—patient relationship improperly are similar to those discussed with respect to the Shettles regime. Issues involving negligence and informed consent are sufficiently different from those in the Shettles regime to warrant continued discussion. Also, issues involving parentage must be discussed because of the novel possibilities presented by artificial insemination.

Because artificial insemination involves both doctor—patient counseling and some rather complicated procedures on

87. Section 31 of The Human Fertilization and Embryology Act, 1990.
88. Sec. 2(g) of Hindu Marriage Act, 1955 prescribes the degrees of prohibited relationship.
89. Section 5 of The Hindu Marriage Act, 1955 states that for a valid marriage the parties should not be within degrees of prohibited relationship.

the part of the physician, the possibility of malpractice suits on grounds of negligence is increased. It is likely that issues involving informed consent would be intermingled with issues involving negligence, as is the case in many malpractice suits.

If the fetus is damaged by the procedure or if the wrong sex is produced, then issues involving the extent to which the physician provided the patient with sufficient knowledge to make an intelligent choice concerning the procedure can arise and compound the legal difficulties of the physician. Sex selection achieved through artificial insemination presents many opportunities for doing damage to the fetus, and very little is known about the likelihood of these occurrences.

It would therefore be prudent for the physician to provide extensive information concerning the steps in the procedure and the possible outcomes, for better or for worse, involved in each step. It is especially important that the possibility of producing the wrong sex be discussed at length. This is because the physician would wish to establish that he is not a guarantor of the success of the procedure and to foreclose the possibility that informed consent issues would be blended with concerns about the actual conduct of the procedure to from a negligence action.

Sex selection through artificial insemination involves the cooperation of more that one person and, therefore, the law must develop rules to determine now much information each interested party is entitled to regarding the procedure and to what extent their individual desires will control the process. Various combinations of four potential classes of people can emerge to form the decision-making unit regarding artificial insemination.

The members of the decision-making unit must be provided with adequate information to be able to make an informed judgment regarding the procedure. The classes of potential people who could be involved in the decision include:

- The mother (the woman who would raise the child),
- The father (the man who would raise the child),
- A surrogate mother (a woman who would be inseminated and give birth to the child in place of the mother), and

- A surrogate father (a man who would donate sperm in place of the father).

The law must evolve rules determining who will make decisions regarding initiating the procedure, who will make decision regarding the disposition of the sperm before insemination, who will make decisions regarding prenatal care and the actual delivery of the child. It is possible that the decision-making unit could change during the process.

For example, the man donating the sperm could be the decision-maker regarding the disposition of the sperm before fertilization, the couple charged with raising the child could make decisions regarding fertilization, and the woman bearing the child, be it mother or surrogate mother, could be entrusted with making decisions regarding prenatal care and delivery.

Other combinations could obtain depending on the controlling legal system. This means that legal rules governing this type of procedure must necessarily the quite complex and almost certainly be very confusing to the physician attempting to implement the procedure.

Any legal system will have to contemplate all of these diverse contingencies and develop a logical, systematic hierarchy of rules to define the decision-making unit, to determine what rights arise during the various stages of the process, and to determine how the parties may contract among themselves to tailor the rights and obligations involved in the process to their particular needs.

Also, if sex selection via artificial insemination is to be controlled through a multiparty contractual relationship, the law must contemplate what remedies will be available to the parties involved in case of breach of contract (e.g., specific performance or damages) and whether the child will be recognized as a third-party beneficiary under the contracting scheme.

Moreover, if the child is recognized as a third-party beneficiary to the contract, the law must determine if the child will have any remedies against the parties to the contract in the case of breach of contract. Otherwise, the issues arising out of disputes between the third-party interest and the other interests are similar to those of the Shettles regime discussed previously.

5. *Liability of Negligence in Assisted Reproduction*

There is very likelihood of the whole process of assisted conception going wrong. It may be that of (i) mixing of the sperms of the husband or donor with that of some else; or (ii) the transplant of gametes or embryo intended for someone else, in the wrong patient; or (iii) use of the gametes or embryo which are discarded for implant in the woman; or (iv) the disposal of an embryo by mistake.

The super ovulatory drugs may develop hyper stimulation syndrome in women going for IVF and other problems like contracting an infection are always possible. Further, complications in delivery prematurely the child may suffer damage at birth or die in the pre-natal period.

'Wrongful life' claims[90] have been allowed under certain legal systems. "Wrongful life" claim is an action for damages brought by the plaintiff child (thus distinguishing the action from the "wrongful birth" which is brought by the child's parents) on the premise that were it not for the negligence of the defendant, the child would not have been born, or would not have born in an unimpaired state of existence.

On the basis of this definition, wrongful life claims fall under two categories, (i) the preconception negligence cases in which the child claims that but for the defendant's negligence he would not have been born; and (ii) the post-conception negligence cases in which the child claims that but for the defendant's negligence he would not have been born in disabled conditions, or would have been aborted if the disabled condition had been for should have been) detected.

Similarly 'wrongful birth' claims may also arise. However, the feasibility of allowing the same remedy to be claimed by a child who suffers a handicap due to the use of faulty gametes or embryos is a moot issue. In case of the donor's failure to

90. Philip Hersch, "Tort liability for wrongful life", 6, *UNSWLJ*, 113 (1983); H. Teff, "The action for wrongful life in England and the U.S.", 34, *ICLQ*, 423 (1985).

reveal his genetic diseases, the problem gets all the more difficult. By strict adherence to the principle of donor secrecy, the child's raising a claim for wrongful life or non-disclosure becomes impossible. In such a case, can the remedy be allowed against the doctor for his failure to find out the disease by testing and thus resulting in deformities to the child? Or can there be a slight deviation from the strict adherence to donor secrecy and in cases of 'wrongful life', the child be allowed to claim damages from the donor for his failure to disclose diseases?

Under the Indian legal system, the whole are needs to be governed by the general law relating to settlement of disputes. 'Wrongful life' claims have not yet been recognized in India. Even in England, where 'wrongful life' claims have been allowed, opinion has been expressed against the availability of such a redressal on the reasoning that the birth of a child is not a cause to brood over.[91]

Though it seems possible now that the parents who availed of the services of the physician can claim remedy, against the doctor under the Consumer Protection Act for deficiency of services, after the ruling of the Supreme Court[92] but it is doubtful whether the child can bring an action under this Act. So the child may go without any remedy, if anything goes wrong while treatment is provided using IVF or other artificial reproduction techniques.

The English Parliament has dealt with the position of the child and provided for his remedy. "A child may sue under this Act if the child is born disabled and the disability results from an act or omission in the course of selection, or the keeping or use outside the body, of the embryo, or the gametes used to bring about the creation of the embryo for a wrongful act against the person who was responsible for it".[93] By section IA the remedy available is against the medical staff any physician.

91. C. Symmons, "Policy factors in actions for wrongful birth", 50, *Mod L. Rev.*, 269 (1987).
92. Indian Medical Association *v.* V.P. Shantha, (1995) 6, *SCALE*, 273.
93. Congenital Disabilities (Civil Liability) Act, 1976, Sec. IA inserted by Sec. 44. Human Fertilization and Embryology Act, 1990. See Section IA(1)(b).

Still, parents have to settle their disputes only under the general laws.

Further remedy against the donor in cases where he fails to reveal genetic disease or infection is provided under the Human Fertilization and Embryology Act.[94] Where a conditions or a defect cannot be revealed by testing, and the doctor is not at fault and the donor is responsible for it, the child might seek to have redressal from the donor.

In such cases, the anonymity or secrecy of the donor might be discarded, on the child applying to the court for an order under section 35 requiring the Human Fertilization and Embryology Authority to disclose information regarding the donor so that the child may sue under section IA of the Congenital Disabilities (Civil Liability) Act, 1976.

With the practice of AI, and IVF using donor gametes going on in India, and the whole field uncontrolled by any legislation, there is every possibility of the process going wrong and resulting in disability, disease or deformity to the child. The existing legal system is not sufficient to provide relief to the child in case of any wrong done as a result of these practices. Hence the situation warrants legislative intervention. Law should provide for remedy to the child either from the donor or from the medical community.

6. *Rights and Duties of Donor*

When artificial insemination by using husband's sperm fails or is impossible. The alternative is by donor sperm. Likewise, an ovum from a donor can be used for artificial insemination or in vitro fertilization. Hence donation of gametes is common phenomenon in medically assisted procreation.

Many legal issues like commercialization of gametes, imposing liability on the donor towards the child, the recipient and the physicians arise when the donor's gametes are used in the treatment of patients.

The first issue is the one concerned with donation of gametes. Thought it is expected that donors have to give their

94. Section 35 of Human Fertilization and Embryology Act.

gametes free of charge, the practice is that it is not so. It has been reported that 'donors' demand a 'fee' for their 'donation'.[95] The payment of a certain amount for donation of gametes, will commercialize the whole filed,[96] and make 'donor's of the sperm turn professional. On the other hand, non-payment of any gratification, may lead to non-availability of people to come forward to donate gametes. This will adversely affect the patients who go for medically assisted conception.

It can be argued that altruism should be the motive behind donation and hence charging of their donation by the donors is against basic human values and policy of the State. But the ovum donor has to undergone by the sperm donor. In India, blood 'donation' on the payment of a fee has not been prohibited. Since blood and sperms are similar in nature, the question is can sperm be allowed in the market.

The legal consequences which arose out of blood transfusion are not subjected to complications whereas the sperm decides the paternity of the child and the genetic order. Hence the commodification of sperm is not approved by the society

Hence it can be stated that in donation of gametes, the driving force should be altruism. The guidelines issued by the Swiss Academy of Medical Science echoes this principle when it states that the donation of gametes must be made free of charge.[97] To ask the gamete donor to donate gametes with pure altruism will be stretching the principle of gratuitous donation to the maximum.

This will detrimentally affect people in need of donated gametes as it will reduce the number of those willing to donate

---

95. Davis Linda, "Surrogate parenting" 134, *New LJ*, 707 at 708 (1984). According to Indira Hinduja of the Hinduja Hospitals, egg donors ask for their 'donation' and amount between Rs. 10,000 to Rs. 30,000. "Human eggs for sale", Flash points, Law teller 3-47 (March 1996).
96. Prakash, Padma, "Regulating reproductive technology", 4, *The Lawyers Collective*, 4 (Feb. 1989).
97. News and Views, "Swiss Academy of Medical Sciences issues medico-ethical guidelines on medically assisted procreation (1990) version", 42(2), *IDHL*, 346 at 349 (1991).

gametes. Hence a practical solution will be that of a combination of altruism with the bearing of medical expenses like those incurred in testing suitability of the donor and in case of the egg donor, the expenses incurred in egg retrieval by the couple intending to use it. Other than and medical expenses (which are to be paid to the clinic in which donation takes place) no charge is to be made for the donation of gametes.

7. *Duties of Donor*

The donor owes a duty to the inseminating physician, recipient's spouse and child to be born as a result of the usage of his gamete..

The main duty of the donor is to assist the inseminating physician in assessing whether he is a suitable donor.[98] He is expected to divulge exclusive details known to him, especially, the genetic disease of either self or genetically related persons. In case of voluntary non-disclosure, the donor has to undergo medical examination, if the physician asks for it.

The Identity of the donor is normally not disclosed to recipients. Secrecy is maintained to protect the interests of all parties and prevent psychological problems that may arise if his identity is made known.[99] But that does not relieve the donor of his responsibilities towards recipients. His consent from has to include surrender of his right, in relation to any child conceived as a result of use of his gamete.

Schedule 3 of the Act states that consent to the use of gametes or embryos must be in writing and it must satisfy the conditions provided under the schedule and other matters which the Human fertilization and Embryology Authority may specify in its directions. Also, that he will not make any attempt to gain knowledge about the identity of the recipients or their child.

The gamete donor is the genetic mother or father, depending upon the ovum or sperm donation of the child. But owing to secrecy, the child as well as its social parents is

98. Domnique, F.J.J. De Stoop, "Human Artificial Insemination and the law in Australia", 50 Aust. L.J., 298 at 307 (1976).
99. The Human Fertilization and Embryology Act, 1990 provides for the donation of gametes and embryo for treatment, research and storage.

unaware of the donor's identity. The donor while consenting to donation has to disown any claim of rights towards the child.

8. *Rights of Donor*

Firstly, secrecy has to be adhered to. The donor must be assured that information about him not pass on to, (i) the recipients at the time of treatment; or (ii) the child born using the gamete. This will minimize the psychological hardships faced by recipients and the donor in knowing each other. But it is not always possible.

If the child needs to learn about the donor's identity to obtain medical information should be provided to him.[100] It is true that, revealing the identity of the donor will upset the family set-up and result in family discord, but in cases where it is necessary it has to be allowed. The better way out will be to maintain records regarding the donors and on an application made by the child to learn about its origin for medical reasons or for knowing about the prohibited degrees in relation to marriage.

As per S. 31, Human Fertilization and Embryology Act, 1990 (UK) on an application made by the child on attaining 18 years of age, information will be provided regarding any person whom the child intends to marry as to the whether the child and the intending spouse would or might be related.

In the same manner any person may request the Authority by an application to provide with information regarding any person who has been born in consequence of treatment services. Whom the applicant intends to marry as to whether the intending spouse is related or not.

The donor should be assured that no responsibilities or liabilities will be bestowed upon him as a result of donation of the gamete. Making him to bear responsibilities like, (i) parental responsibility over the child, (ii) maintenance of the child in case artificial insemination is done by an unmarried

100. Pedro, F. Silva-Ruiz, "Artificial Reproductive Technique, Fertility Regulations : The Challenge of Contemporary Family Law", 34, *Am J Comp L. (Supp.)* 125 at 130 (1986): K. Rudlow, "Legal aspects of artificial insemination", 28, Aust. L.J., 490 at 494 (1954-55).

woman, (iii) claim of inheritance rights by the child, are legal issues raised by the usage of donor sperm.

On the contrary, if the sperm donor is a person known to the woman who artificially inseminates herself without medical assistance, the issue of identity of the donor and his responsibility arise. It becomes more complicated, if the woman is unmarried.

At this juncture, it is to be noted, that the existing control, caters only to problems which arise when medical assistance is used in procreation. There is every possibility and probability that artificial insemination will be done by the woman herself without medical assistance.

In such cases, fixing of parental duties on the sperm donor will deter such prospective donors. Hence in any case of artificial insemination, either with or without medical assistance, the donor should be free from any responsibilities towards the child. But in a case[101] where the court held that the donor of the semen to a lady who artificially inseminated herself without medical assistance, had responsibilities 'towards the child and is the legal father of the child

9. *Duties of Inseminating Physician*

Normally, the physicians owe a duty of care towards their patients. In case of failure to take reasonable care doctors are liable under the existing legal system. The civil liability has been fixed upon the doctor and when he exercises reasonable care and professional skill, he is not liable.[102] But the tendency of the judiciary is that the better wisdom of the medical profession is to be respected and decisions taken by them should not be questioned.[103]

In treatment of patients with the new reproductive techniques, the person who is to avail of the treatment is decided by the physician who is to treat them. The medical

---

101. Jhordon *v.* Mary, K., 224 Cal Rptr 530 (Cal. App. 1986) as referred to in Dominick Vetri 'Reproductive Technologies and United States Law", 37, *Int. & Comp L.Q.*, 505 at 518 (1988).
102. Bolam *v.* Friern Hospital Management Committee, 1957 I WLR 582.
103. R. *v.* Malcherek, 1981 2 ALL ER 421 (C.A.); Airedale NHS Trust *v.* Bland 1993 I All ER 821 (HL).

professional to be the final decision making authority, while stating that the area of control of fertility displays many of the reasons for denying the medical profession role responsibility for decisions making.[104]

In medicine, there is a case wherein the clinic refused to treat a woman who sought IVF treatment based on the criteria formulated by the clinic for offering treatment to couples.[105] Such value judgments are made and clinical freedom of doctors demands that they should not be required to divulge to outsiders every time they take a decision.[106] The courts have also accepted that expert opinion of the physicians should not be questioned.

But many issues arise in the treatment of patients when they go in for medically assisted procreation. Communication between the doctor and his patient needs to be confidential and privileged. Where AIH is to be done? Though the doctor is to stick on to the confidentiality aspect, he is at times compelled to defer and give valuable information about the donor to :

(i) The Recipients, and (ii) Child at a Subsequent Stage

Further, the duty of care and skill of the physician may be put to test when he selects the donors for artificially inseminating the woman. While selecting the donor for use in artificial insemination the duty of care which physicians have to take and their responsibility towards the patients has been laid down by the Judicial Council of the American Medical Association in 1983.[107] The duty of care of the doctor may be questioned when defective donor gametes are used for insemination.

There are virtually no cases in medically assisted reproduction claiming that the doctor is responsible for the

104. 66 Jonathan Montgomery "Power/Knowledge/consent: Medical decision making", 51, *Mod L. Rev,* 245 at 249 (1988).
105. R. *v.* Ethical Committee of St. Mary's Hospital (Manchester) *ex parte* H. 1988 I FLR 512 as referred to in Gillian Douglas, Law, Fertility and Reproduction 120.
106. Douglas Gillian, "Assisted reproduction and the Welfare of the Child", 46, *Current Legal Probs,* 53 at 68 (1993).
107. Dominick Vetri, "Reproductive Technologies and United States Law", 37, *Int. & Comp L.Q.* at 519 (1988).

failure in pregnancy or for the acquiring of disease or deformity by the child either by the child or the requisitioning parents. Obviously these questions will arise in the near future as the future of medico-legal actions are "rights" based, which is a consequence of the "human rights" movement in vogue.[108]

Hence, as the identity of the donor is kept confidential, if the child is born with an inherited defect or deformity, can the physician be held liable for negligence for failure to take due care in donor selection? Or alternatively can there be a 'wrongful life' or 'wrongful birth' claim by the child or its parents respectively against the doctors?[109] However, there is the problem of awarding damages in which aspect, it has been pointed out, and this in itself is a mistake as the child so born with a handicap need not be treated differently from other handicapped children.[110]

Under the human Fertilization and Embryology Act, 1990, the child has been given a statutory right to seek information about the donor so that it can sue the latter for failure to reveal infection or genetic disease.[111]

(c) *Ethical Considerations of AI*

None of the foregoing considerations are without ethical significance. However, it is my contention that the chief ethical issue, upon which hinges one's ultimate decision for or against AIH, has to do with the very nature of marriage and parenthood.

This is the issue that finally underlies our ethical assessment of many of the other considerations discussed above. What is the nature of the marriage bond, and what significance does this have for our assessment of AIH. What is the proper relationship between this marriage bond and the

108. Grubb Andrew, "The Emergence and Rise on Medical Law and Ethics", 50, *Mod L Rev,* 241. (1987).
109. Philip Hersch, 6, *UNSWLJ,* 113 (1983); H. Teff, "The Action for Wrongful Life in England and the U.S.", 34, *Int & Comp LQ,* 423 (1985).
110. Stolker, Carel J.J.M., "Wrongful Life: The Limits of Liability and Beyond", 43, *Int. & Comp. L.Q.,* 521 at 532 (1994).
111. Sec. 35, Human Fertilization and Embryology Act, 1990.

procreation of children? These are the crucial ethical questions in determining our decisions about AIH.

Contemporary ethicists have taken widely different views of these questions. Joseph Fletcher, the father of "situation ethics" takes a view that does not require of the marital bound a physical monopoly. He stresses the "personal" character of the marriage covenant, and goes on to assert that since no personal relationship is entered into with the donor. AIH is acceptable when mutually agreed upon by husband and wife. In such a case there is no broken faith, no infidelity, between them.

The claim that AIH is immoral rests upon the view that marriage is an absolute generative, as well as sexual, monopoly and that parenthood is an essentially, if not solely, physiological partnership. Neither of these ideas is compatible with a mortality that welcomes emancipation from natural necessity, or with the Christian ethic which rises morality to the level of love (a personal bond), above the determinism of nature and the rigidities of laws as distinguished from love?

An act of sexual intercourse is at the same time an act of love and procreative act. This does not mean that sexual intercourse always in fact nourishes love between the parties or always engenders a child. It simply means that it tends, of its own nature, toward the strengthening of love and toward the engendering of children.

The problem occurs by the fact that in AIH, a third person enters into the exclusive psychophysical relationship of marriage even though is only his sperm that represents him. The introduction of donor semen, therefore, violates the mysterious of marital fellowship, the psychophysical unity of husband and wife. "This violation also manifests itself when the fulfilment of motherhood which is not accompanied by the fulfilment of fatherhood breaks down the personal solidarity of the married couple. AIH is therefore rejected even if, the husband consents to the procedure, physical realities are called into play which have a life of their own even apart from his initial motivation (AIH is therefore rejected).

1. *Roman Catholic Theologians*

Artificial insemination in marriage with the use of an

active element from a third person is equally immoral and as such is to be rejected summarily. Only the marriage partner's have mutual rights over their bodies for the procreation of a new life and these are exclusive, non-transferable, and inalienable rights. So it must be, out of consideration for the child.

Roman Catholic theologians in the main have also rejected AIH. The official position of the Roman Catholic Church was stated by Pope Pius XII in 1949. After condemning artificial insemination outside of marriage, he went on to reject AIH within marriage.

By virtue of the same bond, nature imposes on whoever gives life to small creatures the task of its prevention and education. Between the marriage partners, however, and a child which is the fruit of the active element of a third person—even though the husband consents—there is no bond of origin. No moral or juridical bond of conjugal procreation. AIH is thus understood as contrary to the divine plan for marriage and parenthood. It is an essentially disordered act.

II. IN-VITRO FERTILIZATION

(A) Concept of In-Vitro Fertilization

(a) History

In vitro fertilization (IVF) is now practiced by many workers world-wide, in an attempt to treat various disorders in infertility. More than 250 pregnancies have been established in the last 2 years and over 100 babies born, including 62 from Bourn Hall.[112] It is commonly known as 'Test Tube Baby' IVF involves fertilization of an ovum outside the body and consequently transfers of embryo into the uterus of the woman. "In-vitro" is Latin word mean "in glass", which referred as the

112. Fishel, S.B.,"Establishing and Maintaining Pregnancy by In-Vitro Fertilization" a R.G. Edwards, a P.C. Steptoe, b J.M. Purdy a and J. Webster b.
    (a) Physiological Laboratory, Downing Street, Cambridge, and
    (b) Bourn Hall Clinic, Bourn, Cambridgeshire, England.

test tubes, however neither glass nor test tubes are being used; the term is used generically for laboratory procedures.

IVF is probably the most widely practiced assisted conception procedure in the world. The procedure does not need admission at any step and is conducted on an out patient basis. The success rate for each in vitro fertilization cycle is around 20-30%. Many factors affect success rates, including patient age, sperm and egg quality, reproductive health, duration of the infertility, and medical expertise. Because multiple embryos are often transferred, the risk of multiple births is the major complication in IVF.

The technique was developed in the United Kingdom by Doctors Patrick Steptoe and Robert Edwards. The first so-called "test-tube baby", Louise Brown, was born as a result on July 25, 1978 amid intense controversy over the safety and morality of the procedure. Also called test-tube conception medical procedure in which mature egg cells are removed from a woman, fertilized with male sperm outside the body, and inserted into the uterus of the same or another woman for normal gestation.

The first "test tube" baby, Louise Brown, was born in England in 1978. Since then, hundreds of thousands of babies have been born using in-vitro fertilization and related techniques. In vitro (which means "in glass") fertilization (IVF) is often used for women with blocked or malfunctioning fallopian tubes, severe endometriosis, or unexplained infertility.

Prior to IVF, a woman is given synthetic hormones that stimulate the maturation and release of a large number of eggs. The eggs are removed from the ovaries using an ultrasound-guided needle and combined with sperm in a laboratory dish. To increase the chances of pregnancy, four to six embryos are typically implanted into the woman's uterus when they are about three days old. Extra embryos may be frozen for later use.

Since multiple embryos are implanted, there is an increased chance of multiple births and the associated risks to both mother and children. Selective reduction or abortion of one or more fetuses may be used to reduce the number of multiples. IVF is expensive ($8,000 to $10,000 per trial) and the likelihood of producing a child using IVF decreases with increased maternal age. In addition, the success rate is typically less than 20 percent, although it varies by clinic and is improving as the procedure becomes more common.

The first in-vitro fertilization, to produce test tube baby "Durga" in India and second in the world was performed by a Calcutta based doctor Dr. Subhash Mukhopadhyay on October 3, 1978. Both these events caused public debate, criticism and even social professional ostracism of those involved in initiating life outside the body. Besides these obstacles the techniques of IVF has survived as a method of choice for treating some type of infertility.

The first successful IVF treatment in the USA (producing Elizabeth Carr) took place in 1981 under the direction of Drs. Howard and Georgeanna Seegar Jones in Norfolk, Virginia. Since then IVF has exploded in popularity, with as many as 1% of all births now being conceived in-vitro, with over 115,000 born in the USA to date.

IVF may also be used in cases where the husband's semen contains so few sperms that it becomes difficult for them to fertilize an ovum in the fallopian tube. By IVF, sperm of such a person is used to fertilize the ovum in a test-tube. As far as the *shari'ah* is concerned, in-vitro fertilization is allowed as long as it be being done between a married couples. Although in-vitro fertilization with re implantation of fertilized eggs (ova) has long been widely used in animal breeding, the first successful birth of a human child from in-vitro fertilization, carried out by Patrick Steptoe and R.G. Edwards of Britain, did not take place until 1978.

In-vitro fertilization is generally undertaken only after an exhaustive evaluation of infertility has been made. A number of the candidates for IVF are women who suffer from blocked or absent fallopian tubes; others are men with low sperm counts or couples whose infertility is unexplained. IVF procedure includes the recovery (by needle aspiration) of mature eggs and the incubation of the eggs in a culture medium, as well as the collection and preparation of sperm and its addition to the medium. Fertilization generally occurs within 12 to 48 hours. The potential embryo is then placed in a growth medium, where it is observed periodically for division into two-cell, four-cell, and eight-cell stages. During this period the mother receives progesterone to prepare her uterine lining for implantation of the embryo.

The embryo, which at this point is known as a blastcyst, is introduced through the cervix into the uterus, in which the blastocyst seems to float free for about three-and-a-half days. If the procedure is successful, the embryo implants itself in the uterine wall, and pregnancy begins.

Process of *In-vitro fertilization* (IVF) is a technique by which an egg is fertilized under laboratory conditions. After the resulting embryo has developed for a short while it is then placed into the uterus of the woman who produced the egg. If it is implanted into another woman, we speak of embryo donation or embryo transfer. Before fertilization can take place an egg has to be removed from the ovary. In order to increase the chances of a pregnancy, in practice a number of eggs (normally three) are produced with the help of drugs and removed, fertilized, and reimplanted at the same time.

This technique, however, creates the possibility of more embryos being produced than are needed for reimplantation. These "surplus embryos" may be frozen and stored and/or used for research purposes including genetic engineering. The problems arising in this context are dealt with in the next section of this paper. It has to be noted that even if all embryos are reimplanted a number of difficult ethical and legal problems concerning the status and protection of the embryo, etc., remain.

In the concept of test-tube baby the original mother carries the fertilized embryo. For the fertilization in-vitro sperm and the ova may come from husband, wife, sperm donor, ova donor. Here sperm of husband of sperm of donor can combine with ova of any one, i.e. wife or ova donor.

In-Vitro Fertilization and Embryo Transplantation is a medical technique which is available for the treatment of infertility in many parts of the world. It has the potential to benefit both individual patients and society generally, not only by the alleviation of infertility, but also by the possible avoidance of genetic disorders and by enhancing fundamental studies of human reproduction and contraception.

The principles of the World Medical Association's Declaration of Helsinki will apply to all clinical research in respect to in-vitro fertilization and embryo transplantation. Any commercialization by which ova, sperm, or embryo is offered for purchase or sale is expressly condemned by the World Medical Association.

(b) Meaning and Definition of IVF

- In-vitro fertilization (IVF) is a procedure in which eggs (ova) from a woman's ovary are removed, they are fertilized with sperm in a laboratory procedure, and then the fertilized egg (embryo) is returned to the woman's uterus.
- IVF is one of several possible methods to increase the chances for an infertile couple to become pregnant. Its use depends on the reason for infertility. IVF may be an option if there is a blockage in the fallopian tube or endometriosis in the woman or low sperm count or poor quality sperm in the man and IVF will not work for a woman who is incapable of ovulating or with a man who is not able to produce at least a few healthy sperm.
- In-vitro fertilization is a procedure in which the joining of egg and sperm takes place outside of a woman's body.

A woman may be given fertility drugs before this procedure so that several eggs mature in the ovaries at the same time. The mature eggs (ova) are removed from the woman's ovaries using a long thin needle. They are mixed with sperm in a laboratory dish or test tube. (This is the origin of the term "test tube baby"). The eggs are monitored for several days. Once there is evidence that fertilization has occurred and the cells have begun to divide, they are then returned to the woman's uterus.

In-vitro fertilization, hormones are administered to the patient, and then eggs are harvested from her ovaries (A). The eggs are fertilized by sperm donated by the father (B). Once the cells begin to divide, one or more embryos are placed into the woman's uterus to develop and the pregnancy carries the same risks as any pregnancy achieved without assisted technology.

Also called test tube conception medical procedure in which mature egg cells are removed from a woman, fertilized with male sperm outside the body, and inserted into the uterus of the same or another woman for normal gestation and if the procedure is successful, the embryo implants itself in the uterine wall and pregnancy begins.

(c) Methods of IVF

One involves inserting the needle through the vagina (transvaginally); the physician guides the needle to the location in the ovaries with the help of an ultrasound machine. In the other procedure, called laparoscopy, a small thin tube with a viewing lens is inserted through an incision in the navel. This allows the physician to see on a video monitor inside the uterus to locate the ovaries.

(d) Steps Involved in IVF Procedure

An obstetrician-gynecologist (OB-GYN) with specialized training in IVF supervises the activities of IVF. This specialist performs most of the procedures involving the woman. Most IVF activities are performed in a professional medical office. In IVF procedures following steps are taken:

- Ovarian stimulation by hormonal injections to produce multiple eggs Monitoring of the response by ultrasound scans and blood tests.
- Egg retrieval with the help of a needle under local / general anesthesia Fertilization of the eggs in laboratory.
- Transfer of the resulting embryo(s) into the uterus of the woman.
- Blood test performed 15 days after embryo transfer, to assess the establishment of pregnancy.
- If the treatment procedure is successful, one or more of the embryos will implant in the uterus and pregnancy will result, just as it happens in the natural process of conception.

Another aspect of IVF, cryopreservation has in recent times gained popularity. Cryopreservation is the process of cooling and dehydrating an embryo to allow it to be stored for a long period of time. This process has gained popularity because it allows a woman undergoing IVF procedures to use possibly all of her retrieved and fertilized eggs. Cryopreservation eliminates the need to implant all of a woman resulting embryos at once, which something results in multiple pregnancies. In addition, the process reduces the number of times a woman may have to undergo egg retrieval if the first IVF attempts are unsuccessful in producing a pregnancy.

(e) *Assessment of Patients before IVF*

She should be physically fit to carry a resultant pregnancy and IVF and ET will not create any problem:

- Her ovaries should be accessible for oocytes;
- Her uterus should be capable of accepting and sustaining pregnancy for full term of 9 months;
- She should have easily negotiable cervical canal cervix for ET; and
- The male partner should have an appropriate concentration of motile sperms.

(f) *Treatment of Patients of IVF*

The female patients for IVF are required to record the commencement of each of their menstrual cycles for at least six months, so that decision may be taken for admitting the patient in the hospital. Date of urine sampling for Iuteirising hormone (LH) surge and date of administration of human chorionic gonadotrophin (HCG) to control the final stages of follicular and oocyte formation should be noted on record.

(g) *Nature of the Cycle for Follicular Development*

In the stimulated cycle, multiple follicular developments are stimulated by clomiphene, and/or human menopausal gonadotrophin (HMG), but LH surge is spontaneous and detected. The advantage of stimulated cycle is the availability of multiple follicles and oocytes so that several embryos are available for ET, leading to higher success rate.

In the controlled cycle, the development of the follicles is arrested at the optimum state of maturation by the administration of egg. The advantage of its cycle is that oocyte recovery can be performed through laparoscopy (see later) at a time convenient to the doctor and the patient so that the patient's hospital stay and anxiety are reduced. These 2 cycles are known to have given higher success rates in oocyte recovery, embryo transfer and pregnancies achieved.

(h) Technique for Recovery of Eggs

Blood tests and ultrasound scans of the ovaries are used to determine the optimal time to retrieve the eggs from the ovary. This optimal time is just before evaluation when the oocytes are almost ready for fertilization.

At the proper time, an outpatient procedure under local anesthesia will allow the female's egg to be visualized by ultrasound and retrieved from the ovary by placing a needle through the vaginal wall. The mild discomfort that the patient feels has been described as similar to a Pap smear or endometrial biopsy. After a short rest, the patient will be able to go home and resume normal activities.

The fluid from the follicles is examined under the microscope by the embryologist, who locates the eggs and keeps them in the laboratory under physiologic conditions. The embryologist will place the sperm with the eggs when they are ready for fertilization. Usually, the eggs will develop into cleaving pre-embryos, whose cells divide 2 or 3 times to become pre-implantation embryos (pre-embryos). They are maintained in laboratory dishes, in a nutrient mixture which acts as a substitute for the environment that would otherwise have been provided by the fallopian tubes.

Using a special catheter, the couple's pre-embryos will be passed through the vagina and into the uterus at the time the pre-embryos would normally have reached the uterus (2+ days after retrieval). After the pre-embryo placement in the uterus, the patient will lie quietly in a bed for about an hour, and then will return home.

(i) IVF without Surgery/Transvaginal Oocyte Retrieval (TOR)

It uses a sonographically guided needle to replace the surgical procedure which previously was used to recover oocytes (eggs). This procedure, called Transvaginal Oocyte Retrieval, requires neither hospitalization nor general anesthesia.

(j) Some Clarification about IVF

- There is no evidence to suggest that either normal laparoscopy or ultrasound egg retrieval damages the ovaries.
- Ordinarily there will be scar tissue around my ovaries to make it impossible to retrieve the eggs. The surgeon must be able to see the follicles in order to guide the needle to the proper spot for retrieval of the eggs whether by sonographic (ultrasound) or surgical methods.

Once ovulation has occurred it is impossible to retrieve the eggs. The entire team of physician, nurse and embryologist will monitor your cycle very carefully to avoid premature ovulation. If an egg is not retrieved or if the technique does not produce a pregnancy on the first attempt, how soon can the procedure be repeated? This depends on the individual. The primary reason for delay is to allow the patient's normal menstrual cycle to resume, which may take 2 to 3 cycles. There is no specific number. This is determined by the couple together with the physician.

We can have intercourse during the two-week period before an IVF procedure is performed? Doctor recommends that the husband refrain from ejaculation for at least 48 hours, but for no more than 5 to 6 days preceding egg retrieval.

After the IVF procedure, doctor suggests abstinence for two to 3 weeks and to wait to have intercourse. The IVF team recommends that the patient be sedentary for a full 24 hours following pre-embryo placement in the uterus. Strenuous exercises such as jogging, horseback, riding, swimming, etc. should be avoided until pregnancy is confirmed. Otherwise, the patient is free to return to her regular activities. Pregnancy can be confirmed using blood tests about 13 days after egg aspiration. Pregnancy can be confirmed by ultrasound 30 to 40 days after aspiration.

IVF may be covered by insurance companies. Frequently insurance policies will cover infertility but exclude IVF. Consultation with your lawyer may be necessary. For infertility alone, most insurance policies will not provide coverage. Four to five medications normally are given to stimulate the ovarian follicles and to maintain the lining of the uterus prior to implantation of the pre-embryo.

There is also a possibility of multiple births with IVF. When multiple pre-embryos are transferred 25% of pregnancies with IVF are *twins*. (In normal population, the rate is one set of twins per 80 births. Triplets are seen in approximately 2-3% of pregnancies.

There are no known effects for increased chance to birth defects if I become pregnant through IVF. Approximately three weeks are required for whole procedure. Fertility drugs are administered to stimulate the ovaries. Then during the four to six days prior to ovulation, the patient is monitored by ultrasound as well as by hormone levels. A maximum of four pre-embryos will be transferred to the uterus for possible implantation. Patients will have several other options regarding the disposition of the remaining pre-embryos. One option is to freeze pre-embryos for your later use. Other options are to donate or simply dispose of them. Excess pre-embryos, if any, belong to you, and you will determine what is to be done.

(B) Challenges Regarding IVF

- Eggs and Embryos have been stolen from women and given to other or to researchers.
- Fertility drugs have been sold illegally.
- Medical records have gone amiss.
- Women recruited as surrogate mother have refused to part with the newborn baby that they have conceived to assist couples to bear a child. India has been known to play host to visiting foreign IVF fertility experts to carry out such procedures that

have been banned in the home country of visiting experts the case of injecting round spermatic into the egg cytoplasm is a good example of such misdemeanor.

- Sale of eggs and embryos are subtly advertised over the internet by some IVF clinics in India. IVF costs approximately $ 10,000 per cycle, and it takes an average of four cycles to achieve a successful pregnancy.

(C) Global Endeavours for Controlling the Vices of IVF

(a) The Victorian IVF Committee

By the end of 1981 the phenomenon then usually labeled, in a plethora of media reports, comments, accounts and speculations, as the test-tube baby was the subject of serious questions canvassed in the councils of the major Christian denominations in Victoria, and in other groups in the community. Some of these questions had been raised by religious and secular groups nearly a decade earlier in the publication of the first reports of successful laboratory fertilizations of mammalian gametes and the development of mammalian embryos, and the birth, after transfer, of healthy mice, followed by claves, lamb or kids.[113]

Dr. Paul Ramsey, a renowned American ethicist had argued that since there could be no certainly that in-vitro fertilization would result in no harm whatever to a child born from its employment, it should never be done.

The committee fulfilled its obligation to complete an interim report within three months of starting its enquiries. Between June and September 1982 it held nine meetings, interviewing a number of experts in the area of reproductive medicine, infertility counseling, moral philosophy and child psychiatry.

The committee, recognizing the grave concerns (some of which have been mentioned) about the procedure and its outcomes went on immediately to propose that legislation be

113. 'The first test tube baby,' *Time*, 31 July 1978, pp. 46-49.

enacted to provide a system for the approval or licensing of hospitals to undertake IVF programmes, and imposing conditions in relation to such approvals. Counseling for infertile couples admitted to an IVF programme was to be a core condition.

The committee published its second report, Report on Donor Gametes in IVF, in August 1983, its third and final report, Report on the Disposition of Embryos produced by in Vitro Fertilization, appeared in August 1984. Throughout its work, the IVG committee solicited public comments and submissions and made the community aware of the questions it was asking by publishing, in April 1983, an issues paper on Donor gametes in IVF.

(b) Major Recommendations in Its Second Report

- The use of donor gametes and donor embryos in IVF programmes was acceptable.
- Hospitals should be specifically authorized to conduct IVF programmes using donor gametes or donor embryos.
- Donors of gametes should not receive payment (other than medical hospital and traveling expenses).
- Donations of gametes from children should be prohibited.
- Counseling should be mandatory for donors, as well as for infertile couples.
- Non-identifying information about donors should be offered to recipients of gametes or embryos and to donors about recipients and successful pregnancies and live births.
- Comprehensive (that is, identifying) information about donors whose gametes were successfully used in an IVF programme should be stored in a Central Registry maintained by the Health Department of Victory.
- Legislation should be enacted to establish clearly the relationship of father and child, where donor gametes or donor embryos were used to establish a

pregnancy, provide it was with the consent of the spouse who made no genetic contribution to the child.

- Conscientious objection to participation by doctors and allied health professionals in approved IVF programmes should be recognized and protected.

(c) *The Infertility Treatment Act, 1995*

IVF is permissible for genetic parents, with donor eggs and with donated embryos (Intracytoplasmic sperm injection) ICSI. ICSI is also permitted. All are regulated by the Act.

(d) *South Australia*

In March 1988 South Australia joined Victoria in the field of regulation, when it enacted the Reproductive Technology Act, 1988 which provides a system of licensing and control for the state's artificial fertilization procedures. This statute was preceded by the In-Vitro Fertilization (Restriction) Act, 1987 which restricted IVF programmes to those established in three named Adelaide hospitals.[114] In 1989, an IVF Planning Decree was issue with a framework for licensing of in-vitro fertilization.

In February 1994, the then State Secretary for Health accordingly asked the health council to prepare a scientific report on the subject. In June 1996 the committee, which prepared the Report (the Health Council's IVF Planning Decree Review Committee), presented a separate report on ICSL. In February 1997, the report on IVF was published. In 1998 a third and final report dealing with pre-implementation genetic diagnosis, future developments in the field of IVF and research using embryos was published. A new IVF Planning Decree appeared in 1998.

The capacity for IVF is confined to 13 centers, which are supposed to cover the demand for the next 10 years. The Decree formulates amongst others the following conditions:

---

114. In-Vitro Fertilization (Restriction) Act, 1987 (SA) Section 4(2) limits IVF Procedures to:
(a) The University of Adelaide and the Queen Elizabeth Hospital.

- IVF is governed to the Guidelines Indications for IVF' of the Dutch association for Obstetrics and Gynecology.
- At least 15% of the started treatments have to result in a continuing pregnancy.
- The centre complies with the moratorium on ICSI with MESA and TESE of the Dutch association for obstetrics and Gynaecology, the Dutch Clinical Genetics Association.
- IVF in combination with surrogacy is carried out according to the rules laid down in a protocol that has to comply with the Guidelines High Tech Surrogacy of the Dutch Association for Obstetrics and Gynecology and only takes place under the condition that the surrogate mother already has one or more children. Before acting, the doctor must write a statement that the treatment is based on medical grounds and complies with the Guidelines.
- According to the rules laid down in the protocol a written agreement is made about the use and storage time of embryos that remain after the treatment making of embryos and ova available to others is free of charge.
- IVF is taking into account a protocol, of which the Decree indicates some elements. When the centre carries out IVF with ovum donation, the protocol needs to be extended with additional rules. The same applies to ICSI. When IVF is carried out in combination with surrogacy, the Protocol contains rules concerning information to be given to the partners and the surrogate mother about the consequences that result from surrogacy, which include anyway.
- Possible psychosocial consequences for the parties involved and the future child.
- Agreement concerning parting with the child.
- Possible personal and family law or other legal consequences.

In the report of the Health Council on in-vitro Fertilization

(1997) attention is paid to, amongst others, access and risk assessment.

In the report of the health council on in-vitro Fertilization attention is also paid to the interests of the child in the assessment of the individual request for help. The guidelines of the Royal Dutch Medical Association (KNMG) on this subject state that the doctor cannot simply seek to the (would be) parents, but must also take into account the future interests of the (. . .) 'resultant child' (KNMG, 1998). The health council's committee subscribes to this view. This dual responsibility implies that doctors face difficult decision in some cases which may result in the request not being granted in view of the child's interests.

(e) America

Although the first American IVF birth occurred more than fifteen years ago, the field has been largely unregulated by the federal government. The federal government's first significant step into the area was more informational than regulatory: In 1992, Congress passed the Fertility Clinic Success Rate and Certification Act of 1992 (the Wyden Bill), which required an accounting of IVF births. Even this modest gesture, however, had only a postponed effect, since the Department of Health and Human Services declined to fund the project until 1995.

State regulation is similarly sparse. Approximately, sixteen states have laws that even mention human cell transfers. Some of these statutes require certification by state boards, some screening of donors, and some annual reporting. However, most states have been content to let the industry regulate itself.[115]

(f) Del Zio v. Presbyterian Hospital

A 1978 federal district court jury in *New York* awarded prospective parents in an IVF procedure the sum of $ 50,000. The "Parents" claimed they endured great pain and suffering due to the deliberate destruction by the defendant of a potential embryo before fertilization had occurred. There is

---

115. Byers Keith Alan, "Infertility and in-Vitro Fertilization", 18, *J. Legal Med.* 29 (1997).

however, a 90 percent success rate for egg recovery, fertilization, and early embryonic cleavage. As of 1986 more than 130 IVF programs existed in the *United States,* in major cities and even in small towns.

Pennsylvania and *Illinois* have statues requiring the monitoring of the in-vitro fertilization procedure, although in Illinois the physician's restricted liability is based upon custody of the woman's egg and presumably the man's sperm. In many states, the legality of IVF as a medical procedure to overcome infertility is in question.

Half of the infertility clinics in the *United States* in 1987 utilized the in-vitro fertilization technique. As one writer observed,

> *"The IVF clinic represents the end of the road for most of the women here each of us has a long history of disappointment verging on despair. Our pain is private; we keep it to ourselves. . . . I know, like every woman who waits in an IVF clinic, that anything less than 100% is failure. In 1988 the U.S. Congress commenced a study toward regulation of or controlling "unscrupulous fertility clinics": more than half of the 169 clinics in the United States performing in-vitro fertilization in 1987 never produced a baby".*

Pennsylvania is one of the few states that have statutes regarding IVFD. It is designed to monitor the procedure by requiring the IVF clinic to file quarterly report with the State Department of Health, describing the processes involved with the undertakings. The Illinois statute is criminal in nature but does not directly prohibit the IVF procedure: it makes the physician who fertilizes a woman's egg outside her body the custodian of that tissue for purposes of the 1977 child abuse Act. In short, in Illinois, a physician who performs the IVF procedure without wilful endangerment or injury to the embryo during the pre-implantation period will not be prosecuted. The *Illinois* statute grants custody to the physician and makes no provision for the parents to regain custody.

In New York, in the unreported case of *Del Zio* v. *Columbia,* Presbyterian Medical Center, the prospective parents of the IVF baby were compensated for emotional distress caused by the willful destruction of the embryo.

Is IVF being oversold? Its national success rate is said to be only 15 percent. To maintain uniformity and to improve IVF techniques, federal regulation has been recommended: all IVF laboratories would be certified, its personnel licensed, and its success rate verified. However, it should be observed that IVF is most effective in surmounting tubal problems and endometriosis or sperm scarcity. Indeed, it may be procedure of choice of only 5 to 10 percent of those seeking infertility treatments.

(D) Ethical and Legal Issues of IVF and Judicial Response

Normally the participants in IVF will be a married couple who will donate the eggs and spermatozoa. After receiving adequate explanation of the IVF and ET procedures from the clinician they will give their informed consent.

Superficially this seems a straightforward matter. The right of every person to have a child is enshrined in the Declaration of Human Rights (Geneva, 1948) and the doctor's role in the relief of suffering, of which infertility is a manifestation, has been recognized science the techniques of Hippocrates (400-500 BC). In this situation, however, the adult participants are consenting to a proposed action, which is not centered on themselves but on the embryo and child-to-be.

If IVF is extended to include the eggs or spermatozoa donated by a third party or implantation of the embryo in the uterus of a woman not the egg donor, consent to what is done with the donated gametes or transferred embryo introduces the question of the consent of the third party. Should the gamete-donor or host mother have any rights of consent in determining what might be done with the embryo or child? It might be argued that the rules governing adoption of a child could also apply in these circumstances but the matter still requires clarification.

Already, we have seen that consent of the adult participants in IVF has called into question the situation of the embryo and whether the "parents" can consent to IVF on the future embryo's behalf. This is a convenient juncture at which to deal with the moral status of the embryo.[116]

(a) Resolution of Ethical Problems

To do nothing about the problems is tantamount to making a decision to ignore the complicated moral, legal, social and economic consequences of an IVF programme that are inevitable in due course. It would also be to ignore the concerns of those in the community who have expressed opposition to IVF. Both would be irresponsible acts and unworthy of the best traditions of medicine.

In the USA, there is a presidential commission for the study of ethical problems in medicine and biomedical and behavioral research. This is a national body—unlike the one in Australia mentioned above, which is a State committee. We do not have a national body of this type in Australia but the already established Australian Law Reform Commission could serve this function. Mr. Justice Kirby, president of this commission, has urged Australian to respond to the ethical challenge of IVF and its possible future applications by ending a paper on "Law for the Test Tube man?" with the words: "Let it not be the epitaph of our generation that we proved ourselves brilliant in a dazzling filed of scientific Endeavour but so morally bankrupt and legally incompetent that we could not bother or did not have the courage to sort out the consequences for our society and for the human species".[117]

(b) Legal View-Point

Legal problem of Test-tube Baby is like that of A.I. and surrogate mother. In a case of divorced couple, the British Medical Council stated that the woman has the right to conceive child through the embryo preserved before marriage. But also in AIH, the child will be illegitimate conceived by the procedure of Test-tube baby.

---

116. Walters, William A.W., "The Role of Ethics In The IVF Programme", Department of Obstetrics and Gynecology, Monash University, Queen Victoria Medical Centre, 172, Lansdale Street, Melbourne, Victoria, Australia 3000.

117. *Ibid.*

Now the issue arises on utilization, preservation and destruction of the embryo. British Government set-up a Committee of enquiry in 1982 under the Chairmanship of Lady Warnock and that has submitted a report with 65 recommendations. Some of them are as under:

- A statutory licensing body should be set-up to monitor infertility services and I.V.F.
- I.V.F., A.I.D., egg donation, sperm freezing, embryo freezing and the sale and purchase of these should be permitted but subject to regulation by the licensing body.
- Embryos could be produced for and used in research up 7 to 14 days after fertilization preferably with the consent of the couples who generated them.
- Embryos from trans-species I.V.F., must not be allowed to service beyond a two cell stage. It would be criminal offence to transplant a human embryo to an animal uterus.
- No human embryo that had been the subject of research experiments must be implanted.
- No male or female must provide eggs or sperm for more than 10 children.
- No agency or professional third party must be involved in surrogacy arrangements.

These recommendations were accepted by British Parliament while passing human fertilization and embryology Act, 1990. I.C.M.R. Code has also mentioned some recommendation regarding the utilization preservation and destruction of embryo but there is no particular statute law to enforce the same. India needs a law on this point.

The law needs to move along with medical advancements and should be suitably framed not to give rise any type of dilemmas of harsh situation. In India Law should take active part to make an act on this issue. It is therefore, imperative to legislate for regulating following things-

- The status of the surrogate mother who carries pregnancy even though she does not contribute the egg to resultant rights and liabilities arising out of surrogate motherhood.

- The parental legal status of a child in a situation where the sperm is contributed by a donor other than the legal husband.
- To monitor and regulate the contractual relationship arising between the surrogate mother and the donor.
- To protect marketing and production of produce compounds.
- To permit to practice foreign Lawyers in National Courts and Forums.
- To permit foreign accounting firm and companies.
- To improve quality check procedure.
- To regulate the policy for giving foreign construction companies.
- To protect and provide effective Tele-Communication province.
- To improve and regulate Copy Rights and Parents Law.
- To make more stringent Trade Marks Legislation to protect the rights of Trade Marks owners.
- To provide strong and serious legislative provisions including criminal actions for breach of AIH proposed laws.

III. SURROGATE MOTHERHOOD

(A) Concept of Surrogate Motherhood

(a) Historical Background

Motherhood is a relation of blood and emotions born out of carrying a foetus and it can never be perceived when the baby is grown in a rented womb. Surrogate motherhood (S.M.) is a newer development in the management of infertility. It assists infertile couple to procreate by different techniques. The advantage is that a woman without a uterus but with functioning ovaries may have her child with the help of a surrogate mother. The concept of surrogacy is not new. It is old but issues are new and amplitude is wider.

Before the advent of modern assisted conception techniques, natural surrogacy was the only means of helping certain barren women to have children. Before artificial insemination, babies were conceived the natural way. Later as artificial insemination (AI) was accepted, this became the usual means of achieving pregnancy in cases of infertility, being more socially acceptable than the natural way. When assisted conception methods such as in vitro fertilization (IVF) become available, it was a natural step to use the eggs of the women wanting the baby donor woman and the sperm of her husband/donor male, to create their embryos in vitro and transfer these to a suitable host.

The concept of "*rent a uterus*" in fact may be readily acceptable in the more analytical frame of the mind with the argument "*at least the baby is made with our gemmates even though nourished in a rented body*". With sisters, sister-in-law and even mothers lending a hand or rather a uterus, it received greater acceptability (even if future consequences arose, it could resolved very easily and the helping hand of near and close relative my not be taken out after delivering the child).

Although offering to become a surrogate mother for an unfertile couple might appear to be an uncomplicated altruistic act, it is not an easy course of action. Equally the intended parents may see surrogacy as the answer to their prayers, but they are also likely to have concerns over the implication of their decision before proceedings.

(b) *Instances of Surrogate Motherhood in the Ancient World*

There are no authentic documents survived up to contemporary times. Information is to be collected from chronicles, legends, myths, epics and even the folk songs that have survived from oral transmissions from generation to generation. The concept of surrogate motherhood was well known in the ancient world. Some of the instances are traced as under:

1. *Ancient India*

Surrogacy is as old as the Mahabharata, Ramayana and the Bible. Surrogacy was known and practiced in ancient times.

In the Mahabharata, Gandhari, wife of King Dhritarashtra, conceived but the pregnancy went on for nearly two years; after which she delivered a mass (mole). Bhagwan Vyasa found that there were 101 cells that were normal in the mass. These cells were put in a nutrient medium and were grown in-vitro till full term. Of these 100, developed into male children (Duryodhan, Dushashan and the other Kauravas) and one as a female child called (Dusheela).

There are other well-quoted examples that refer to not only IVF but also to the idea that a male can produce a child without the help of female. Saga Gautama produced two children from his own semen—a son Kripa and a daughter Kripi, who were both test tube babies.

Likewise, sage Bharadwaj produced Drona, later to be the teacher of the Pandavas and the Kauravas. The story reflects the supernatural powers of the great sages. King Draupada had enmity with Dronacharya and desired to have a son strong enough to kill Drona. He was given medicine by Rishi and after collecting his semen, processed it and suggested that AIH should be done for his wife who however refused. The Rishi then put the semen in a Yajnakunda from which Dhrishtadyumna and Draupadi were born.

There is another story, which refers to embryo transfer. This was regarding the seventh pregnancy of Devaki, by the will of the Lord; the embryo was transferred to the womb of Rohini, the first wife of Vasudev to prevent the body being killed by baby Kamsa.

2. *Ancient Mesopotamia and Egypt*

Surrogacy has been around a long time and dates back to biblical times. An interesting biblical scenario is Sarah, the wife of Abraham. Sarah could not have children in the beginning. She gave her handmaid Hager to Abraham to produce them a child.

The method used was copulation. The outcome in this arrangement did not prove to be a productive one and ended in disaster.[118]

118. http://www.yale.edu/ynhti/curriculum/units.

Traditionally the generational or surrogate mother is a close relative who agrees to carry a pregnancy to term and had the baby over to the childless couple. Those days pregnancy was by sexual intercourse. Since the late 1970's in-vitro fertilization (IVF) has been used to achieve pregnancy in Petri, dish.

Now surrogate mother is a woman who accepts pregnancy and bears child either by way of artificial insemination or by way of implantation of in-vitro fertilized ova at the blastocyte state, till normal delivery, for another woman who is incapable to carry child. Surrogate mothers are paid for their expenses and receive an additional fee. Agencies and/or lawyers are often involved in the process.[119]

The late 1970s saw the birth of the first *"test tube babies"*, conceived in-vitro (*"in glass"*) under laboratory conditions. In-vitro fertilization normally begins with the extraction of an ovum, or egg, and the fertilization of the ovum in a laboratory dish. The fertilized ovum is then introduced into the uterus, where it develops normally. In itself, in-vitro fertilization is not particularly problematic, since it can and often does involve simply fertilizing an ovum from the woman who will carry the child. It becomes problematic, however, when the woman is a surrogate mother.

Surrogate motherhood was first reported from Britain on 4th January, 1985. For $ 7475, Kim Cotton agreed to bear a child. She was a 28 year old married woman with two children. She was inseminated with the hiring husband's sperm form an American couple. Within hours of the birth, the social Service Director, Alan Gorst, the Council Authority in North London borough of Barnet, said the Council was responsible for the welfare of all the babies born in the area and opined that any money transaction involving a child would be unlawful.

The first recorded birth in Australia took place in 1988. Between 1989 and 1991 eleven requests for IVF surrogacy were made to the Monash IVF programme and in 1994 a failed attempt at such a procedure in Victoria was reported.

119. Nordenberg Tamara, "Overcoming Infertility", *FDA Consumer,* 31, No. 1 (1997): 18.

(c) Recent Example of Surrogate Motherhood

Nirmala, a poor housewife from Chandigarh raised a basic issue, by asking the court to permit her to bear a child for a childless couple on consideration for a sum of money. Forced by poverty and illness of her husband, Nirmala (30 years old) asked the court to allow her to rent out her womb. For the first time in the history of the country the law was faced with a peculiar situation where the woman pleaded before the Chandigarh court to declare her proposal to *"rent out her womb"* as legal and constitutional. She also demanded *"legitimacy"* for the 'yet to be born child'. Her husband, Chand Ram was bedridden for a couple of years after being incapacitated by a paralytic attack following a bout of high fever. Faced with penury and no means to pay for the expensive medicines prescribed by the doctors for her husband, Nirmala agreed to enter into a contract with the childless couple. 'They approached me to bear his (a retired Airforce Officer) child and offered to pay Rs. 50,000 a decent place to live and sufficient food for the family'. Nirmala said that the Simplest solution perhaps is a permanent job for Nirmala and areolation for the couple she wants to bear the child for.

Surrogate arrangements are made usually through close friends or relatives of the childless couple. However, the practice of commercial surrogacy has increased greatly during the last decade. Man major cities have surrogate agencies that maintain lists of potential surrogate mothers and help match these with couples wanting to have a baby. These agencies are often run by doctors or lawyers and may be found through listings in telephone books. Commercial surrogate agencies typically charge a fee of $ 10,000 or more to make the arrangements, which is in addition to the surrogate mother's expenses and fees.

These agencies are not legal in all states. Most commercial surrogacy are handled through a contract between the prospective parents and the surrogate mother. The contracting couple agrees to pay the surrogate mother's expenses during the pregnancy and delivery plus a fee for the surrogate's services. The fee can vary between $ 10,000 and $ 10,000 per pregnancy.

The surrogate mother also agrees to terminate her parental rights to the infant and turn it over to the contracting couple after birth. A vast majority of the surrogacy arrangements proceed without difficulty, occasionally problems arise concerning custody of the child. Since the concept of commercial surrogacy is relatively new, there are few laws and legal precedents concerning this contrast. In some states these contracts are illegal and are considered null and unenforceable by the courts.

There are no laws or guidelines in India as yet. This is why the element of trust b/w the couple and the surrogate mothers are so important. Surrogacy has a bond with both the genetic mother and the surrogate mother.

Bradley 5 the bond between these two women and this child is permanent and cannot be changed by law. The law can only govern which woman has the legal right to raise the child.

(d) Meaning and Definition of Surrogate Motherhood

The word surrogate, from Latin Surrogatus (substituted) means "to *rent out her womb*". A surrogacy arrangement is one in which one woman (the surrogate mother) agrees to bear a child for another woman or a couple (the intended parents) and surrender it at birth. This provides an opportunity for those woman who are unable to carry a child themselves to overcome their childlessness".[120] As per Oxford Dictionary a surrogate is a substitute for a person in a specific role or office".

"Surrogate Mother is the term generally used to describe a gestating mother, who lets her womb out". It is the practice whereby a woman carries a child for another with the intention that the child should be handed over after birth either for a fee or voluntarily. This carrying of a child may take different forms. A mother who cannot bear a child for herself may commission another woman to carry a child for her.

1. Commissioning Mother (CM)

"The mother who asks another to carry the pregnancy for

120. Definition inserted from http://www.answers.com/topic/surrogate mother.

her is called C. Mother and the woman who does pregnancy for her is called C. Mother".

2. *Carrying Mother (CM)*

"The woman who agrees to bear the child in her womb is called the carrying Mother".

3. *Genetic Mother (GM)*

"The commissioning mother may provide the egg, so she is called the Genetic Mother".

4. *Genetic Father (GF)*

"The Genetic father is the husband of the commissioning mother or an anonymous donor".

- Surrogacy involves artificial insemination, where the carrying mother is the genetic mother inseminated with the semen of the infertile woman's husband. In case the egg and semen come from the commissioning couple through in-vitro fertilization and the resultant embryo is transferred to and implanted in the carrying mother, it is surrogacy involving artificial insemination.
- "A person acting the role of mother, a woman who bears a child on behalf of another woman from her own egg fertilized by the other woman's partner".
- "Surrogate mother is a means for conceiving procuring a child genetically related to at least one person of the childless couple".
- The word surrogate means substitute or replacement and a surrogate mother is one who lends her uterus to another couple so that they can have a baby.
- Surrogate motherhood is when one woman carries to term the fertilized egg of another woman. This procedure is chosen by marred couples who can not conceive a child in the "natural way". In some occasions the mother may be able to produce an egg, but has so womb or some other physical problem, which prevents her from carrying a child. Whether or not the husband can produce a large amount of

sperms is not a problem. Once the egg and sperm are combined in a petri dish fertilization is very likely to occur. The couple will then choose a surrogate mother and make an agreement in which she will carry the baby and release it to the emetic parents after the birth.

- S. M. assists infertile couple to procreate by different techniques the advantage is that a woman without a uterus but with functioning ovaries may have her child with the help of a surrogate mother.
- A surrogate mother is a woman who carries a child on behalf of another woman, who will become the child's social mother. The social mother will also be the child's genetic mother if she donates the ovum.
- Surrogacy is an arrangement whereby one woman carries a child for another woman with the intention that is should be handed over after birth. Surrogacy is used more and more by gay couples and single men who cannot otherwise have their own offspring. Surrogacy agreements may involve different methods of procreation such as natural or artificial insemination, egg or embryo donation. Usually it is a married couple that enters into the arrangement with a surrogate mother who will be either artificially inseminated with the husband's semen or who will receive the embryo after IVF. In most cases the surrogate mother agrees to do this only for a fee but there are also agreements without financial implications. Surrogacy agreements intend that the genetic mother (who produced the egg) will also be the nurturing mother after the child's birth, and that the surrogate mother will only function as carrying mother and surrender the child immediately after birth to the nurturing mother.
- "S. Motherhood involves the artificial insemination of a women with a man's sperm is his wife is infertile or does not want to carry a pregnancy. The surrogate mother receives a tree and relinquishes the child to the contracting couple immediately after birth".

(e) Types of Surrogacy

1. Total or Gestational Surrogacy
2. Partial or Traditional Surrogacy
3. Commercial Surrogacy
4. Non-Commercial Surrogacy

1. Total Surrogacy or Gestational Surrogacy

"Is when the women bears a child that has been formed form the garments of another woman and man and implanted in her body".

In order for a pregnancy to take place, a sperm egg, and a uterus are necessary. In gestational surrogacy, the surrogate mother has no genetic ties to the offspring: Eggs and sperm are extracted from the donors and in vitro fertilized and implanted into uterus of the surrogate. The child will be given back to the donor of the ovum. This is an expensive procedure, again, the unused embryos may he frozen for further use if the First transfer does not result in pregnancy.

2. Partial or Traditional Surrogacy

"Occurs when the birth mother contributes the sperm is introduced by artificial incardination, she is a biological parent of the child".

One commissioning father donates a sperm which is introduced by insemination for in-vitro fertilization with the oocytes of woman, the surrogate mother. The insemination can be natural or artificial. The custody of the child will be surrendered to the biological father, who donated the sperm(when the sperm count is low). In either case the surrogate's own egg will be used. Genetically the surrogate becomes the mother of the resulting child. This is the common method of surrogate motherhood. This is called partial surrogacy, because the genetic origin is found in one of the commissioning parents.

3. Commercial Surrogacy

Means a "business like transaction where a fee is charged for the incubation period". If the surrogacy involves payment of money it is termed as "commercial surrogacy".

4. *Non-Commercial Surrogacy or Altruistic Surrogacy*

"In Non-Commercial Surrogacy there is no formal contract when surrogacy does not involve payment of money it's called Altruistic Surrogacy. It arises out of friendship involving only friends and for relatives.

(a) Essentials of Altruistic Surrogacy

- The Practice of altruistic surrogacy cannot be stopped; therefore, there is little point passing legislation to regulate it;
- Altruistic surrogacy is more acceptable as it occurs between friends and relatives father than strangers (i.e. commercial surrogacy is potentially more devastating for parties to such an agreement as friends and relatives are more likely to have regards for each other welfare); and.
- Altruistic surrogacy does not threaten our perceptions of the role of women, marriage and the family to the same degree as commercial surrogacy.

(f) Three Means of S.M.

- Carrying of child from father sperm and rented mother's egg.
- Embryo of couple.
- Having sex with the husband.

(g) Who might use Surrogacy?

Some women are unable to carry a child to a term. A variety of causes account for this, including:

- Failure of embryo to transplant.
- Hysterectomy or pelvic disorder.
- Dangerously high blood pressure.
- Heart or liver disease.
- Women who has no uterus, i.e. absent form birth (Mullein an agenesis) or removed surgically: Hysterectomy for life saving reasons, such as excessive bleeding during a caesareans

- Multiple Miscarriages.
- Who have tailed repeated IVF attempts for unexplained reasons.
- Uterine Cancer.
- Ovarian Cancer.
- Sister, mother or close turned of the couples.
- Financial remuneration.
- Woman, with or without children.
- Known or unknown to the couple.
- Rents her womb for a free.
- A woman who cannot retain the conceived foetus due to spontaneous abortion.
- To fulfil her dream of having a child.
- Kidney cineastes or multiple sclerosis.
- Figure couscous woman to desire that some other woman should bear a child for her.

Due to above reasons, pregnancy would entail serious risk for them. Some people may come to terms with their childishness. Others may find adoption or fostering an acceptable alternative.[121]

(h) Criteria for Becoming a Surrogate Mother

- A surrogate mother must be in good overall health.
- No medical problems which could lead to complication with pregnancy.
- She should not be overweight, heavy smokers, drinkers or substance abusers are not suitable as surrogate mother, because of the associated risk both to the woman and to the baby.
- Surrogate mothers should have borne at least one child previously and preferably have completed her own family.
- She should give her own consent.
- She should be below age group of 35 years.
- Being a surrogate mother is an emotionally and

121. http://www.yale.edu/ynhti/curriculum/units

physically demanding task. So there should be a backing of partner, family or friends.

- Careful consideration must be given to the medical, emotional, legal and practical issues.
- Is the potential surrogate healthy and free from disease.
- Is the surrogate's genetic material compatible with the contracting couple's expectations.
- Is the surrogate candidate emotionally and psychologically stable.
- Does the potential surrogate live in a stable situation which positively influence the pregnant.
- Does the potential surrogate have a family history of genetic defects that might adversely affect the baby?
- Thought must also be given to the effect of any existing children, the potential surrogate mother's partner, family and friend.

(i) What is Parental Order and who can Apply for it?

A parental order, which is obtainable by application to the Courts, makes the intended parent child's legal parents. This has the same effect as adoption, but allows a quicker route in case of surrogacy. In order to apply for the parental order, the following criteria must be met:

- The child must be genetically related to one or both of the intended parents.
- The intended parents must be married to each other and must both be aged 18 or over.
- The legal mother and father (i.e. the surrogate mother and her partner, if she has one) must consent to the making of order (this consent can not be given until six weeks after the birth of the child).
- No money other than reasonable expenses has been paid for the surrogacy arrangement unless a Court has authorized the payment.
- An application must be made within six months of the birth of the child.[122]

122. http://www.bma.org.uk/ap.nsf/content/considering surrogacy.

(B) Challenges Regarding Surrogate Motherhood

A surrogate mother is a woman who carries a child on behalf of another woman, who will become the child's social mother. The social mother will also be the child's genetic mother if she donates the ovum. The problem is that three roles normally borne by one woman—genetic mother, childbearing mother, and social mother—are now divided between two.

In addition, the sperm may come from the husband of one of the women or from another man. Because of these complications and the emotional strain on both mothers (and potentially the child), surrogacy has been made illegal in some countries. In others, it is becoming institutionalized, and laws are being changed in order to define precisely the rights and obligations of parents and children in this situation.

Surrogate arrangements[123] have created a lot of confusion in legal circles, posing new challenges. The bifurcated role of woman in surrogate arrangements is prompting renewed assessment of the meaning of motherhood and the designation of maternal rights.[124] From the human rights point of view the underpinning issues involve right to individual autonomy, procreative liberty, right to dignity, right to privacy, commercialization of human body, etc.

However, reproductive technologies also bring with them complex social, psychological, and ethical considerations, and the multi-billion-dollar industry has little regulation. Egg, sperm, and embryo donors may worry about anonymity or being sued for child support. Children may want the right to know their medical history and perhaps their biological parents and siblings. Genetic or surrogate parents may want to claim the children they have helped produce. Couples may argue about custody of frozen embryos or disposal of extra or inferior

123. Surrogacy arrangements are agreements under which a woman agrees to bear a child for a couple (or, less frequently, a single person) often called the "commissioning" couple or person. The woman is either artificially inseminated with the sperm of the commissioning man (or a donor) or she is implanted with the embryo produced in-vitro from the gametes of one or both.

124. Stumpf Andres E., "Redefining Mother: A Legal Matrix for New Reproductive Technologies", 96, *The Yale Law Journal,* 186 (1986).

embryos. Others may question the ethics of selling eggs, sperm, and "womb space.

Surrogate motherhood is a by-product of the artificial insemination. It has created great controversy in the legal and ethical circles around the world. This procedure of human reproduction is adopted when a woman has a problem in carrying her child to its full term. From the *shariah* point of view, surrogate motherhood as portrayed above is not allowed because it involves the insertion of a sperm of another person into the woman's uterus. This goes against the verse of the Quran which says that the believing women should guard their private parts except from their spouses.

The late 1970s saw the birth of the first "test tube babies", conceived in-vitro ("in glass") under laboratory conditions. In vitro fertilization normally begins with the extraction of an ovum, or egg, and the fertilization of the ovum in a laboratory dish. The fertilized ovum is then introduced into the uterus, where it develops normally. In itself, in-vitro fertilization is not particularly problematic, since it can and often does involve simply fertilizing an ovum from the woman who will carry the child. It becomes problematic, however, when the woman is a surrogate mother.

(a) Individual Autonomy

The principle of autonomy is often invoked as a justification for allowing surrogacy. This principle states that people have the freedom to decide what to do with their bodies provided that no harm is caused to others. The fundamental fallacy of the autonomy argument lies in the fact that the decision a woman makes to have a child (i.e. to do something with her own body) is not the issue in case of surrogacy but rather the decision to give the child to some else who happens to want it.

(b) Procreative Liberty

As courts have struggled to define the parameter of procreative choice, the right of procreation has received its most extensive legal expression as a right not to procreate.[125]

125. Griswold *v.* Connecticut, 381 U.S. 479 (1965); Roe *v.* Wade, 410 U.S. 113 (1973).

Included in the right to procreate is the right to conceive. Abortion is a right to conceive followed by a protected option—a right not to procreate. Surrogate motherhood is the inverse: a right to conceive that should also be followed by a protected option—a right to procreate. In the abortion case, the mother's conception is only biological in origin.

In the surrogate mother's case, the initiating mother's conception is only mental. Different kinds of protection are required for conceivers to realize different kinds of procreative intent.[126] Courts in abortion cases must balance the rights of a mother and a child, whereas courts in surrogate cases must balance the rights of two mothers and a child. However, in both cases, the fundamental right of conception as a predicate of the right to procreate is at stake.

Because even infertile mothers can exert their right of psychological conception, they too have a procreative right that courts should preserve. Conscious and intentional exertion of the right to procreate should be accorded more protection than an accidental and unintended procreation.

(c) *Inviolability of Surrogate Mother*

Once the embryo is implanted in the womb of the surrogate the process enters a realm of privacy which entails substantial personal freedom for gestating mother. The inviolability of this personal realm prohibits enforcement of the surrogate contract through specific performances during gestation.

Damage remedies against the surrogate mother for non-performance must be severely limited to reserve the fundamental rights of privacy and procreative autonomy. The terms of the contract should serve primarily as indications of the parties' intent including a willingness on the part of the surrogate mother to abide by the terms. However, punishing the surrogate mother for "inadequate" birth is misplaced in the traditional scheme of maternity, which accords pregnant woman the freedom to lead their life without fear of sanction.[127]

126. Stumpf Andres E., "Redefining Mother: A Legal Matrix for New Reproductive Technologies", 96, *The Yale Law Journal,* at p. 200 (1986).
127. *Id.* at pp. 202-03.

Surrogacy arrangement have different implications on different societies having distinct culture, social values, religious and social set-up, etc. But human rights issues relating to surrogacy arrangements have universal character. These issues can be addressed by effectuating the basic human rights through legislation. The human rights instruments should be translated in tune with the current pace of assisted reproductive technologies.

The problems involved in cases of AID are multiplied in the technique of surrogate motherhood. In AID, sexual intercourse is separated from reproduction. Now, in surrogate motherhood, there is further desegmentation in the process of pregnancy depending upon the arrangement involved. The three different processes involved in Surrogate Motherhood are:

- A woman having the capacity to produce normal egg cells but lacking the capacity to bear a child, can have her eggs removed, fertilized in-vitro and implanted into the womb of a carrying mother.
- The second procedure involves in situation where a woman has no capacity to produce normal egg cells but has the capacity to bear the child. In this, woman donor's egg cell is fertilized through AI and the embryo is implanted in the womb of the recipient carrying mother.

The above two procedures raise the basic question as to what constitutes motherhood? Is it the process of gestation or bearing which constitutes the motherhood? This is a highly complicated question that may deny any satisfactory answer.

The third and the most commonly used forms at surrogate motherhood is where the woman in question is both the gestational and bearing mother but she gives up the child to the couple who has engaged her services for a pre-determined fees. While this process does not involve the complicated question of what constitutes motherhood, it brings about its own queries.

The surrogacy contract raises a question as to whether the contract amounts to contract of service or contract for service. If a contract of service where somebody is employed as apart of business and his/her business is done as an integral part of the business, the surrogacy arrangement falls under the of contract category of service and, hence, would be outside the scope of the Consumer Production Act, 1986.

The surrogacy arrangement gives rise to man matrimonial challenges, for e.g. if the husband of infertile woman engages the services of surrogate mother who has been artificially inseminated with his sperms does it amount to adultery if his wife is opposed to such an agreement? As the AI does not involve actual sexual intercourse, it does not amount to adultery but will certainly amount to be matrimonial cruelty. The same answer may be extended to a situation where the surrogate mother has agreed to the arrangement without her husband's consent.

In a situation where the woman who has agreed to be a surrogate mother, but has refused to oblige the contract, will she be guilty for breach of contract? Can the man of couple involved insist upon the specific performance of the contract? This raises the fundamental question as to whether the contract is valid contract or not? Public policy demands that such contracts be treated as void for two reasons—

- Surrogate motherhood arrangement leads to child trafficking.
- Commercial surrogacy arrangements though offers respectable status when compared to prostitution, fosters physical, emotional and economic exploitation of women reducing their status further to be no more than being a commodity.

In this context, New Jersey Supreme Court's statement in *In re Baby M. Case*[128] may be mentioned in which the court specifically held that "the right to procreate very simply is the right to have natural children whether through sexual intercourse or artificial insemination. It is no more than that". The decision thereby had given sanction to AI but denied the same to surrogate motherhood. It is the opinion of the author

128. 109 J.M. at 448, 537 A to D at 1253.

that the distinction between AI and surrogate mother hood based upon 'naturalness' is misleading.

Both the techniques are equally natural or unnatural. The simplest way of denying legal sanction to surrogate motherhood arrangement is as being opposed to public policy.

(d) Problem about Consent

Moreover, the extensive medical involvement in this process, especially in the light of profit motivation, scientific curiosity and professional rivalry needs to be regulated. It is necessary to evolve a legal regime for fixing up technological resistibility. It is highly essential in view of the fact that the women often are provided with false information as to rates of success and the side effects or the treatment. There are also situations where the possible side effects have not been known and yet the treatment goes on as experimentation.

Thus, where the consent given by the woman for undergoing treatment is obtained due to the absence of accurate information or due to false information either deliberate or unsure, such consent can never be treated as consent proper.

Owing to the fact that professional judgment cannot be always precise and accurate and that there is possibility of facing false allegations leading to diminished professional competence, it is very much desirable that the fixation of legal responsibility on medical profession should proceed with due precaution.

In the opinion of the author, medical services may be categorized into essential and non-essential services bringing the latter into the purview of stricter legal standards of responsibility. Artificial reproductive technologies can safely be categorized under non-essential services in view of the fact other alternative such as adoption is possible for an infertile couple

(e) Problem about Parenthood

Legal experts said that it is unique in making more than two people responsible for a child. It also brings into question when a sperm donor is liable for support, though at least one expert said the ruling shouldn't worry truly anonymous donors. While these contributions have been voluntary, they evidence a settled intention to demonstrate parental involvement far beyond merely biological.

Robert Rains, who teaches family law at Penn State Dickinson School of Law in Carlisle and is a co-director of the school's family law clinic, said the decision should not intimidate men who contribute to sperm banks.[129] This should be entirely different from a guy who goes to a sperm bank and makes a donation with the understanding that he will remain anonymous.

So what is this really about? It's about a panel of judges who rule that there are more than two parents involved in the raising of the child. This ruling is not about implicating anonymous sperm donors as parents, who are now liable for the child. Rather, it is an interesting study of how the courts might start acknowledging that more than two people can claim to be parents. It is also a case that highlights how reproductive technology practices are changing family law.

Lori Andrews, a Chicago-Kent College of Law professor with expertise in reproductive technology, said as many as five people could claim some parental status toward a single child if its conception involved a surrogate mother, an egg donor and a sperm donor. "The courts are beginning to find increased rights for all the parties involved", she said. "Most states have adoption laws that go dozens of pages, and we see very few laws with a comprehensive approach to reproductive technology".[130]

The state Supreme Court is considering a similar case, in which a sperm donor wants to enforce a promise made by the mother that he would not have to be involved in the child's life. That biological father was ordered to pay $ 1,520 in monthly support. About two-thirds nations of the world have adopted versions of the Uniform Parentage Act that shields sperm donors from being forced to assume parenting responsibilities.

---

129. Rains Robert; Mother Machine, London (1985), Women's Press, London.
130. Morgan, D. and Lee, R.G.; Guide to the Human Fertilization and Embryology (1991), Blackstone Press.

Presently a few intellectuals related to the field of law are seeking to amend the constitution to declare that personhood extends from conception to natural death. With regard to this Constitution and the laws that emanate from it, a person is any human being from conception until natural death, and the State will guarantee to him the complete enjoyment and exercise of all of his rights.

(f) *Selective Parenthood*

Abortion is illegal for most purposes in every state in India. Although abortion carries criminal penalties in India, the criminal code contains an exception in rape cases.

In China, India, and other Asian countries, there is a strong preference for boys, Mosher says. This combination of a preference for boys and modern technology—the ultrasound machine—has proven deadly for millions of baby girls.[131]

Amniocentesis makes it possible to detect the sex. There are also techniques available whereby it is now possible to implant only embryos of chosen sex. These techniques have got primary advantages of disease prevention, population limitation and the emotional satisfaction which a 'wanted child' may experience. But these techniques are more misused than utilized which is evidence from the practice of amniocentesis leading to female foeticide.

The sex-selection would result in marked shift in the sex ratio in favour of male population. Moreover, the knowledge of foetal sex allows the people to form strong gender role expectations. Selective parenthood takes away the precious value of the true parenthood in accepting the child as it is.

(g) *Health Risks to the Surrogate Mother*

The risk of transmitting infection, such as I-IJV or Hepatitis, to the surrogate mother from the infected parents has been discussed above. Testing can reduce this risk and lithe sperm or embryos are quarantined, the risk is very small.

In full surrogacy, when more than one embryo is replaced into the surrogate mother uterus, the risk of multiple

131. SIOUX FALLS, SD, July 24, 2008 (Life SiteNews.com)

pregnancy increases. Around 20 to 25% of the pregnancies resulting from in-vitro fertilization will result in a multiple pregnancy of twins or triplets, depending upon the number of embryos replaced. This carries associated risk for both mother and babies and there are serious implications for the intended parents of raising children from a multiple pregnancy. Careful consideration should be given to the number of embryos to be replaced.[132]

(h) Social Problems Regarding S.M.

- Identity Crisis
- Child Commodification
- Quality of product

First the child's mother is doubtful in surrogacy; the law is incapable of deciding the basic question, i.e. which of the two women is the real and legal mother of the child. Child's life, future and social existence would become a very complex problem in the absence of a correct identification.

That is commercialized and child is commodified by tagging a price card to the just born child or for the gestating mother's womb. Once you introduce a market mechanism for acquiring a child, it fosters and generates a demand for "Product quality". The commissioning couple, paying large sums of money to obtain a child may reject an imperfect child.

(i) Advantages of Surrogate Motherhood

This procedure can be effective solution for men with a low sperm count or poor sperm motility, where the sperm can't make the long journey to the egg. It is a good treatment option for couples who have problems because the man's sperm can't get through the woman's cervical mucus, perhaps because of an immune reaction. It can only work for couples where the woman has no fallopian tube blockage. Donor sperm can be used in cases where the man is producing no sperm at all.

---

132. http://www.bma.org.uk/ap.nsf/content/considering surrogacy.

(j) Disadvantages of Surrogate Motherhood

Because timing of insemination is so crucial, your partner must be able to produce a sperm sample quickly by masturbating into a cup at your doctor's office or clinic. The procedure can also be uncomfortable for some women.

When couples find themselves childless because of male infertility, they have several choices. They can remain childless and learn to cope with their disappointment, or they can adopt someone else's child. A child alternative is artificial insemination.

(k) Surrogate Motherhood and Human Rights

Sharma[133] highlights the problem of surrogate mothers, pre-birth determination of sex. In India, young girls, whether educated or uneducated, succumb to the allurements and inducements of the 'would be husbands' and sometimes conceive a child from such person.

In most of cases, the girls go for abortion. But in a number of cases, the unwedded mother prefers to give birth to the child, who does not have any right of succession from his father except against a hood wink or a free-lancer. The same is the problem with the surrogate mothers who bear children for consideration and by artificial insemination.

So far as only very few cases have come to light but in the coming future if this reproduction method picks up it may require a suitable legislation just as the problem of determination of pre-birth sex of the foetus, is being tackled in some states through legislative measures.

(l) Positive Impact of S.M. on Human Rights

- One Achieving parenthood to a few couples who could never have a baby by any other mean.
- 2 Genetic features like good height characteristic features, beautiful teeth live and a fair complexion.
- Help childless couple to get a child.

---

133. Sharma, S.R., "Protection to Women under the Law some Strategies" in the seminar on Women and Law, Centre for Women Studies, University of Rajasthan, Jaipur (1987).

- Prevent from suffering of Human being.
- Widening the Concept of Human Right.
- Broad interpretation of "Right to Life".
- Upgradation of Human Life.
- Advancement of Human Rights Jurisprudence.
- New Direction to Human Rights Jurisprudence.
- Concept of noble cause for service of mankind.
- Protecting the right of family.
- Fulfilment the sentimental feeling of couples.

(m) Negative Impact of S.M. on Human Rights

- Exploitation of poor women.
- 'Mother machines' to bear babies.
- Practice of commercial surrogacy has increased.
- Women to surrender her entire instinct of motherly love.
- Free play for brokers and service agencies to advertise in the classifieds columns of the newspapers.
- Near future one may find a column in the classified ads "Womb for sale" or "Womb for lease".
- Exploitation of woman in a new way.
- Problems including the health may develop.
- Breach of agreement to retain the child.
- Genetic defect.
- She is not the owner of the genetic material.
- Carrying mother has neither a role nor a right over the child acc to the contract.
- Marital home may be broken.
- Social stigma for ever and may result in an identity crisis of the child.
- Health hazards relating to pregnancy.
- Distorts the timely unit in to contractual agreement.
- Dismantles society's initial base.
- Destruction of an already corrupt world.
- Wicked manipulation of privacy and procreative rights.
- Devaluation of parenthood.

- Violation of right to person, right to bear a child tight to motherhood.
- Split motherhood in to genetic mother and social mother.
- Contrary to the unity of marriage dignity and the procreation of the human being.
- Offends the dignity and the right of the child to be conceived nurtured and carried in the womb by its own mother.
- Social, Ethical, Medical and moral implications.
- Replace the conjugal act would be morally illicit.
- Technological adultery.
- Violation of Natural rights.
- Violation of individual rights.
- Violation of right to life of fetus.
- Experimentation on Human being.
- Against human valued.
- Degradation of Human dignity.
- Gross violation of Human rights.
- Misuse of medical science against human ethics.
- Effect on future generation.
- Violation of right to health.
- Legally void.
- Violation of Right of Privacy.
- Concept of Human Factory and man as machine.

(C) Surrogate Motherhood and Law in India

It is advantageous to be well in formed of your rights before deciding to become a surrogate. Therefore, seeking legal counsel is a necessity. The lawyer will assist the surrogate in defining her right, prior to signing any document. It is important for the surrogate to be knowledgeable of her rights as well as the rights o the infertile couple. Once the contract is agreed upon and signed, a lot of the surrogate's privacy is done away with. The infertile mother is privileged to accompany the surrogate to her medical appointments and be present when certain examinations are conducted.

In spite of the fact that the mother makes a much larger contribution to the birth of the baby, the baby is considered illegitimate, if the mother is not the legal wife of the man.

Surrogacy denies eve the recognition of women's biological contribution.

As it is already seen in traditional surrogacy in either cake, the surrogate's own eggs are used. Genetically the surrogate becomes mother of the resulting child. That time, she may refuse to hand over the child. And she can as such there is no any law. In married surrogate, the spouse is a necessary party and many states presume him to be the genetic father.

In the traditional scenario of an unmarried surrogate with a semi-permanent significant other, some states may allow him the rights of a common law husband arid he is at liberty to contest the legal proceedings. In either case the surrogate's spouse or significant other would have to agree to sexual abstinence during the duration of fertilization or embryo transfer. These men are also subject to infectious disease testing. Diseases could be problematic during pregnancy or delivery.

When it comes to compensation to the surrogate, this issue comes under close scrutiny. The surrogate is usually paid $ 10,000.00 for her services upon completion of her contract. If the contract is not fulfilled she gets nothing (if she backs out). If the pregnancy results in a miscarriage the surrogate receives partial payment. If for any reason remuneration is out of order, it is looked upon as baby selling (reproductive prostitution, baby trade, selling body and parts, prostitution, renting uterus) by the pregnant woman. The law frowns upon baby selling and in many states it is classified as a felony and punishable by heavy fines and many years in prison.

In the adoption procedure the amount of money exchanged is disclosed along with purposes for which ills intended. In an informal adoption procedure the amount that is allowed are restricted to the reimbursement of medical fees, cost of living and legal fees. Adoption agencies are flexible in allowing reimbursement expenses. Wages lost due to illness may not be allowed. All compensation issues must be reported.

In the State where the child is to be born if the surrogate just happens to be passing through has a sufficient connection and has to issue the birth certificate. It is also a legal matter as to whose names are listed on the birth certificate.

It is a requirement of some states that a contract be drawn up among the parties involved in birthing arrangement. All points in the contract should be carefully and fully explored. Parties that should be present are:

(a) The surrogate (spouse/significant other)
(b) The infertile couple
(c) Legal counsel.

In order to avoid disputes, most infertility clinics require a contract. Legal counsel is recommended in order that all involved. To ensure that local laws are kept in compliance.[134]

Spouses are at liberty to contest the legal proceedings. In either case, husband slay feel emotional attachment with unmarried surrogate as she had fulfilled his wish, which his wife could not. This could lead to divorce.

Consideration must be given in advance as to how to proceed if a severe abnormality is detected. If, i.e. the intended parents feel that they will be unable to look alter a child with severe disability, the surrogate mother is opposed to termination, the parties need to decide arrangement should not proceed, cases may occur where one party has a change of mind when situation arises but discussing the matter in advance should minimize the likelihood of this happening.

- If the surrogacy had been made with the help of agency, then agency has to arrange contract of life insurance for the surrogate's family if surrogate mother dies during pregnancy or during delivery. They also must provide life insurance for the child, is contracting couple does before the child is born.

In all the consequences, both have to decide in the contract because the surrogate may be forced to terminate the pregnancy if so desired by the contracting couple and she will not be able to terminate it. If it is against the desire of couple, she has difficulty in keeping her own baby. There have been

134. http://www.yale.edu/ynhti/curriculum/units

instances where the contracting individual has specified the sex of the baby as well as refused to take the baby, if it was normal and filed a suit against the surrogate saying she had broken the contract.

In relation to the complex socio-legal situation of surrogacy considered under the vast medical development, we have still to consider the following ethical and religious points carefully:

(a) Even we are bypassing its natural method of conception and creating life in the laboratory.
(b) Some women may participate in surrogacy to save their marriage.
(c) A single women or same sex couple may wish to bring up a child or a man may consider the possibility and this would meet the approval of those who wish for dissent without any involvement of the other sex or any association involving obligation this surrogacy pattern is changing traditional role of parenthood.
(d) Handing over a child after delivery for a fee is "baby selling" or not.
(e) Products of the human body must not be traded for profit, leading to restrict the right to intercede to only a few individuals.
(f) There is religious objection to surrogacy pattern because the child's right to be born of a father and mother known to him and bound to each other by marriage to call him as legitimate child.
(g) In 2001 a French woman received worldwide publicity when she posed as the wife of her brother in order to give birth to a donor egg fertilized by his sperm. Some saw this as form of incest: others thought it would prove psychologically unhealthy for the child when he learned how he was delivered.
(h) In a few case a laboratory mix-ups misidentified gametes, transfer of wrong embryos have occurred leading to legal action against the IVF provider and complex paternity suits. As example is the case of a woman in California who received the embryo of

another couple and was notified of this mistake after the birth of her son.[135]

(i) It is left up to the laws of a particular state to determine the mother or father of the child prior to the birth. All parties must agree to provide affidavits, a Court appearance and testimony to effectuate the designated mother and father of the unborn fetus. The Courts will honor contracts and agreements between surrogate and intending parents unless circumstances significantly change that will jeopardize the best interest of the child, the gestational bond is not an issue. The decision is always for the best interest of the child.

A recent news piece that has caught everyone's eye is that an Israeli homosexual couple has got a surrogate child from India. Everywhere, people seem to be pleased about it, but when analyzed legally, it leaves us in a very befuddled state of mind.

Doctor Allahabadi, who made the couple's dream of having a child come true, confirmed that almost 16 homosexual couples of different nationalities (such as Swedish, French, etc.) have approached him for the surrogacy. Reasons for choosing India as a destination are also quite obvious—less paper work and also, cost of whole treatment is much lesser than other countries.

In the light of the aforesaid, it is pertinent to note that under Section 377 of Indian Penal Code, 1860 (IPC), "Whoever voluntarily has carnal intercourse against the order of nature with any man, woman or animal shall be punished with imprisonment for life, or with imprisonment of either description for term which may extend to ten years, and shall also be liable to fine".

Since as per IPC homosexuality is treated as an act that entails criminal liability in India, how can a foreign homosexual couple be legally allowed to get a surrogate child? It is often alleged that Section 377 of IPC violates the

135. http://www.answers.com/topic/in-vitro-fertilisation.

fundamental rights of homosexuals in India. Despite the existence of literature drawn from Hindu, Buddhist, Muslim as well as modern fiction to testify the presence of same-sex affinity in various forms, homosexuality is still considered a taboo by both the civil society and the government in India.

(a) Surrogate Motherhood and Muslim Religion

There are, however, certain procedures in marriage system which would allow some form of surrogate motherhood. For example, if a woman is having problems in carrying her husband's child to its full term, then the husband may marry another woman on a temporary or permanent basis and then an ovum of the first wife fertilized by the husband's sperm can be injected into the womb of the second wife with her approval.

To which of the two wives will the child belong? Does it belong to the genetic mother (the first wife) or the biological mother (the second wife)? According to Ayatullah al-Khumayni it depends on the age of fetus. If it was inseminated in the womb of the second wife after four months, then it belongs to the first wife the second wife is just a receptacle. If it was inseminated before its fourth month, then it is difficult to say that the child belongs to the first wife.

However, there is another way of looking at this relationship. In the present case from Islamic point of view, the common people have a perception about child-mother relationship. The *'urfi* would say that the woman who "gives birth" is the mother.

As for the relationship between the child and the first wife, I would say that although she is not a biological mother, but her status as a genetic mother places her above a *riza'i* mother. A *riza'i* mother is a woman who did not give birth to the child but breast-fed him or her. There are some other similar practices, like Fostering, Embryo Adoption, etc.

(b) Fostering

Fostering is the practice of using a parent or set of parents to care for someone else's child on a long-term basis. Often the child's own parents have died or have been declared legally unfit to look after him. Modern government social services and some private agencies place such children with families they believe will give them good homes.

(c) Adoption

Fostering is often a first step toward adoption. Although both practices involve the assumption of parental roles by persons who are not the child's biologic parents, adoption involves legal considerations not found in fostering.

The original ancient Roman notion of 'adoptio' or "adoption", was simply one of passing legal authority over an individual from one person to another, often for the purpose of making alliances and securing the inheritance of property. In Roman times the person who was adopted was most often an adult male who continued, even after his adoption, to retain ties of love and duty toward his own living parents. In modern society these ties are normally broken in favour of ties of affection between the adoptive parents and children. The modern notion of adoption, then, combines legal aspects of the Roman notion with the affective aspects of both fostering and biologic parentage.

Adopted children in most countries today enjoy the same privileges as natural children. They are treated as fully part of the family into which they are adopted. Adoption gives couples who are unable to produce children of their own the chance to rise children, who themselves might not otherwise find a home.

(d) Embryo Adoption

Embryo adoption is a procedure in which an embryo created from the egg of a woman and the sperm of a man is transferred into the uterus of another woman to be raised by her and her partner. Embryos for "pre-birth adoption" may be surplus frozen embryos from IVF donated by the genetic parents or embryos created specifically from egg and sperm donors.

In both cases, the embryo has no genetic relationship to its parents. Fostering is often a first step toward adoption. Although both practices involve the assumption of parental roles by persons who are not the child's biologic parents, adoption involves legal considerations not found in fostering.

(D) Global Endeavours for Controlling the Vices of Surrogate Motherhood

In many western countries surrogacy is an accepted; mode of having a child. In the *U.K.*, it was legalized in 1990 for infertile couples, whereas in the *USA* surrogacy arrangement even on commercial basis is also allowed.

(a) Legal Control in Different Countries Regarding S.M.

1. The Current Legislation

There have been 10 committees of inquiry in *Australia* into for surrogacy and related reproductive technologies. All but one of these committees either "expressed grave reservations about the practice or recommended that it be prohibited" it is therefore not surprising that the legislation regulating surrogacy, although not uniform, does contain similarities. In particular, the legislation in each jurisdiction:

- Prevents advertising, thus effectively reducing the spread of people to whom surrogacy is available and preventing the emergence in Australia of commercial surrogacy agencies such as those which exist in the United States.
- Renders surrogate arrangements unenforceable, with the results that the surrogate mother to either a commercial or an altruistic agreement cannot be required to give away relinquish custody of the child to the commissioning parents.
- Applies not only to the situation where a woman becomes pregnant pursuant to a surrogacy agreement but also to the situation where a woman is already pregnant and then agrees to give the child away. Additionally, the legislation distinguishes between the concepts of altruistic and commercial surrogacy as explained below.

2. Australia Enactments in Relation to Surrogate Motherhood

Six states in Australia regulated surrogate motherhood by enactments. These laws distinguish commercial or paid surrogacy form unpaid or altruistic surrogacy, while providing penalties for paid surrogacy. There are different laws in these six states, yet they have similar objectives. The enactments (i) prevents advertising of surrogacy and emergence of commercial surrogacy agencies such as those exists in the United States; and (ii) make surrogacy agreements unenforceable. The provisions of these states are as follows:

3. *Victoria*

(a) Sec. 13(3)(d)(i) of Infertility (Medical Procedures) Act, 1984 (IMP Act)

Both commercial and altruistic surrogacy arrangements void and therefore unenforceable criminal penalties to a commercial surrogacy while altruistic agreement are not penalized:

> "The surrogate mother must be infertile to receive IVF treatment and therefore precludes fertile women from acting as surrogates".

The Act renders both commercial and altruistic surrogacy arrangements void and unenforceable.[136] The Act distinguishes between commercial and altruistic surrogacy in that criminal penalties are imposed upon the parties to a commercial surrogacy agreement while parties to an altruistic agreement are not penalized.

Although altruistic surrogacy arrangements have not been specifically prohibited by the Victorian legislation. However, an exception in the IMP Act provides that IVF procedure can be accepted only when a recipient is unlikely to become pregnant.

But the commissioning couple who get a child through artificial insemination will come under the prohibition clause of

---

136. Section 30(3) of Infertility (Medical Procedures) Act, 1984, 'A contract or agreement (Whether made before or after the commencement of this section) under which a woman agrees with another person or persons to act as a surrogate mother is void'.

Section 10(c) of *The Status of Children (Amendment) Act, 1984 (Victoria)*, which deems the resulting child of surrogacy agreement to be that of the surrogate mother and her husband, while denying the relationship between the child and the commissioning sperm donor.[137] As a consequence, commissioning couple have to resort to adoption or guardianship provision.[138]

This becomes complicated by the strict requirements of *The Adoption Act, 1984* (Vic) which prohibits private adoption and discourages adoption by relatives. However, it is frequently suggested that it is relatives who are most likely to participate in an altruistic surrogacy arrangement.

The situation is further complicated because the distinction between commercial and altruistic surrogacy is undefined in the legislation. For example, in the case of an 'altruistic' surrogacy arrangement should the woman who has agreed to be the surrogate mother is allowed health care costs, home help throughout the pregnancy or, alternatively, no assistance whatsoever?

Section 30(2) of the *Infertility (Medical Procedures) Act, 1984 (Vic)* states that a person shall not:

> "(b) make, give or receive, or agree to make, give or receive, a payment or reward for or in consideration of the making of a contract, agreement or arrangement under which a woman agrees to act as a surrogate mother; or
>
> (c) receive or agree to receive a payment or reward in consideration for acting or agreeing to act as a surrogate mother".

Section 30(2) of *the Infertility (Medical Procedure) Act, 1984* prohibits surrogacy agreements involving any kind of payments or an attempt for it. It may include costs of medicine, treatment and even delivery leaving the surrogate mother in lurch. Even in case of altruistic surrogacy arrangement, the surrogate mother would be left with no assistance at all, as that

137. See also The Family Act, 1975.
138. Sec. 12, Adoption Act, 1984 (Vic.).

would be treated as commercial element, which vitiates the arrangement.[139]

On a literal interpretation, even compensation for medical expenses may be caught under these provisions. On a broader interpretation, it may be argued that these provisions aim to prohibit the payment for the use of reproductive services and thus payment not made directly for such services may not be penalized under the Act. Indeed the Waller report states that in an altruistic surrogacy agreement an arrangement that the surrogate mother's "medical, hospital and traveling expenses be paid would not result in [the arrangement] being labeled as commercial". However, the legislation in its present form remains ambiguous on this point.

4. *Australian Capital Territory*

In the Australian Capital Territory, *The Substitute Parent Agreements Act, 1994,* renders substitute parent agreement void.[140] it is an offence for anyone who does not intend to be a party to a substitute parent agreement to procure another person to enter an agreement with a third party

Perhaps most importantly, the Act further distinguishes between commercial and altruistic surrogacy by making it an offence for a person to knowingly provide any professional or technical services to a woman to facilitate a pregnancy with respect to the former, while leaving the latter unregulated.

In essence commercial surrogacy is considered a criminal act in the Australian Capital Territory while altruistic surrogacy is allowed to proceed. Additionally, if advertising is made with respect to a commercial substitute agreement the penalty is a fine or a period of imprisonment of both. If the advertising is made for the purposes of altruistic surrogacy the penalty is a fine only.

Because non-commercial surrogacy are between people who know each other well; who have a long standing relationship, that is often sisters, counsels, etc. who trust each

139. Family Law Council, Creating Children: A Uniform Approach to the Law and Practice of Reproduction Technology in Australia, AGPS, Canberra, 1985.

140. Sec. 9, Substitute Parents Agreement Act, 1993 (Act).

other and who have a clear commitment to each other's well being: and who have the support of their families and who are informed about the procedures and the consequences and who are willing to participate, in other words, it is their consent such altruistic surrogacy should be allowed to proceed".

A "non-commercial" or altruistic agreement includes those agreements under which the expenses of the surrogate mother are paid. One reason for doing so was stated in parliamentary debate by Mrs. Carnell:

> This Act allows payment of expenses of the surrogate mother in altruistic agreements, while making commercial surrogacy an offence. According to this Act, altruistic surrogacy arrangements are unenforceable in a court of law. This means that while entering an altruistic surrogacy agreement is not an offence, the agreement is legally ineffective and the surrogate mother will be the legal mother as is no agreement has been made.[141]

What is important to note however, is that the Act does explicitly allow and, to an extent, encourages the formation of such arrangements? The penalties for advertising for altruistic surrogacy are not severe and technical services may be provided to parties to such an arrangement, including medical services and legal advice.

However, while the effect of the Act is to allow altruistic surrogacy agreements to proceed, practically any such agreements will face hurdles. More specifically, the current law in the Australian Capital Territory indirectly raises impediments to the realization of substitute parent. Therefore, the commissioning parents will have no claim over the child in such an agreement. Additional impediments arise following the

141. This is because parenthood of the child is established by other Legislation. See for example, The Birth (Equality of Status) Act (Act); The Family Law Act, 1975 (Cth) And The Adoption Act, 1993 (Act). For a discussion of the effect of this Legislation See The Act. Attorney General's Dept., Discussion Paper on Surrogacy Agreements in the Act, 1993.

birth of the child when issues such as the name on the birth certificate and adoption arise. For example under.

(a) Section 19 of The Adoption Act, 1993

All adoption applications are subject to review by an approved adoption agency before a grant of adoption by the Court and in any proceedings relating to a child born from a surrogacy agreement "the welfare and interests of the child born as a result of a pregnancy that was the subject of the agreement shall be regarded as the paramount consideration".

(b) Section 5(1) of The Artificial Conception Act, 1985

Where a married woman given birth to a child as the result of artificial conception (either artificial conception by donor or IVF) with the consent of her husband, the donor of the gametes will have no legal relationship with the child and the husband is presumed to be the father of the child. Therefore, the commissioning parents will have no claim over the child.

5. *South Australia*

In South Australia, a surrogacy contract and a procreation contract are not allowed. "Surrogacy Contract" as 'A contract under which (a) a person agrees (i) to become pregnant or seek to become pregnant; and (ii) to surrender the custody of, or rights in relation to a child born as a result of the pregnancy; or (b) a person who is already pregnant agrees to surrender the custody of, or rights in relation to a child born as a result of the pregnancy"[142]

"Procreation Contract" as 'A contract under which (a) a person agrees to negotiate, arrange or obtain the benefit of surrogacy contract on behalf of another: or (b) a person agrees to introduce prospective parties to a surrogacy contract'.[143] Hence, a surrogacy and a procreation contract are illegal and void[144] in South Australia.

---

142. Section 10(f) of Family Relationships Act, 1975 (Sa).
143. *Ibid.*
144. Sections 10g(1) and 10g(2) of Family Relationships Act, 1975 (Sa).

(a) The Family Relationship Act, 1975

Commercial agreements making it an offence to be involved in a commercial surrogacy agreement, while not penalizing parties to an altruistic surrogacy agreement. It distinguishes between altruistic and commercial surrogacy agreements making it an offence to be involved in commercial surrogacy agreement[145] while not penalizing parties to an altruistic surrogacy agreement.

10(d)(1) of the Act states that where a child is born to a married women as a result of the artificial insemination by, donor and her husband has consented to the procedure, the woman's husband is presumed to be the child's father. This means that even if the commissioning couple produced the sperm and are therefore biologically connected to the child they will be prevented from asserting any right to parenthood.

A parliamentarian *Honorable R.S. Ritson* gave out the reasons.[146]

"One cannot legislate to prevent private agreements amongst people to arrange for the pregnancy and birth of the child, and for a friend to have custody of that child as if that person were the parent. Is guess that it will go on to a certain extent, but we need to prevent some of the distressing and unhappy litigations that have occurred in the other countries and prevent in particular, the Transatlantic trade which has occurred, where agencies in the UK have advertised surrogacy services and people from North America have, crossed to England to take advantage of those services".

As in other jurisdictions, parties to an altruistic surrogacy agreement in South Australia, face unintended obstacles to the successful completion of such an arrangement.

6. *Queensland*

(a) Surrogate Parenthood Act, 1988

A prescribed contract is void.[147] Sec. 2(2) of The Surrogate

145. This is punishable by a Fine or Imprisonment. See Sec. 10(H)(A&B) of Family Relationships Act, 1975 (Sa).
146. Parliamentary Debates (Hansard) Third Session of the 46th Parliament, 16.02.1988, 2764.
147. Sec. 4(1), Surrogate Parenthood Act, 1988 (Qld).

Parenthood Act, 1988 defines a 'Prescribed Contract' as a contract made between two or more persons. Whether formally or informally and whether or not for payment of reward, under which it is agreed (a) that a person shall become or shall seek or attempt to become the bearer of a child and that a child delivered as a result there of shall become and be treated.

Whether by adoption, agreement or otherwise, as the child of any person or persons other than the person first mentioned in this paragraph (a) or (b) that a child delivered from a person who is the bearer of the embryo, foetus or child at the time when the prescribed contract is made shall become and be treated, whether by adoption, agreement or otherwise, as the child of any person or persons other than the person first mentioned in this paragraph.

The parties who enter in to or offer to enter into a prescribed contract may be liable for a fine, imprisonment or both and the same restrictions as to advertising apply to both altruistic and commercial surrogate contracts.

In Queensland the major provision of the Surrogate parenthood Act, 1988 are identical with respect to commercial and altruistic surrogacy contracts. For example.

Although the legislation does not overtly distinguish between altruistic and commercial surrogacy in the same manner as other jurisdictions such as Victoria and the Australian Capital Territory. It appears that such a distinction will be read into the legislation by the Queensland court. Queensland is the only Australian Jurisdiction which has witnessed a judgment on surrogate motherhood in this judgment.

The magistrate in sentencing the defendant stated that "there is not the slightest suggestion that you sought to gain or did gain personal enrichment form these actions. There could be nothing, in my view, so abhorrent as trading in babies. Some might say not even abortion but where babies become chattels to be sold at will".

The judgment appears to distinguish between the concepts of commercial surrogacy and corresponding ideas of profit for gain and altruistic surrogacy and notions of kindness and thoughtfulness viewing the former as worthy of more severe punishment than the latter. The distinction is interesting as it assumes that personal enrichment on the part of the defendant centers upon monetary reward and ignores any other motivations which may give personal gratification. For instance, in this case evidence was led not only illustrating the defendant's desire to assist another but also that the defendant "was a person vehemently opposed to abortion" who would presumably gain personal gratification from seeing pregnant women agree to become surrogate mothers for infertile women rather than have their fetus aborted.

7. *USA Enactments in relation to Surrogate Motherhood*

Regulation of surrogate arrangements varies from state to state. Nevada amended its Adoptive Statutes in 1988 but failed to specifically address the issue of surrogacy contracts. However, there is a reference in this amendment to "Illegal Surrogacy Contracts".

8. *Taiwan Enactments in Relation to Surrogate Motherhood*

Taiwan has imposed a total ban on all surrogacy arrangement, 1997. Health Minister Chan-Chi-Shean proposed to life the ban on surrogate mother-hood as his first major policy announcement on 12 September, 1997. According to the Department of Health, the surrogate mother contracts must be certified by the courts and cannot be used for commercial purposes. Also surrogate mothers must be healthy married women between the ages of 20-40 years who have previously had at least one child of their own. Divorced women and those whose children have died are not eligible to be hired as surrogate mothers under the new policy. These restrictions aim to avoid disputes that would occur over possession of the new bourns.

According to the Department of Health Statistics, one out of every seven Taiwan couples is unable to bear children. The condition is mainly a result of the female spouse being unable to conceive due to problems with her womb. In Taiwan, the procedure to surgically important a prem or a fertilized off into the surrogate mother cost about $ 3500. Also the couple has to pay the surrogate mother's contract fee, the child birth expenses at the hospital and the related health care costs.

9. *U.K. Enactments in Relation to Surrogate Motherhood*

An order of the court made under section 30 of the Human Fertilization and Embryology Act, 1990 provides for a child to be treated in law as the child of the parties to a marriage if the child has been carried by a woman other than the wife as a result of human assisted reproduction. Application must be made with six months of the child's birth and the child's home must be with the husband and wife at the time of the application.

After a series of cases that highlighted the way legislation was failing to prevent commercialization, the Health Minister, Tessa Jowell announced on June 12, 1997 that laws to impose greater controls on surrogate motherhood would be considered by an independent inquiry to be set-up by the Government. There was public concern over the case of Karen Roche, who was understood to have received £ 12000 in expenses from a Dutch couple to have a baby for them. She later decided to have the child and kept it. The Dutch family made the arrangement with the help of COTS, an organization set up by Kim Cotton, Britain's first surrogate for childless couples.[148]

Laws of England and judicial decisions of the Privy Council have always been guidelines for all the countries within the Common wealth. Let us have a birds eye view upon the novel medico-legal situation which the U.K. Legislation has successfully tackled. The Surrogacy Arrangement Act, 1985 combines with sections of The Human Fertilization and Embryology Act, 1990 to provide a workable framework within which such arrangements can take place. One area of particular concern relates to the financial reward a surrogate may receive. The Surrogate Arrangement Act makes it a criminal offence for commercial surrogacy to be arranged, punishable by a fine and or up to three months' imprisonment.

10. *Tasmania Enactments in Relation to Surrogate Motherhood*

In Tasmania, both altruistic and commercial surrogacy contracts are void and unenforceable. "Surrogacy Contract" is defined as 'a contract, agreement or arrangement, with or

148. New Laws May Curb Surrogate Mothers, Times 12 June 1997.

without payment or reward, under which (a) a person agrees to become or is already pregnant and agrees to surrender to another person the custody or guardianship of, or rights in relation to child born as a result of the pregnancy; and (b) the other person agrees to accept custody or guardianship of such a child.'[149] It punishes only commercial contracts.[150]

There is no corresponding adoption registration in Tasmania prohibits a person from entering into a private adoption arrangement and a woman who gives birth to a child as a result of the carrying out of an artificial conception procedure is deemed to be the mother of the child, whether or not the child is biologically.

Thus commercial surrogacy is penalized more severely than altruistic surrogacy, as it is the payment of a fee to the surrogate mother, which has raised the most objections because of high priority given to morality and orthodox social set-up, the practice of surrogacy and related issues have wider ramifications.

(b) Current Legislation in Different Countries Regarding S.M.

Indiana passed a Law in 1988 declares all surrogacy agreement written or oral, which provide compensation to be unenforceable. It does not criminalize them. Kentucky also enacted a law-making compensation for surrogates and surrogate brokers illegal and surrogate contracts unenforceable. Penalties for violation of this law came from the Child Selling Statutes and include $ 500 to $ 2000 fines and six months' imprisonment". Washington D.C. prohibits Surrogate parenting contracts. In Minnesota it is a criminal offence to enter into or arrange surrogacy contracts.

Nebraska's Law makes surrogacy contracts null, void and unenforceable if compensation is involved. Surrogacy contracts

149. As per The Surrogacy Contract Act, 1993.
150. This distinction is interesting given the Tasmanian Committee to investigate artificial conception and related matters (1985) which concluded that "Surrogate Motherhood" in general and commercial surrogacy arrangements in particular are unacceptable to the Tasmanian.

are not illegal but they are unenforceable as per the New Jersey Law.

Surrogacy can be accepted as an option for a married couple with an infertile wife, as per American Bar Association up to 180 days of conception, surrogate mother can cancel the contract; after 180 days, the child belongs to the married couple, if the contract is not cancelled. *France* has banned surrogate motherhood as violating bodies of women and subverting adoption. *Germany* imposed a total ban on all forms of surrogacy.

(c) Who is the Legal Mother?

Israel Law states that Genetic Mother is the legal mother of the child without the need for legal adoption. *Virginia* Law declared Surrogate Mother as the real mother and the child will be deemed to be the legitimate and natural child of the surrogate mother. And *California Civil Code* states that the genetic mother is the legal mother. In *England* Genetic mother as the real mother.

Arkansas law creates a presumption that the mother of a child conceived by artificial insemination and born to an unmarried surrogate is the intended mother. Only by a judicial order signed before the pregnancy, the parental rights will vest in the intended parents.

(E) Ethical and Legal Issues of Surrogate Motherhood and Judicial Response

Surrogacy is an arrangement whereby one woman carries a child for another woman with the intention that it should be handed over after birth.[151] Surrogacy is used more and more by gay couples and single men who cannot otherwise have their own offspring. Usually it is a married couple that enters into the arrangement with a surrogate mother who will be either artificially inseminated with the husband's semen or who will receive the embryo after IVF. In most cases the surrogate

---

151. Cusine Cf. (note 1 above), pp. 143 ff.; Cusine (note 3 above), note 2, page 30 ff.; Michael Freeman, "Is Surrogacy Exploitative?" in McLean (note 1 above), p. 164 ff.

mother agrees to do this only for a fee but there are also agreements without financial implications.

Surrogacy agreements intend that the genetic mother (who produced the egg) will also be the nurturing mother after the child's birth, and that the surrogate mother will only function as carrying mother and surrender the child immediately after birth to the nurturing mother. In practice, however, the genetic mother or parents might change their minds during pregnancy, the surrogate mother might wish to keep the child after birth, or both mothers might wish to abandon the child and the nurturing mother would then be a third woman.

The case of the surrogate mother is an even more complex example. In this case, the law must develop; rules to determine the extent to which it will recognize contractual arrangements between the mother and father and the surrogate mother regarding the time and place of fertilization, prenatal care during pregnancy, right to terminate the pregnancy, conditions governing delivery, and parentage of the child once it is born.

Once the child is born to a surrogate mother, is the child to be considered the natural child of the surrogate mother who is then adopted by the mother and father contracting for her services, or is the child considered to be the natural child automatically of the woman (or couple) contracting for the birth? Another interesting question is whether the mother (or couple) contracting for the birth can refuse to accept the child if the child is defective or of the wrong sex. A more complicated question is whether a father can contract with a surrogate mother to produce a child without the involvement of the mother (the woman who will actually raise the child, presumably the wife of the father).

If one adds a surrogate father to the question of a surrogate mother, then the legal questions become complicated indeed. This is because the decision-making unit swells to its largest size both in regard to the processes under which the child is produced and the eventual parentage of that child.

No doubt assisted reproduction is a great scientific achievement, consequently, the emotional, social, legal and ethical problems arising from surrogacy agreements are extremely complicated and have become aggravated by the increasing involvement of commercial agencies which are faced by the couple, the surrogate mother, the child, the society, the donor as also by the doctor.

(a) Legal Implications of Surrogacy

Offering money to the woman concerned for surrogacy may lead to an invasion of their private lives. It may, thus, result in exploitation of woman in a new way. Another question is whether renting out the womb is against public policy, if it permits transfer of money for the use of woman's organ, womb? The other problems including the health may develop. In case of abortion, several other complications may not be possible to be easily assessed, and every payment could be a point of dispute.

The carrying mother may develop affection towards the child born and may breach the agreement to retain the child, resulting in new questions of law. On the other hand, the commission couple may reject the baby born out of the carrying mother for any reason, including genetic defect, if any.

A part from this, the surrogate mother may claim the custody rights or any other legal relationship with the child she is carrying or give birth to. The basic problem being that the sperm and ova are drawn from two different persons, as she is not the owner of the genetic material, her relationship cannot be easily described.

Except the contractual relationship, the carrying mother has neither a role nor a right over the child according to the contract. But her physical motherhood and umbilical bond, if not genetic, with the child give new dimensions to the legal dispute, if any. Surrogacy remains a complex problem either in the presence or absence of any express provision of law.

Apart from the above, surrogacy may result in several complex socio-legal problems in the family of the surrogate mother. At times, her marital home may be broken, or it may remain a social stigma forever and may result in an identity crisis of the child. The commercial element of surrogacy on one hand and the genetic complexities on the other hand are two issues which made "surrogacy" unique puzzle of law.

(b) Contractual Arrangement

As it involves two couples for this kind of non-coital

preproduction, there is a need for surrogate motherhood contracts. Whether a woman has the right to enter into a contractual agreement to bear a child and receive month for the service? What is the public policy as to the enforcement of these contracts? Does it interfere with the autonomy of a woman? It involves definitely the interference with the person of the woman and so it is an interference with her personal right. The right to life is a comprehensive one. Does it include the right to procreate children? Whether these contracts of surrogate motherhood and their enforcement of prohibition is a violation of that right to procreate?

There are two schools of thought. One says that as the woman has the right to her person, it includes the right to procreate which facilitates surrogate motherhood contracts too. Once she has a right to enter into a contract to procreate children for other childless couples, it should be enforceable. The second type of opinion is that it amounts to interference of a third person into the private partnership of the couple and changing the process of procreation. The private conjugal life of a validly married couple cannot be interfered with as a matter of law and any interference can be viewed as a violation of the privacy of the couple and of the woman too.

Another important problem is that as a consequence of this surrogate motherhood contract, the relationship between the mother and the child gets distorted, leading to several social problems of identity. From moral and religious point of view, the very concept of conception and purpose of marriage, which is regarded as the procreation of children for continuing the line of the clan, gets basically changed with this unprecedented scientific invention of new styles of reproduction. There are two basic questions:

- Who is the legal mother?
- Are contracts for surrogate motherhood enforceable?

According to Israel law, genetic mother is the legal mother of the child without the need for legal adoption.[152] But there are

152. Michael Bell, Law Society's Gazette (London), Human Embryology Legislation, 2nd March 1988 at 25.

two contentious arguments; one saying that genetic mother is the real mother and the other saying that the surrogate who given birth is the real mother.

American jurisprudence also has not reached a consensus on surrogate motherhood. There is neither a Federal law nor a decree by the Supreme Court of USA. *Virginia law* declared surrogate mother as the real mother and the child will be deemed to be the legitimate and natural child of the surrogate mother. Alternatively, *California Civil Code* states that the genetic mother is the legal mother.

England proposed to define mother as the woman who has carried the child as a result of the placing in her an embryo or of sperm and eggs and no other woman is to be treated as the mother of the child. This proposal was highly criticized by the Bar in England. The bar advised to consider the commissioning mother as the real and legal mother. The Bar also condemned the provision making the husband of the surrogate mother the legal father of the child.[153] After the Bar's recommendation, the House of Commons added a provision providing the court to declare genetic mother as the real mother.[154] Would the doctor be liable in law, following the birth of a defective child or failure of the process of AI?

In *Lamaritata* v. *Lucas,*[155] the donor and the recipient entered into a contract whereby the donor provided sperm to the recipient with the expectation that she would become pregnant through artificial insemination. The agreement provided that if childbirth resulted, the donor would have no parental rights and obligations associated with the child.

The donor, in an attempt gain parental rights of the twin boys who were born to Mr. Lamaritata argued that he was not a sperm donor but instead the biological father, and thus should be afforded parental rights. Issue is does a sperm donor

153. Cumbria County Council *v.* X. THE TIMES (London), 25 June 1990, quoting Human Fertilization and Embryology Bill proposed in front of the House of Commons on 9th June 1990.
154. Michael Bell, Law Society' Gazette (London), Human Embryology Legislation, 2nd March 1988 at 25, Citing Glanville Williams (Ed.) Criminal Law, 1978 at 678.
155. Lamaritata *v.* Lucas (823 So. 2d 316 (2002).

have any legal parental rights. Court held that in an attempt to avoid the enforcement of the contract, Mr. Lucas argued that he was not a sperm donor. Instead, he argued that he was part of a commissioning couple with the mother. A commissioning couple is defined as the intended mother and father of a child who will be conceived by Steinbock means of assisted reproductive technology using the eggs or sperm of at least one of the intended parents.

There were no facts to establish this, and the intent of the parties was established by contract. A person who provides sperm for a woman to conceive a child by artificial insemination is not a parent. Thus, the sperm donor here has no legal parental rights.

In *Strand* v. *Strand,*[156] the husband had been given visitation rights in a divorce petition, but the wife later tried to have these rights rescinded in the ground that her child was illegitimate. She, however, admitted that she had undergone AIH with her husband's consent. The court held that the husband should retain his right and because he had consented for AIH the child was not illegitimate. According to the decision of the court the child had been potentially adopted or semi-adopted? by the husband, thus, he was entitled to the same rights as those acquired by a foster parents, who has formally adopted a child.

In another case *Gursky* v. *Gursky*[157] the Supreme Court of New York ruled that a child on the basis of an implied contract on his part or the doctrine of equitable-estoppels.

Anonymous v. Anonymous[158] a husband had consented to his wife's therapeutic impregnation. On the wife's claim for alimony the husband pleaded that the child was illegitimate. Rejecting his plea, the court awarded the alimony on the ground that consents in writing carried with it an implied promise to furnish support for the resulting progeny.

In *People* v. *Sorenson*[159] a man from California was, convicted of criminal non-support, sentenced to jail for one

156. *Harvard Law Review,* 73rd Vol., p. 692.
157. Gursky *v.* Gursky ((1963)242 N.Y.S. 2d 406.
158. Anonymous *v.* Anonymous (1964) 246 NYS 2d 835.
159. People *v.* Sorenson (1967) 62 Cal. Rep. 462.

year on probation with an order to make support payments for a child born to his wife consequent to AIH after his written consent during the wedlock. On appeal however, the court held that for the purposes if the criminal statute the husband was not the child's father.

(c) Other Legal Problems Regarding Surrogate Mother

- What will you do if the surrogate insists on keeping the child?
- How much should you pay the surrogate?
- If she gets ill as a result of the pregnancy who will pay the medical costs?
- Is possible to put the receiving mother's name as mother's name on the birth certificate
- Will you tell the child about the surrogacy?
- Will surrogates undertake pregnancy for profit?
- What happens if the child is handicapped and is unwanted by the couple and the surrogate mother?
- What happens if the surrogate dies during child birth?
- Whether or not the commissioning parents have the right to tell surrogate mother how to live?
- Can the couple ban smoking, control alcohol and other substance intake?

IV. CLONING

(A) Concept of Cloning

(a) Historical Background

Cloning is fundamental to most living things, since the body cells of plants and animals are clones ultimately derived from the mitosis of a single fertilized egg. More narrowly, a clone can be defined as an individual organism that was grown from a single body cell of its parent and that is genetically identical to it. Also spelled clone population of genetically identical cells or organisms that are derived originally from a single original cell or organism by a sexual methods.

Plants those are able to propagate by asexual means produce genetically identical plants that are clones. Cloning has been commonplace in horticulture since ancient times; simply obtaining cuttings of their leaves, stems, or roots and replanting them clone many varieties of plants. A vast array of fruit and nut tree varieties and innumerable ornamental plants represent clones.

The body cells of adult animals and humans can be routinely cloned in the laboratory. Adult cells of various tissues, such as muscle cells, that are removed from the donor animal and maintained on a culture medium while receiving nutrients manage not only to survive but to go on dividing, producing colonies of identical descendants. By the 1950s scientists were able to clone frogs, producing identical individuals that carry the genetic characteristics of only a single parent. The technique used in the cloning of frogs consists of transplanting frog DNA, contained in the nucleus of a body cell, into an egg cell whose own genetic material has been removed. The fused cells then begin to grow and divide, just like a normal fertilized egg to form an embryo.

Mice were first successfully cloned in the 1980s, using a procedure in which the nucleus from a body cell of a mouse embryo is removed from the uterus of a pregnant mouse and transplanted into a recently fertilized egg (from another mouse) whose genetic contents have been evacuated. The cell is cultured artificially until it divides and becomes an embryo. The embryo, which is composed entirely of cells derived from the single implanted nucleus, is artificially implanted into the uterus of another mouse that brings it to term.

Cloning a new animal from the cells of an adult (as opposed to those of an embryo) is considerably more difficult, however. Almost all of an animal's cells contain the genetic information needed to reproduce a copy of the organism. But as cells differentiate into the various tissues and organs of a developing animal, they express only that genetic information needed to reproduce their own cell type. This tended to restrict animal cloning to the use of embryonic cells, which have not yet differentiated into blood, skin, bone, or other specialized cells, and which can more easily be induced to grow into an entire organism.

The first success in cloning an adult mammal was achieved by a team of British researchers led by Ian Wilmut at the Roslin Institute in Edinburgh, Scotland, in 1996. After having already produced clones from sheep embryos, they were able to produce a lamb, named Dolly, using DNA from an adult sheep; Dolly was euthanized in 2003 after being diagnosed with a severe lung infection. To create the clone, the nucleus of a cell from the mammary gland of an adult sheep was implanted in another sheep's unfertilized egg whose nucleus had been removed. The key to the procedure is to synchronize the cell cycle—i.e., the ordered sequence of events that occur in a cell in preparation for division—of the mammary cell with that of the egg. To achieve this, before implantation the mammary cell is deprived of nutrients; this stops its cell cycle, thus preventing it from dividing. The nucleus is then implanted into the recipient egg and fused to it, and an electrical current is applied to simulate the burst of energy that occurs during fertilization. The egg begins dividing normally and becomes an embryo, which is implanted into another ewe. The lamb that is born is a clone of the donor of the original mammary cell.

The practical applications of cloning are economically promising but philosophically unsettling. Animal breeders would welcome the chance to clone top-quality livestock. Genetically engineered animals could be cloned in large numbers to increase the production of drugs or human proteins that are useful in fighting disease. Clones are also highly useful in biological research because of their genetic uniformity.

In November 2001, scientists from Advanced Cell Technologies (ACT), a biotechnology company in Massachusetts, announced that they had cloned the first human embryos for the purpose of advancing therapeutic research. To do this, they collected eggs from women's ovaries and then removed the genetic material from these eggs with a needle less than 2/10,000th of an inch wide. A skin cell was inserted inside the enucleated egg to serve as a new nucleus. The egg began to divide after it was stimulated with a chemical called ionomycin. The results were limited in success. Although this process was carried out with eight eggs, only three began dividing, and only one was able to divide into six cells before stopping.

Within conceptual and experimental contexts, the term "cloning" has taken on different meanings that in turn presume different technical procedures as well as different aims.

The production of a nucleic (DNA, RNA), a protein,or a cell line starting from a single or a few copies of each of these entities. As no individual life is concerned, there are no peculiar ethical and legal questions on these processes.

The generation, in an asexual artificial way, of one or more biological individuals belonging to sexually-reproducing species (plants, animals and humans). As animals and humans are concerned, this can be done either by disaggregating or sub-dividing an embryo ("Embryo splitting") in its early stages of development or through the transfer of a diploid nucleus of a cell from an embryo, a fetus or an adult individual to a denucleated oocyte.

In the latter case, if successful, after activation the reconstructed oocyte will develop into an embryo that is capable of further development to term. Regardless of its destiny, a cloned embryo is a cloned individual of a given species at the beginning of its life.

The cloning of human beings is a subject fraught with ethical and moral controversy. If cloning can ensure the infinite replication of specific genetic traits, a judgment would need to be made as to which traits are desirable and therefore worthy of perpetuation. The persons empowered to exercise such judgment would be in a position to change the course of human development.

Up till now attempts to clone a human being have not been successful. Claims of cloning of people like the Italian fertility doctor Severino Antinori and the Realian sect have not been proved. The world is yet to see a clone of a human being. Many animals like pigs, cows, cats, goats, mice, rabbits, etc. have been cloned since the birth of Dolly the sheep in 1996. However, we are yet to perfect the art. We still encounter abnormalities like excessive birth weight, malformed hearts, livers and other organs. Birth defects occur at the rate of 20% to 30% as compared to 1% or 2% in case of natural births. There are issues regarding the safety of the procedure.

Therefore, the question which arises is whether the reproduction of a clone organism from an individual gene, used to produce mice and sheep, be allowed in the case of human beings?[160] Many countries have altogether banned cloning.

What exactly is cloning? Cloning is a scientific technique to create genetically identical molecules, cells or organisms. It is probably an answer to a couple who having lost their child, want him back. But does one really want a person who is dead, back. That's eerie.

(b) Meaning and Definition of Cloning

- Cloning Means "Production of identical daughter cells from a parental cell. The process of cloning can be used to derive either multiple cell types or an entire individual being. This process can start from either an egg cell or from stem cells. Stem cells are cells derived from 1-14 day old embryos".
- Cloning as: human asexual reproduction, accomplished by introducing nuclear material from one or more human somatic cells into a fertilized or unfertilized oocyte [an egg] whose nuclear material has been removed or inactivated so as to produce a living organism (at any stage of development) that is genetically virtually identical to an existing or previously existing human organism.[161]
- Cloning in itself refers to the production of a biological entity which is genetically identical or very similar to the one from which it originated.
- Human cloning is the scientific technique by which a human being is generated. The early but unavoidable result of both embryo splitting and nuclear transfer cloning is the reproduction of a human being at its embryonic stage of development. Thus, human

160. Symonides Januszed", Human Rights: New Dimensions and Challenges", Ashgate Publishing, Dartmouth, 1998, p. 19.
161. The US Human Cloning Prohibition Act of Feb. 2003.

cloning and human embryo are identical with one another.

- Generally cloning refers to a precise genetic copy of molecule/cell/plant/animal or human being.
- "Clone can be defined area individual organism that was grown from a single body cell of its parent and that is genetically identical to it".
- "The use of recombinant DNA technology to manipulate and change genes is sometimes called gene cloning".
- Cloning is to create a generally identical complete human being from a fully differentiated adult, cell, i.e. a fully specialized mature cell such as the mammary cell that was used to create '*Dolly*'.
- A clone is an individual or group of individual that discard through asexual reproduction from a single individual.
- The Human Genetics Advisory Commission (HGAC) and the Human Fertilization and Embryology Authority (HFEA) (HGAC/HFEA, 1998) defines cloning as 'copying and propagation without altering the genome'. When the genome—the complete genetic identity of any individual—is cloned or copied) a genetically identical individual is created. Cloning *per se* does not necessarily involve copying a complete genome.

(c) Concept of Cloning

Cloning has been commonplace in horticulture since ancient times many varieties of plants are cloned simply by obtaining cutting of their leaves, stems, or roots and replanting them. A vast array of fruit and nut tree varieties and innumerable ornamental plants represent clones.

Cloning in Bacteria's can be classified in to:

- Gram negative bacteria
- Gram positive bacteria

Gram negative bacteria can be used as hosts for plasmids, phages and cosmids vectors, gram positive bacteria can be used as hosts for only plasmids. Chimeric vector is inserted into bacterial cells and transformed bacterial colonies are selected and used for multiplication in suspension culture. The Chimeric DNA is retrieved, whenever required

Among eukaryotes, DNA cloning has been done in yeast, mouse and to some extent even in some higher plant species. In yeast, a plasmid called 2a DNA (63bp) is found, which is an appropriate cloning vehicle

1950s scientists were able to clone frogs, producing identical individuals that carry the genetic characteristics of only a single parent. The technique used in the closing of frogs consists of transplanting frog DNA, contained in the nucleus of a body cell, into an egg cell whose won genetic material has been removed. The fused cells then begin to grow and divide just like a normal fertilized egg, to form an embryo.

Mice were first successfully cloned in the 1980s, using a procedure in which the nucleus from a body cell of a mouse embryo is removed from the uterus of a pregnant mouse and transplanted into a recently fertilized egg (from another mouse) whose genetic contents have been evacuated. The cell is cultured artificially until it divides and becomes and embryo. The embryo, chich is composed entirely of cells derived from the single implanted nucleus, is artificially implanted into the uterus of another mouse that brings it to term.

The first success in cloning an adult mammal was achieved by a team of British researchers led by Sir Ian Wilmut and Campbell at the Roslin Institute in Edinburgh, Scotland, in 1996. After having already produced clones from sheep embryos, they were able to produce a lamb, named Dolly, using DNA from an adult sheep; Dolly was euthanized in 2003 after being diagnosed with a severe lung infection. To create the clone, the nucleus of a cell from the mammary gland of an adult sheep was implanted in another sheep's unfertilized egg whose nucleus had been removed. The key to the procedure is to synchronize the cell cycle—i.e., the ordered sequence of events that occur in a cell in preparation for division—of the mammary cell with that of the egg. To achieve this, before implantation the mammary cell is deprived of nutrients; this stops its cell cycle, thus preventing it from dividing.

The nucleus is then implanted into the recipient egg and fused to it, and an electrical current is applied to simulate the burst of energy that occurs during fertilization. The egg begins dividing normally and becomes an embryo, which is implanted into another ewe. The lamb that is born is a clone of the donor of the original mammary cell.

In the wake of Dolly 1997 Dr. Richard Seed Alarmed the world by announcing his intention to clone humans using the same technique.

"He has since received 100 of letters from *inter alia,* infertile or homo sexual couples seeking to be cloned as an alternative to sexual reproduction and the terminally ill".

After the cloning experience of Dolly the sheep human cloning is theoretically and technically possible. The procedure would consist of taking an egg, removing its chromosomes, and then fusing it with a somatic, all from the individual to be cloned.

Consider the situation of a homosexual man who feds fractured with his incapacity to bear children and wants to be cloned consider the couple that wants to have a baby but the husband is sterile assuming that cloning is an alternative the couple decides to clone the husband and the wife would contribute as a surrogate mother.

This Development as profoundly troubling. President Clinton's immediate response to 'Dolly was to announce an urgent enquiry into the ethical and legal implications of cloning to be carried out by the US National Bioethics Advisory Commission (NBAC). This was accompanied by a statement that 'no federal funds shall be allocated for cloning of human beings'.

"Recommended legislation to ban research in the cloning of complete people".[162] The House is now considering 2 separate bills from the Democrats and Republicans. Both Bills seek to ban the use of somatic cell (not destined to become a sperm or egg cell) nuclear transfer technology, although both parties claim the other's, Bill is seriously, flawed.

The Republican Cloning Bill Prohibiting implantation and make the ban permanent, thus preventing embryo creation per se using nuclear transfer.

162. The NBAC Report, 1997.

(d) Purpose of Human Cloning

- Cloning Human embryos as a way of making babies.
- Cloning Human embryos as a mean of producing stem cells.
- Cloning Human embryos as a tool for studying genetic and epigenetic processes.

A clone of a candidate for an organ transplant would, like an identical twin, be a perfect tissue match. There would be no risk of rejection because the clone would certain the same genetic material as the organ recipient; the clone would essentially be a younger version of the patient, cloning for this reason would obviously be extremely beneficial. As former ethicist for the NISH, John other, commented, "[t]he reasons for opposing this is not easy to argue".

Human clones as organ donors arose in 1997. Scientist announced that they had created a headless frog embryo named Freddy. Scientists may be able to apply the same technology used to create headless grogs to human embryos, in effect creating headless human clones for the purpose of increasing the supply of organs and tissues for transplantation.

Same technology used to create headless frog embryos may also one day lead to the growth of individual human organs and tissues in the laboratory. Some scientists believe that "the technique could be adapted to grow human organs such as hearts, kidneys, livers and pancreases in an embryonic sac living in an artificial womb".

Cloning individual organs would overcome the organ shortage and rejection problems, as well as avoid some of the moral and ethical concerns surrounding human reproductive cloning.

Cloning technologies can also be used for other purposes besides producing the genetic twin of another organism. A basic understanding of the different types of cloning is key to taking an informed stance on current public policy issues and making the best possible personal decisions.

- Reproductive Cloning
- Therapeutic Cloning

- Nucleus Reprogramming

(e) Reproductive Cloning

"When the targeted result of cloning is the creation of a new human being, it is called reproductive cloning.

When a cloned human embryo is implanted in the uterus of the woman to which the generating egg belongs or of a surrogate mother, the delivery of a newborn baby is expected following pregnancy, as has been demonstrated by mammalian cloning. This use of human cloning has been improperly called "reproductive cloning" since its ultimate goal is to reproduce an adult human being.

Reproductive cloning is a way of creating an exact replica of a person, i.e. a live human clone. There are various steps involved in it.

Firstly, doctors remove the DNA rich nucleus from an egg and replace it with the DNA of the person they want to clone. Then the donor DNA fuses with the egg, causing it to spontaneously start dividing into an embryo. The embryo then develops based on the instructions from the implanted DNA. It is then implanted in a woman's womb and the growing embryo develops into a foetus. Having developed from the implanted DNA, the baby is a virtual genetic copy of the person who donated the genetic material.[163]

This procedure which we have been unable to perfect till now means the constant killing of life it means human experimentation on live persons.

Reproductive Cloning is a technology used to generate an animal that has the same nuclear DNA as another currently or previously existing animal. Dolly was created by reproductive cloning technology. In a process called *'somatic cell nuclear transfer'* (SCNT), scientists transfer genetic material from the nucleus of a donor adult cell to an egg, whose nucleus, or genetic material, has been removed.

Human reproductive cloning is banned in most countries. Such methodology is also available in the cultivation of plants.

---

163. *Newsweek*, Attack of the Clones, January 13, 2002, pp. 40-41.

Human justify such agricultural technology as being necessary to meet the growing needs of an increasing population deprived of vital food resources.

Reproductive cloning is condemned by critics for ethical reasons and because of the predicted risks to the health of the clone.

(f) Therapeutic Cloning

When the targeted result of cloning is the creation of a new human being, it is called reproductive cloning. Once the human embryo is cloned, its further development is arrested before implantation usually at the blastocyst stage. Thereby destroying the further development of the embryo. This is called therapeutic cloning.

Therapeutic Cloning, where the embryo is only grown for a few days or weeks in order to harvest stem cells, is believed to have great medical potential. Cloned stem cells would not be rejected after implantation into the original donor. Therapeutic cloning is that the process actually kills one life to save another.

Therapeutic cloning, also called 'embryo cloning,' is the production of human embryos for use in research. The goal of this process is not to create cloned human beings, but rather to harvest stem cells that can be used to study human development and to treat disease. Stem cells are important to biomedical researchers because they can be used to generate virtually any type of specialized cell in the human body. Stem cells are extracted from the egg after it has divided for 5 days. The egg at this stage of development is called a blastocyst.

The extraction process destroys the embryo, which raises a variety of ethical concerns. Many researchers hope that one day stem cells can be used to serve as replacement cells to treat heart disease, Alzheimer's, cancer, and other diseases.

Indeed, to produce embryonic stem cells a living human embryo has been deliberately created and destroyed.

(g) Methods of Cloning

- Molecular and Cellular Cloning.
- Blastomere separation somatic nuclear transplantation cloning (SNTC).

- Artificial Embryo twining.

"Molecular cloning involves copying and simplifying DNA gene fragments in a host cell to produce large quantities of the DNA for use in experiments".

Cellular Cloning occurs at the Cellular Level, by growing Cells in culture in a laboratory to produce a cell. It cannot be used to produce a cloned human.

Blastomere Separation involves splitting an embryo soon after fertilization while it is in the two-to-eight cell state). Each resulting cell is capable of producing an entire organism, genetically identical to the others.

Somatic cell nuclear transfer (SCNT) both pairs of chromosomes in embryo acquire from somatic cells. Dolly Ship was made on this technique.

In Artificial embryo twining fertilized ovum zygote divided in to two embryos and then it was transplanted in uterus of surrogate mother.

(h) Reasons for not Cloning Humans

- Biological analysis of the cloning process.
- Anthropological, social, ethical and legal reflection on the negative implications that human cloning has on the life, the dignity, and the rights of the human being.

(B) Challenges Regarding Cloning

It is said that we are made in the image and likeness of God. Imagine if all the people in this world were clones of each other. We would probably die of boredom. For this very reason we are not replicas of each other.

Everyone has the right to enjoy the benefits of scientific progress and its applications. However, certain advances may have potentially adverse consequences for the integrity, dignity and human rights of the individual.

Cloning like most scientific discoveries has a positive and a negative aspect to it. It can be used and misused. Cloning is of two kinds—reproductive and therapeutic. Reproductive cloning is a way of creating an exact replica of a person, i.e. a live human clone. There are various steps involved in it.

Firstly, doctors remove the DNA rich nucleus from an egg and replace it with the DNA of the person they want to clone. Then the donor DNA fuses with the egg, causing it to spontaneously start dividing into an embryo. The embryo then develops based on the instructions from the implanted DNA. It is then implanted in a woman's womb and the growing embryo develops into a foetus. Having developed from the implanted DNA, the baby is a virtual genetic copy of the person who donated the genetic material.[164]

This procedure which we have been unable to perfect till now means the constant killing of life it means human experimentation on live persons.[165]

(a) Caution

As reproductive technologies assist couples in establishing families, there must be a serious and detailed analysis of the reasons why reproductive cloning it gives cause for concern. The birth of a cloned human being has not yet been achieved. The possible consequences of such a procedure are not entirely clear. There is in the view of the experts, a general need for caution in considering a legal response. Premature attempts at prohibition and comprehensive regulation would have disadvantages that would be difficult to correct once an international convention was adopted.

The technique, which could be adapted to help female infertility by growing eggs in a lab, would raise the prospect of children being born through entirely artificial means. If the technology were abused, men could be completely sidelined.

It also raises the prospect of being able to take bone marrow tissue from women and coaxing the stem cells within the female tissue to develop into sperm cells. Creating sperm from women would mean they would only be able to produce daughters because the Y chromosome of male sperm would still be needed to produce sons. The latest research brings the prospect of female only conception a step closer.

---

164. *Newsweek,* Attack of The Clones, January 13, 2002, pp. 40-41.
165. Laws, Cloning: Are we on the Right Path?, March 2003, p. 15.

A forthcoming shake up the Britain's fertility laws could see minister outlaw the use of lab grown sperm and eggs in IVF treatment—even in research. The scientist says it would be wrong to ban such a possibly life-altering treatment before its potential has been established. It centers on stem cells-blank cells which have the power to turn into other cell types, creating a repair kit for the body. Removed from the human bone marrow, they were grown in a lab and then coaxed into turning into the cells which produce sperm. These particular cells did not go on to produce sperm.

The artificial sperm fertilized eggs and seven baby mice were born. While they suffered health problems and died prematurely, the research published last summer was seen as an important milestone in the race to find a cure for infertility. The latest research avoids the ethical problems associated with embryonic stem cells, by using cells taken from the bone marrow. Using a patient's own cells also removes the possibility of lab-grown material being rejected by the body.

(b) Scientific and Moral Implications of Cloning

While there is no apparent ethical offence in cloning a carrot, or even a frog, such is not the case with people. Each person is unique by virtue of his unique genetic make-up barring naturally occurring identical twins. In 1997, there was much notoriety surrounding the cloning of Dolly, the Sheep in Scotland.[166]

Mammalian cloning, through somatic-cell nuclear transfer process, has resulted in the birth of hundreds of organisms to date.[167] However, significantly more cloned animals and ruminants fail during pregnancy than would fail in sexual reproduction, and a substantial majority of cloned animals that have survived to birth have had significant birth defects.

The most common objection to cloning humans is that the current technology is unsafe. The animal clones that have survived after birth have a high chance of dying from heart

---

166. Wilmut, I., Schnieke, A.E., Mcwhir, J. *et. al.* Viable offspring derived from fetal and adult mammalian cells. *Nature,* 1997; 385; 810-13.
167. Campbell, K.H.S., Mcwhir, J., Ritchie, W.A. *et. al.* Sheep cloned by nuclear transfer from a cultured cell line. ,1996; 380, 64-6.

and blood vessel problems, malformed arteries, diabetes, immune system deficiencies and physical deformities.

There is no reason to believe that the outcome of attempted human cloning will be any different.[168] It is a well-known tenet of science that a single observation is not to be codified until confirmed by some one in some credence when well- controlled or of a unique nature, or both. It is the lack of any confirmation that provokes our skepticism.

By undertaking asexual reproduction, the gene pool will by narrowed and humanity's ability to over come disease will be constrained. As such, motives for human cloning are based on increasing personal notoriety rather than the greater good.[169] Cloning represents an unprecedented control over the genetic make-up of another individual.

Indeed, this concept of control over the genetic make up of successive generations is evocative of practice of eugenics, science of altering human evolution so as to encourage desirable traits and discourage undesirable ones, which was rejected by the world community after the Second World War.[170]

Opponents fear that wide spread practice of somatic cell nuclear transfer cloning will encourage a form of eugenics as people would be able to decide which traits are desirable.

Over a period of time, cloning might become a preferred practice and parents who choose to play the lottery of old-fashioned reproduction would be considered irresponsible. Cloning is said to breach a fundamental right to individuality. Uniqueness of identity and individuality are some of the most deep-felt and inherent signifiers of self. Just as a great artwork would lose its value in identical reproduction, so human beings can be said to lose their intrinsic inimitability in reproductions of themselves.[171] Cloning cannot be undone. We cannot destroy

168. Jaenisch, R., Wilmut, I., Don't clone humans. *Science Magazine*. 2001; 291, 2552-54.

169. Watson, J., Moving towards the clonal man, *Atlantic Monthly*, 1971; 227; 50.

170. Kelves, D.J., Eugenics and Human Rights, *BMJ*, 1999; 319, 435-38.

171. Gogarty, B., what exactly is an exact copy? And why it matters when trying to ban human reproductive cloning in Australia, *J Med. Ethics*. 2003; 29; 84-89.

our mistakes or purge the world of any baby born via means we disagree with. Political and academic ostracization and even expelling of the cloners from the International Infertility Association would do little to deter them from their objectives. What we need is an unambiguous international law on human cloning.

Till date, cloning laws and policies are far from uniform across the globe and the legal position in some countries remain uncertain. The Indian council of Medical Research has declared that research on cloning with intent to produce an identical human being, as of today, is prohibited but has not declared therapeutic cloning to be so prohibited.[172]

Some scientists might take an undue advantage by creating an embryo for the purpose of obtaining stem cells, which could be used for a number of degenerative diseases like Parkinson's disease, Alzheimer's disease, etc. Ultimately, it raises the moral status of an embryo, if any.

A recommendation in favour of this idea was publically rejected by President Clinton in December 1994.[173] An embryo has moral standing not so much for what it is (at conception or later) but because it is the result of procreative activity. People have a direct interest in the status and fate of every embryo formed from their gametes because such embryos carry their children. In this respect, the embryo is not only a symbol; it is real.

In order to curb the abuse of the medical technology, reproductive cloning should be controlled internationally till the global community including the scientists, ethicist and theologians finds out answers to morality of human cloning thoroughly and satisfactorily.

Cloning like most scientific discoveries has a positive and a negative aspect to it. It can be used and misused.

---

172. Indian Council of Medical Research. Ethical Guidelines for Biomedical Research on Human Subject, 2000; New Delhi, p. 48.
173. Schwartz, J., Devory, A., Clinton to ban US funds for some Embryo Studies, Washington Post, 1994; 3 December, 183 *JIAFM*, 2005; 27(3). ISSN 0971-0973.

(c) Reproductive Human Cloning and Human Rights—Challenges or Issues

The meaning of human cloning is often misunderstood. Although genes are recognized as influencing behaviour and cognition, "genetically identical" does not mean altogether identical because some important genes are also present in the mitochondria of the egg-cell. It could spell problems in stem-cell treatment for a good deal of diseases where compatibility is essential because of the risk of rejection. With additional experimentation on other animals we can enhance the accuracy of therapeutic cloning.

The temptation to manipulate another human life is almost irresistible for some as the history is replete with practice of eugenics in some parts of the world. The genesis of the 21st century is a period of unequaled medical technological prowess combined with unparalleled moral vacuity.

Human cloning is the creation of a genetically identical copy of an existing human or growing cloned tissue from that individual. The term is generally used to refer to artificial human cloning; human clones in the form of identical twins are common place, with their cloning occurring during the natural process of reproduction. The word "clone" derives from the Greek term Klon, meaning, "sprout" or "twig". It refers to a method of reproduction apart from the parental sexual-mating process that is characteristic of most organisms.

Cloning a human being would involve the following process: The cell nucleus of an adult person would be removed from an ordinary body cell e.g., a skin cell. Since the nucleus of each cell excepting RBCs, contains all of the genetic information in the form of DNA for a complete human being, a nucleus extracted from a donor would be transplanted into an unfertilized host egg cell whose nucleus had been removed. The resulting embryo at a later stage is implanted into the uterus. Finally, a baby clone will supposedly be born who would be an exact copy of the person who's original DNA provided the "Starter". Theoretically, hundreds of identical looking clones can be created by this method.

Reproductive human cloning[174] is seen as a flagrant violation of basic human rights. It is usually taken for granted that reproductive human cloning is a clear violation of basic tenets of like—individual autonomy, procreative liberty, identity, individuality, etc.

This presumption, without a wholesale inquiry into the domain of human cloning is never justified in the age of human rights. The logical battle in pros and cons over this issue requires a deep discussion in the light of recent transformations in the human values and social norms. As things stand now in animal models, cloning technology is not feasible. The recent death of 'Dolly', the first cloned sheep due to problem of ageing and genetic abnormality reveals this fact.

However, human cloning, if realized, would force us to redefine the notions of individuality, human dignity, personal identity, family and procreative liberty, etc. The central contention used to support legislative prohibitions against human cloning is that creating an individual with a genome nearly identical to a living or dead person is an affront to human dignity.

For example, article 11 of UNESCO's Universal Declaration on the Human Genome and Human Rights states: "Practices which are contrary to human dignity, such as reproductive cloning of human beings, shall not be permitted". Arguments used to support this view are that a clone would not have a "genetic individuality" and that his or her individual autonomy would be greatly compromised.[175]

It is, however, a fallacy because in the case of naturally occurring twins it is explicitly clear that genetically identical individuals are far from being identical people, they may differ from one another physically, psychologically and in personality.

---

174. In reproductive cloning an entire animal or human being is produced from a single cell by asexual reproduction. The creation of Dolly falls in this category. Human reproductive cloning would involve the creation of human being who was genetically identical to another.
175. Timothy Caulfield, "Cloning and Genetic Determinism—A Call for Consistency", 19, *Nature Biotechnology*, 403 (2001).

People's uniqueness and individuality is a normative belief in the intrinsic value of each individual person.[176]

The potential danger relating to human reproductive cloning is that it will lead to children being treated as means to parental ends of not as end in themselves, thus violating the Kantian maxim to treat people as ends and not merely means.[177] Human reproductive cloning also creates confusion regarding the family lineage and kinship. Michael Freeman, however, argues that while concerns about the commodification of children in the era of new reproductive technologies are legitimate, they are mostly, 'speculative and alarmist.[178] Here it is important to know that despite the fact that first in vitro fertilization baby, Louise Brown, was born only twenty-five years ago in 1978, the resulting forms of kinship and family to which in vitro fertilization has given rise have been largely assimilated by our culture.

Another human right issue concerned with the reproductive human cloning is procreative liberty. Procreative liberty is generally thought to be an important instance of personal liberty. It has been argued by some scholars that human cloning might seem like a week candidate for constitutional protection because it does not implicate the full range of liberty interests normally associated with natural. reproduction, such as bodily integrity and intimate association. The right to an abortion, for example presents a compelling liberty interest in bodily integrity.[179]

Freedom from government intrusion into the matters of intimate association and sexual conduct is another important liberty interest that supports the protection of some reproductive activities. Arguably, human cloning does not

---

176. Brock Dan W., "Human Cloning and Our Sense of Self", 296, Science 315 (2002).
177. Robertson John A.," Liberty, Identity and Human Cloning", 76, *Texas Law Review*, 1418 (1998).
178. Dean Bell, "Human Cloning and International Human Rights Law", 21, *The Sydney Law Review*, 219 (1999).
179. Planned Parenthood *v.* Casey, 505 US 833 (1992) at 852, 857, 896.

implicate the same quantity of liberty interests as do other forms of reproduction.[180]

In debates around human rights and cloning, human dignity is used to describe the essential quality which cloning is seen to violate. But what is human dignity? Surprisingly—for such a central concept in international law, there has been virtually no commentary on human dignity, its source, content and boundaries. Traditionally this has not been of great importance because international human rights law has not relied on violation of human dignity, but rather on the breach of a specific right which itself derives from the duty to respect human dignity. Human dignity has been retained at the conceptual keystone in international instruments, namely, the Council of Europe's Convention on Human Rights and Biomedicine and UNESCO's Universal Declaration on Human Genome and Human Rights.

So in the case of reproductive human cloning, at present, the risk outweighs the benefit. However, if it becomes feasible it will pose various problems regarding private laws relating to marriage, divorce, maintenance, inheritance, etc. and destabilize established social norms and family lineage. However, the opposition against reproductive human cloning is largely predictive.

Therefore, the situation warrants a deep analysis of the problem. Any legislation regarding the reproductive human cloning should not be made in haphazard way but taking into account its potentials and pitfalls.

So far as the legislative efforts are concerned, in U.K. reproductive human cloning is prohibited under Human Fertilization and Embryology Act, 1990. Similarly, many other countries have banned the reproductive human cloning. However, there are countries that do not currently have legislation relating to cloning, which provides ample opportunities for the misuse of cloning technology. So there requires an international consensus and co-operation for uniform regulatory mechanism in this regard.

---

180. "Human Cloning and Substantive Due Process", 111, *Harvard Law Review*, 23-57 (1998).

Human cloning—for reproductive purposes in particular - is perhaps the area of biotechnology with the highest potential for controversy at the moment, as evidenced by the high level of attention in the media and of policy-making at the international and national levels. Recent developments in technology suggest that the reproductive cloning techniques, used somewhat successfully in relation to animals, might soon be applied to human beings. Were they to be successfully applied, a clone-child could be produced which would have a genetic make-up identical (or virtually identical) to that of another individual or embryo.

The concerns these possible developments raise for the general public are understandable. Were individuals to be given a real power to create genetic copies of themselves or of others, fundamental issues concerning human dignity and identity arise?[181] To be balanced with these concerns are a number of serious questions. The response to the problems arising from reproductive human cloning should not confuse the issue of cloning technology in general, and the possibilities offered by therapeutic cloning in preventing and fighting disease.

(d) Impact of Cloning on Human Rights

1. Positive Impact of Cloning on Human Rights

- Cloning objectifies human sexuality and commodities the bodies of woman.
- Advancement in science and medicine.
- Common good for the present and future generations.
- Keno transplantation and Transgenic Animals.
- Beneficial in corking the problem of trafficking of human organs.
- Clones are useful in biological research for genetic uniformity. Treatment of old age.
- Treatment of severe diseases.

---

181. Lasker, Judith N., and Susan Borg, *In Search of Parenthood* Philadelphia, PA: Temple University Press, 1994.

- Transplantation of defected body organs.
- Avoiding the unable parents from mental torture by providing opportunity of child.
- Recovery of the damaged body organ due to some accident.
- Treatment of genes (healthy human).
- Re-generation of abolishing birds and animals.
- Timely Treatment at initial stage.

2. *Negative Impact of Cloning on Human Rights*

- Contrary to the Dignity of Human beings and their right to life.
- Unnatural sexual reproduction.
- Women are deprived of their innate dignity by becoming suppliers of eggs and wombs.
- Threatening to life or his or her unique identity.
- Imposes the genetic make-up of an already existing person on the cloned person.
- Constituting a violent attack on the clone's personal integrity.
- Assaults against the dignity and integrity of the human person.
- Destruction of nascent human life in the name of scientific discovery.
- Violates moral, ethical and legal considerations to protect the individuality and integrity of human being.
- Deny the fundamental rights of like and self-determination.
- Deny person's basis out logical claim that write and imp to the rest of the human family.
- Inevitable discrimination against those born through the natural process.
- Used for medical research and other objections.
- Commercially viable and obviates the necessity for a woman to physically engage a man in order to become pregnant.
- Curbing of scientific freedom.
- A researcher is free to destroy an embryo.

- Create only specific organs that are financially viable.
- Trade human organs in the black market.
- Unethical organ trade, especially kidneys from live donors.
- Recent e.g.: Cloning of credit cards in Jodhpur, Jaipur and Agra.
- Question mark on the role of male.
- Against the laws of nature.
- Against the Human Values.
- An instrument of rich people only.
- Chances of woman exploitation.
- Man shall be treated as machine.
- Encouragement to crimes (double clone).
- Foeticide.
- Violation of human rights.
- Social Imbalance.

(C) Cloning and Law in India

Right to life as guaranteed under Article 21 of the Indian Constitution is the basis of all human rights. Within its ambit, it includes the right to live with dignity. If a person has the right to live, he has the right to live his life well. The developments in science and technology cannot endanger our basic rights as humans.

Cloning a recent discovery in the field of science has prompted a worldwide debate on its permissibility. South Korea's discovery of the stem cells has further precipitated the matter. Cloning, if allowed raises serious questions concerning its impact on human rights, on human dignity and integrity. A clone is not a biological child. Technically it has no human parents as it does not have to be formed from an egg and sperm.

The cloning of human beings represents a gross violation of fundamental human rights and norms including the right to life, which has been recognized as the most important right by every country in this world.

In a world where we are trying to curtail experimentation on animals, we have human beings being treated like animals. The animals cloned have displayed a wide variety of birth defects due to which they cannot survive for long. Cloning of human beings means consciously bringing somebody into the world, who is suffering from abnormalities. One can kill a deformed animal but not a human being.

(a) Indian Council for Medical Research (ICMR)

Indian Council for Medical Research is currently in the process of framing guidelines on transfer of embryonic stem cell lines for foreign collaborations. There is no regulation on cloning and the use of 14 day old embryos for research is not banned.

(D) Global Endeavours for Controlling the Vices of Cloning

The last decade of the current millennium saw a long-standing fantasy theory becoming manifested in the form of cloning. Clone is an organism that has the same genetic configuration as another organism. The technique of procuring a genetically identical duplicate of an organism is broadly called as cloning.[182]

The new scientific achievement is full of controversial effects specially in relation to human cloning. Very few countries in the world have enacted law to regulate it, that too half-heartedly. It will be wise to enact a comprehensive law to regulate cloning after thoroughly examining the controversies to reap the benefits of this modern technology and to avoid a legal vacuum in case of some negative outcome in future.

(a) Law Aspect

Medical experimentation on human subjects as pointed out below. Is a crime under international law? This prospect is morally and ethically repugnant even to those who generally favor scientific research. There currently exist alternative methods of scientific cell research that accomplish the same potential objectives without the need to clone a human embryo that will inevitably be faced with destruction. To create life with the planned intention of destroying it violates the basic

182. Sinha, S., Gupta, S., Sharma, R.K., Pande, J.N., Cloning: A review article, Medicolegal update 1998; 3(1, 2): 16-21.

norms and moral, ethical, and legal considerations designed to protect the individuality and integrity of each human being.

Freedom of research cannot be absolute and it can be circumscribed in necessary situations. Such a necessity arises when research violates respect for human dignity, which is at the basis of all human rights, including the right to scientific research must be weighed against the heavy costs of humanity. We have a moral obligation not to transgress the genetic heritage of humanity. Therefore, certain practices, contrary to human dignity, such as reproductive cloning of human beings should be absolutely prohibited as it violates our fundamental human rights. Cloning leads to the loss of human dignity and what it means to be a human being.

Even with sensible laws, there's always a chance of cloning technology being misused. One question that we continue to face is what kind of legislation is required? How restrictive? How protective?

(b) Human Cloning Contravenes Basic Precepts of International Law

Various international instruments acknowledge that the dignity of the human person is at the center of international law. Regardless of the objective for which it was done, human cloning conflicts with the international legal norms that protect human dignity.

First of all, international law guarantees the right to life to all not just some human being. Facilitating the formation of human beings who are destined for destruction, the international destruction of cloned human beings once the particular research goal is reached, consigning any human being to an existence of either involuntary servitude or slavery, and being submitted to involuntary medical and biological experimentation on human beings are morally wrong and inadmissible.

Human cloning also poses great threats to the rule of law by enabling those responsible for cloning to select and propagate certain human characteristics based on gender, race, etc and eliminate other. This would be akin to the practice of eugenics leading to the institution of a "super race" and the inevitable discrimination against those born through the natural process. Human cloning conducted for any end is contrary to the rule of law.

(c) Existing National Legislation on Cloning

Following 'Dolly' the UK government was quick to assert that existing legislation prohibited application of the new technique to create human clones. However, the Human Fertilization and Embryology Act, 1990 (HFE Act) does not expressly forbid human cloning and some commentators suggest that the nuclear transfer technique is not encompassed by the HFE Act (Korek, 1997).

The central problem regarding nuclear transfer cloning derives from the inclusion of the word 'fertilization in the Sec. 1(1)(a) definition of 'embryo'. Although Sec. 3(3)9(d) purports to prohibit nuclear transfer cloning it refers to 'replacing a nucleus of a cell of an embryo taken from a cell of any person.

The reconstructed 'cell' that grew into 'Dolly' was never fertilized. Instead, it was induced to divide by a short electric shock (for a review of the nuclear transfer technique, see the *New Scientist*, 1997). Thus, the way in which 'embryo' is defined in the Act, depending on judicial interpretation, could prevent Sec. 3(3) applying to nuclear transfer (Korek, 1997). Also, Sec. 4(2) governs the storage and use of gametes (egg and sperm).

On a literal statutory interpretation, concern has been expressed that the word 'use' was intended to refer to use of the whole gamete for purposes of IVF. Although part of an egg (the outer membrane, cytoplasm and mitochondria) was used to create 'Dolly' it could be convincingly argued that this portion is not a 'gamete' within the context of the Act. Indeed, to submit otherwise would be analogous to arguing that an egg devoid of its yolk is still an egg.

Notwithstanding semantics, every person undertaking procedures involving the creation or use of human embryos must obtain in license from the HFEA. This is the statutory body charged with regulatory responsibility for the Act and was born from recommendations made by the Warnock Report (1985). Performing a procedure governed by the HFE Act without a discretionary HFEA license is a criminal offence.

The HFEA has re-asserted that embryonic human clones might be created for medical research but 'reproductive cloning' of individuals will remain illegal for the foreseeable future (*Financial Times*, 1998c). Despite this assurance, the licensing criteria listed above are not mutually exclusive and more may be added by the Secretary of State for Health (HFE Act, Sec. 45). This discretionary power, combined with deep-rooted ethical, moral and religious concerns, has generated suspicion that human cloning may, at some time in the future be licensed for economic or other prevailing reasons. Another, possibly more realistic, concern is that research proposals which are in reality aimed at human cloning will be able to 'fraudulently' obtain HFEA approval by masquerading behind a legitimate purpose.

In the scenario outlined, it is submitted that reliance on the 1961 Act to prevent the procedure would, at least, be problematical. Cells are the functional units of tissue and, theoretically, just one nucleus extracted from a single cell would suffice to produce a clone using the 'Dolly' method. The nucleus is a sub-cellular fraction and therefore is unlikely to be caught by legislation expressly enacted to prevent tissue removal.

Turning now to legislation in other European jurisdictions, it appears that *Denmark* was the only European country to have anticipated 'Dolly', having enacted legislation expressly forbidding nuclear substitution (Act No. 503 on a Scientific Ethical Committee System and the Handling of Biomedical Research Projects, 1992).

(d) *Enforceability*

Whether implemented at a national or international level, crucial to the efficacy of any legislation enacted to control cloning is the vexed issue of enforceability, particularly in relation to the EU. Disregarding the issue of const, the potential problem within the EU is well illustrated in Blood. Mrs. Blood sought a discretionary export license from the HFEA enabling her to be artificially inseminated with sperm collected from her husband, now deceased.

The HFEA is able to approve export even if the purpose for which the sperm will be used once it leaves the country is contrary to the HFE Act (*Deech*, 1997). EU treaty Article 59 protects the freedom to provide services and gives EU citizen the right to seek medical treatment in any MS. Giving his judgment in the Court of Appeal, Lord Woolf made clear that no derogation would be allowed on the grounds of public policy and thus export was not preventable.

The aforementioned EU harmonizing directive should avert the recurrence of similar situations specifically regarding cloning. More troublesome, however, is the problem of jurisdiction in non-MS exemplified by Dr Seed, who expects to create a human clone by 1999 (*Financial Times*, 1998b). Until US legislation prohibits human cloning *per se* the practice is legal, providing private, as opposed to federal, funds are utilized.

In anticipation of imminent change in the law, Dr Seed blatantly intends to circumvent US prohibition by relocating his operation to Mexico, apparently with the endorsement of the Mexican government. Increasing globalization and, in particular, the internet may render obsolete anything short of a ratified 'global treaty' to prevent human cloning. In its absence, a black market may develop where 'customers' are forced to purchase services illegal in their domestic jurisdiction from providers elsewhere.

Already, human sperm is available for sale on the internet. For just $200 customers may select sperm from a catalogue of donors, depending on which characteristics they most value for their progeny. This service, however abhorrent it may seem, is clearly commercially viable and obviates the necessity for a woman to physically engage a man in order to become pregnant.

It allows consumer influence over the probable genetic characteristics of progeny—as might be expected; sperm prices reflect popular donor attributes. When and if, human cloning becomes viable, commercial cloning services are likely to the widely advertised on the internet.

"Contract to clone" could be negotiated in cyberspace, subject to any defined legal jurisdiction specified by the parties.

Those jurisdictions burdened by prohibitive anti-cloning legislation will simply be avoided.[183]

(e) Federal Embryo Protection Act, 1990

Prima Facie, this adequately encompasses cloning and Germany claims that its legislation is stricter than the amended European Convention on Human Rights (ECHR) protocol (post) (Independent, 1998) which prohibits all research on human embryos. However, it is submitted that a loophole exists in the German legislation that could be exploited unless closed.

The potential problem derives from the words 'genetically identical'. It will likely be argued that a clone produced by nuclear transfer cannot be genetically identical to the parent. The mitochondrial DNA contained in the host cell will be non-identical to the mitochondrial DNA of the donor cell.

Thus, strictly speaking, no clone created by nuclear substitution can ever be genetically identical to the animal cell form which the nucleus was extracted—only the nuclear, but not the mitochondrial, DNA will be identical. In the US there is still no law expressly prohibiting cloning.

The National Bioethics Advisory Commission (NBAC) of USA (1997) report recommended legislation to ban research into the cloning of complete people with a clause to review desirability of cloning after five years. The House is now considering two separate bills from the Democrats and Republicans.

1. International Instruments

However, in the context of the United Nations, a momentum appears to have formed concerning the need for an international legal instrument dealing with reproductive human cloning. The General Assembly has decided to establish an *ad hoc* committee to 'consider the elaboration of an international convention against the reproductive cloning of human beings'.[184] The experts noted with satisfaction that

183. Wood Peter G. "To What Extent Can the Law Control Human Cloning?" BSC Diplaw, Pear Tree Farm, Dunham Hill, Helsby. Cheshire WA6 OLX.
184. GA Res. 56/93 of 12 December 2001.

OHCHR participated as an observer in the meetings of this Committee, and encourage continued participation in the Working Groups of the Sixth Committee which will carry on the work of the *ad hoc* committee.

Since the founding of the United Nations, the centrality of the welfare and protection of all human beings to the work of this organization is beyond question. The safekeeping of present and succeeding generations of human beings and the advancement of fundamental human rights is critical of the work of the UN.

The Universal Declaration of Human Rights [UDHR] reiterates the sanctity of all human life and the compelling need to protect it from harm. In this regard, Article 3 of the Declaration asserts that everyone has the right to life. With life comes hope in the future—a hope that the Universal Declaration protects by acknowledging that all human beings are equal in dignity and rights. With the right to life comes liberty and security of the person. To ensure this, the Universal Declaration confirms that each human being is an entity who is guaranteed a future filled with the hope of self-determination. To further this end, conditions that degrade any human being with servile status and deny the fundamental rights to life and self-determination are reprehensible.

To better understand these points, it would be prudent to take stock of our human nature at this stage. Each of us, regardless of nationality, gender, race, ethnicity, or religion, share the same origin and are destined to develop as members of communities beginning with the family, the natural and fundamental unit of society. We strive to further our goals for self, family, and country, but we also, as fellow human beings, are called to further the common good for the present and future generation across the globe. We do this to protect all who share and participate in the human condition. However, if some human beings are destined to serve interests that do not take account of these fundamental principles of human nature that are at the center of the UN's concern, they are reduced to a servile status that denies them the fundamental claim to life and self-determination guaranteed to all.

To clone a human being—regardless of the goal—is to deny this person's basic ontological claim that unites him or her to the rest of the human family. This human being has no hope in a self-determining future because his or her individuality will be destroyed to further some research purpose or to enhance the narcissism of a person who has already existed. In either case, the cloned human being is reduced to enslavement that contravenes the fundamental nature of human existence—to be free and to live as a unique individual capable of contributing to the development of the self and society.

We must reject attempts to use humans as objects of lethal experimentation. Cloning reduces the class of human beings to the status of objects and property. It is an insult to the dignity of the person. Although it is not legally binding, *Article 11* of the *Universal Declaration on the Human Genome and Human Rights (UNESCO, 1997)* now states that 'Practices which are contrary to human dignity, such as reproductive cloning of human beings, shall not be permitted' and was adopted in November 1997.

In the EU, Members of Parliament (MEPs) expressed concern about recent developments. In a resolution adopted in January 1998, the EU called upon the member states (MS) and the United Nations (UN) to implement a legally binding universal ban on human cloning.

The EU clearly acknowledges that some MS have no national legislation prohibiting the cloning of humans and that it must take the lead in promoting full public consideration of the issues. The resolution also urges MS to ban human cloning at all stages of formation and development, regardless of the method used, and to impose penal sanctions for violation.

It assigns a supervisory role to the Commission, who will report any cloning research carried out and check whether cloning could form any part of research programmes financed by the EU. The same document also established the European Union Ethics Committee, whose role it will be to assess ethical aspects of developments in human cloning technology and related fields.

In January 1998 the *European Convention on Human Rights and Biomedicine* was amended to include a total ban on human cloning. The preparatory resolution states, "Cloning of human beings for any purpose whatsoever cannot under any circumstances be tolerated by any society, because it is a serious violation of fundamental human rights, contrary to the principle of equality as it permits a eugenic and racist selection, it offends against human dignity and it requires experimentation of humans.

Although it allows the cloning of cells for research purposes, this represents the first international ban on human cloning and was signed by 19 European, countries from the 40 member Council of Europe (*Independent*, 1998). The UK government is consulting on aspects of the protocol before deciding whether to sign up to the agreement (HGAC/HEFA 1998).

The cloning of human beings is also a violation of the *Nuremberg Code*, which was written in response to the atrocities committed by the Nazi regime. According to the code,

> "No experiment should be conducted where there is an a priori reason to believe that death or disabling injury will occur".

Further *Article 1(1)* of the *Additional Protocol to the Convention for the Protection of Human Rights and Dignity of the Human Being* with regard to the Application of Biology and Medicine on the Prohibition of Cloning Human Beings states:

> "Any intervention seeking to create a human being genetically identical to another human being, whether living or dead is prohibited".

Ideally, what is required is a global harmonizing treaty asserting that eugenic reproductive human cloning will not be tolerated in any jurisdiction and breach will result in severe penal sanctions. Pragmatically, efforts to restrict access to nuclear technology and the limited success of international treaties, such as the Geneva Convention, suggest a panacea will be unattainable. However, undeterred, progress towards this goal has been made in response to the alarm caused by Dr Seed.

2. Other Legislation on Cloning

In the U.S. there is still no law expressly prohibit cloning. The EU Resolution, ban human cloning at all stages of formation and development and to impose penal sanctions for violation.

The Directives on cloning states that Cloning is essentially biological, thus it cannot be the subject of patent protects in and therefore patents cannot be used to restrict the proliferation of cloning technology.

In addition to, and distinct from, the Directive on Cloning, the controversial draft Bio-technology Directive includes measures on human cloning, '*Official Journal,* 1997(b). This harmonizing directive was intended to enhance the internal market in patented biotechnological products and to protect free movement of goods in accordance with Article 30, thus encouraging European research.

The principal objective of the directive was to clarify the distinction between what is patentable and what is not, and to confirm that 'discoveries' may not be regarded as patentable inventions. Significantly, it also provides that inventions are unpatentable—if their exploitation would be contrary to public policy or morality. International Law says human cloning conducted for any end is contrary to the rule of law.

The Standing Committee of the Catholic Bishops Conference of Japan states that human cloning is a violation of human dignity and the basic principles of human reproduction.

Old paradigms are rapidly vanishing and new ones are but slowly emerging from the mists that shroud the very origins of life itself.

The Human Tissue Act, 1961, which concerns removal of body parts from deceased humans., has also been examined in relation to cloning (Korek), where cloning a cadaver is intended for instance, grieving parents may want to clone a child recently killed in a road crash. Such a procedure would require removal of cells from the child.

The Warnock Report 1985 says this should be so even if this is seen as impinging clinical or a academic freedom.

The Human Fertilization and Embryology Act 1990 (HFE Act) does not expressly forbid human cloning. To prohibit nuclear transfer cloning it refers to replacing a nucleus of a cell of an embryo taken from a cell of any person.[185] And "Reproductive cloning of individual will remain illegal for the foreseeable future".

The Federal Embryo Protection Act, 1990 says that it is an offence to create an embryo genetically identical to any other embryo, foetus or living or dead person. "Reproductive cloning of human beings shall not be permitted".[186] European Ethics Committee 1998 states that one must ban cloning and the genetic manipulation susceptible to altering the character of the human species. The Euro Convention on H.Rt's and Biomedicine, 1998 impose total ban on human cloning. Although it allows the cloning of cells for research purposes. In Jan. 2001 The United Kingdom legalized creation of cloned embryos for therapeutic stem cell research purposes only. The Human Cloning Prohibition Bill, 2001 says: "Cloning confounds the meaning of 'father' and 'mother' and confuses the identity and kinship relations of any cloned child, and thus threatens to weaken existing notions regarding who bears which parental duties and responsibilities for children.

The Human Cloning Prohibition Act, 2003 makes it unlawful for any person to perform, attempt to perform, or to participate in an attempt to perform human cloning. The Watered-down Declaration, 2005 condemns all forms of human cloning but is not legally binding.

(E) Ethical and Legal Issues of Cloning and Judicial Response

The possibility of human cloning, raised when Scottish scientists at Roslin Institute created the much-celebrated sheep 'Dolly', aroused worldwide interest and concern because of its scientific and ethical implications. The feat, also generated uncertainty over the meaning of 'cloning'—an umbrella term traditionally used by scientists to describe different processes for duplicating biological material.

The same problems would be expected in human cloning. In addition, scientists do not know how cloning could impact mental development. While factors such as intellect and mood

185. Sec. 3(3)(d) (HFE Act) 1990.
186. Art. II of The U.D. on the Human Genome & H.Rt's, 1997.

may not be as important for a cow or a mouse, they are crucial for the development of healthy humans. With so many unknowns concerning reproductive cloning, the attempt to clone humans at this time is considered potentially dangerous and ethically irresponsible.

(a) Potential Applications of Cloning

Cloning has the potentials of providing a clone to those individual in which other methods of reproduction have failed to provide a healthy children. It is also a technique to select, control or alter the genome of offspring.[187] Cloning may be chosen by couples who, because of infertility, a high risk of severe genetic disease or other factors, cannot or do not with to conceive a child. In place of sperm, egg or gamete donation to infertile couples, they may opt for cloning of either of them, as the child would biologically related to one of them, even when this goal cannot be achieved through sexual reproduction.

Cloning can also become a good alternative to gamete donation, to seek adoption, or to remain childless to the couples at high risk of offspring's with severe genetic diseases.[188] If they already had healthy child, they might choose cloning to create a later born twin of that child and in distant future it may also become possible to correct the genetic material with gene therapy during cloning. Cloning may also be used to enable a couple to clone dead or dying child so as to have that child live on in some closely related form, to obtain sufficient number of embryos for transfer and pregnancy, or to eliminate mitochondrial disease.

The most controversial application relates to obtaining tissue or organs for transplantation. A child who needed an organ or tissue transplant might lack a medically suitable donor. Couples in this situation have sometimes conceived a child with a hope that the child born would have the correct tissue to serve e.g. as a bone marrow donor for elder sibling.[189]

---

187. Robertson, J.A. Genetic Selection of Offspring Characteristics, *Boston Univ. Law Res* 1996; 76: 421-82.
188. Robertson, J.A. Human Cloning and the Challenge of Regulation, *N Engl J Med,* 1998; 339 (2): 119-21.
189. Robertson, J.A. Children of Choice: Freedom and the New Reproductive Technologies, Princeton N.J., Princeton Univ. Press, 1994.

Cloning a person's cells up to the embryo stage Might provide a source of stem cells or tissue for the person cloned. Using cloning, it may also be possible to elucidate the mechanism that makes tot potent cells differentiate, which could allow diseased or damaged tissue to be encouraged to regenerate in-vivo making transplantation, with the inherent risk of rejection largely unnecessary.[190]

Another potential area of use of cloning is in vaccine development having the biggest advantage of not requiring cold chain which is a must for an effective present day vaccines. Efforts are also being made to develop transgenic fruits which could be used as eatable vaccine. In India, attempts are being made to create the so called Fertility Control Vaccine using closed genes.

Some of the labs are also trying to isolate and then clone a gene from insect cells that would enhance cell life and thus ensure longevity.[191] Cloning is useful in producing large number and better variety of livestock. The goal of transgenic livestock is to produce livestock and ideal characteristics for the agricultural industry and to be able to manufacture biological products. Scientists are also trying to clone the endangered species to increase their population. The cloned livestock can also help treating diseases like diabetes, Parkinson's disease, cystic fibrosis, etc. Biologists are also working to develop transgenic animals which could be used as bio-factories for the hormones.

Clones are also highly useful in biological research because of their genetic uniformity. The cloning of human beings is a subject fraught with ethical and moral controversy. If cloning can ensure the infinite replication of specific genetic traits, a judgment would need to be made as to which traits are desirable and therefore worthy of perpetuation. The persons empowered to exercise such judgment would be in a position to change the course of human development

Cloning has been controversial since early 1970s when Hans Jones noted that it does not matter whether an exact

---

190. Wood Pg. To What Extent Can The Law Control Human Cloning? *Med Science Law,* 1999; 39(1): 5-10.
191. Singh, Dhiraj., Clonial Ambitions, *Hindustan Times,* 19 June 1999.

duplicate of an existing person is impossible. What matters is that the person is chosen to be cloned because of some characteristic he or she possesses. He argued that cloning is always a crime against the clone, the crime of depriving the clone of his or her "existential right to certain subjective terms of being" particularly, the "right of ignorance" of facts about his or her origin that are likely to be "paralyzing for the spontaneity of becoming himself or herself.[192] Eugenic reproductive human cloning has been condemned all over the world as it is totally unethical and against the principle of nature. Various organizations and countries have started making legislation to ban/regulate this technique.

Presently, no steps have been initiated to regulate human cloning in majority of the developing countries including India, since the technique is not reported to be developed in them. But the days are not far, when the technique may become available. Therefore, a debate must be initiated to regulate cloning in our country also.

Further, it is an age of globalization and in particular the internet has made international communication/trade easily feasible. Already, human sperm is available for sale on the internet and a day may come when the human cloning may become feasible and commercial cloning services may be available via internet.

One of the major negative consequences of wide scale cloning envisaged is that it would lead to marked restriction in the diversity of human gene pool. Such a limitation would endanger the ability of our species to survive major environmental changes/diseases as genetic homogeneity in mildly compatible with major environmental change and new diseases.

It is further argued that cloning would be a poor method indeed for improving on the human species. If widely adopted, it would have a devastating impact on the diversity of the human gene pool.

---

192. Jonas, H., Philosophical Essays: From Ancient Creed to Technological Man, Eaglewood Cliffs, N.J., Prentice Hall, 1974: 162-3!

Cloning, would select for traits that have been successful in the past but that will not necessarily be adaptive to an unpredictable future. There is also risk of developing imperfect clones, who will take the responsibility of such clones is also a question to be answered.[193]

There are two different ethical questions, with need an immediate answer. The first, whether cloning for reproduction should be allowed? This is settled; as reproductive cloning is a clear violation of human rights. Issues regarding parenthood, legal identity, the rights of the clone don't have a satisfactory answer.

Also because cloning can involve DNA manipulation, the ability to create individuals with certain admirable qualities and to leave out less than perfect qualities is a possibility. This could lead to the stigmatism that "natural" children are in some way inferior. Cloning would also violate the human dignity of children. It is thought that since clones would be "made" instead of "created by two individuals" society would treat them more as commodities than as individuals.[194]

The question regarding stem cell research also demands a plausible solution before it is allowed across the board. No doubt, the benefits from therapeutic cloning are numerous. On the other hand, reproductive cloning which creates humans has no role in curing disease.

(b) Human Cloning and Right to Life

Even if, cloning is pursed with the aim of making a human baby that will mature into adulthood so that there is no destruction of the human embryo, this activity is will an affront to the dignity of the human embryo, this activity is still an affront to the dignity of the human person. As a form of unnatural sexual reproduction it represents a radical manipulation of the constitutive relationship and complementarily that are at the origin of human procreation as a biological act and an exercise of human love.

193. Stern, K. Strict Liability and the Supply of Donated Gametes. *Med Law Review*, 1994; 2: 261-82.

194. On the internet: www bellonline.com/articles/art1203.asp

Cloning objectifies human sexuality and commodities the bodies of women. Moreover, women are deprived of their innate dignity by becoming suppliers of eggs and wombs. The dignity of the person cloned is similarly threatened because other persons and technological powers exercise undisputed dominion over the duration of this person's life or his or her unique identify.

Reproductive cloning threatens biological individuality and imposes the genetic makeup of an already-existing person on the cloned person. In turn, the cloned person is commandeered by another's external and internal profile thereby constituting a violent attack on the clone's personal integrity.

(c) Legal Aspects of Cloning

The content of the Rule of Law cannot be fixed for all times and all the circumstances are a matter not for lament but for rejoicing. It would be really, unwise and improper if the law were so petrified as to be unable to rise to the situations and constant challenge of evolutionary and revolutionary changes in the society.

Few definitions of the Rule of Law must be founded upon realities of contemporary society. It ought to evolve sound strategies for strong protection against the misuse and abuse of authority and of private and public power.

Law is a creature of society. Whereas, society shown no signs of returning to simpler way of life and habits of olden days or of advancing towards a state of utopian perfection. Therefore Law, legal system and Legal process should continue to occupy central place. Legal system must continue to bend and turn in response to social change. Rule of law should prevail through judicial reinterpretations, reorientation of Law and precedents. Law and Legal system should not only articulate but must create creative contours of major social changes and not only quantitative but also qualitative, such as:

- The Regulatory Statutory process for the record of sperm banking.
- Effective provisions in Intellectual Property Protection Laws.

- Product only and not process patent must be available.
- International code to meet with the challenges of 21st Century.

Indeed the required statutory provisions ought to be explored, expeditiously. Socio-Medico-Legal imperatives, arising out of Bio-Technological growth for the Welfare of the one and all concerned bearing in mind that Law and Medicine as instruments of serving humanity and providing solutions in the context of increasing complexity of modern research and technological growth.

The need of the hour is to reform the existing laws upon the new research for solving new problems, otherwise, we shall be dispensing with justice rather than dispensing of justice itself. With regard to modern trends and new-waves, in the realm of Bio-Technology research and the Genetic Engineering advancement warrant various regulations at the National as well as, international level. Amongst the legal questions raised, questions highlighted here, warrant expeditious attention for arresting NEO, Socio-legal challenges.

It therefore, becomes necessary for all thinkers like, jurists, academician, sociologists to understand, how, these problems cope up in the functioning of different eventualities and social structures to study the operation of various patterns of, inter-relationship. In the society, how people are affected by them and observe how social system needs to be reorganized and restructured in dealing with them.

The role of sociologists and public services-oriented people and institutions in a social problem is to create awareness about social problems to analyze the causes of social problems. Sociologist by himself cannot solve a social problem. Much depends on officials, politicians and NGOs. It is in this context, law plays a very important role to meet with such social problems and the challenges arising out of change in the social structure and basic norms.

The law has due functions. One is of a Legal Order, as a reactor to and increasingly as an initiator of social change. Therefore, interaction of legal and social change must be adopted as a continuous exercise. The controversy between those who believe that law should essentially follow, not lead, and that it should do so, slowly, in response to clearly formulated social problems and those who believe that the law should be determined agent in the creation of the new forms.

However, one thing is certain that law is an instrument for effective and efficient social changes. It can never be forgotten that the maintenance and sustenance of 'Rule of Law' is a 'sine qua non' for any welfare State.

It must be remembered that 21st Century has already been announced the Bio-Tech Century. Bio-Tech, obviously, will give birth to various challenges. Therefore, scientists, activists, jurists, legal academicians and sociologists must start an exercise of exchanging thoughts and tips of finding the latest threats and challenges present and prospective as they know or anticipate. It is obligatory for the Welfare States and mandatory for United Nations to examine and state the problems related to bio-technology past, present and future so as to safeguard the human rights.

(d) Ethical Issues of Cloning

Before setting out the official position of the Catholic Church on this issue, we present the principal ethical reasons western society advances against artificial reduplication of human beings. The Catholic Church is basically an agreement with these reasons. The Catholic Church is opposed to this kind of research for the following reason as well.

First of all, a human being is born of the union between a man and a woman and is endowed with the right to be reared by his or her parents. The duty and responsibility of guarding this right rests on the parents. This is the dispensation of providence. Indeed, this duty and responsibility rests not only on the parents but on society itself. But who will bear this responsibility for a human person who is the product of cloning? A human person is meant to grow up soundly in the home provided by one's parents, and eventually to take one's place in society. A cloned person would be deprived of all these privileges.

Even supposing a human being to be born a product of a cloning experiment, it must not be forgotten that he or she will be a person endowed with absolute worth and dignity. Such a person will be a perfect human being and genetically in the same position as a natural identical twin. Just as identical twins enjoy absolute values and dignity, so also would a cloned human being. However, the creation of human beings blessed with that absolute worth and dignity is a right that belongs to God alone. It is not entrusted to human ingenuity.

(e) Should Cloning be Banned?

This is predominantly an ethical question and arouses passionate conjectures both for and against cloning. Most commentators agree that the nightmare vision of eugenics predicted by Huxley (1932) is undesirable and should be vigorously opposed by the law. The Warnock Report (1985) went as far as asserting that this should be so 'even if this is seen as infringing clinical or academic freedom'. Others, who see no justifiable reason to deny people whatever means are available to enable them to have children, adamantly reject this view.

There are certainly legitimate uses for reproductive and therapeutic human cloning. Notwithstanding the immense philanthropic contribution cloning could make to our physiological knowledge concerning the genotype, it may also offer the chance to create significantly improved models of human diseases.

The United Nations has given up its attempt to introduce a worldwide legal ban on some or all types of human cloning. On Tuesday, 15.5.05 its deeply divided general assembly voted to adopt a watered-down "declaration" that condemns all forms of human cloning but is not legally binding.

The declaration, which was passed by 84 votes to 34, with 37 abstentions, prohibits "all forms of human cloning inasmuch as they are incompatible with human dignity and the protection of human life". But it has been widely criticized for being imprecise and meaningless.

"It lacks precision, it lacks clarity and it is certainly not a guide", says Bernard Siegel, head of the Genetic Policy Institute in Coral Gables, Florida, US, which has lobbied the UN in favour using human cloning to develop new medical therapies. "It masks the ultimate failure of the UN to produce at document with legal teeth".

The proposed ban on cloning is not intended to prohibit the use of cloning techniques to obtain a number of biological entitles (Molecules, cells, and tissues other than human embryos, to generate plants, or to produce non-human embryos and non-chimaeric (human-animal) embryos.

Other Assisted Reproductive Technologies

Assisted Reproduction Technology (ART) has helped to fulfil the dreams of many an infertile couple. Innovative techniques have been introduced to achieve pregnancies in various types of infertility and also to improve existing pregnancy fates. However, pregnancy rates are still unacceptably low and the cost of technology very high.

Alternative techniques in ART have been introduced from time to time with the intent of achieving pregnancy while avoiding the high cost of ART. Some techniques have an acceptable pregnancy rate while others do not. In countries like India the social pressures on a couple to reproduce are very high, the per capita income is low and no funding is available for treatment, hence the use of these measures where indicated, is very relevant. This chapter is an attempt to look at these techniques in the Indian context and to see, which of these procedures can or should be used where in-vitro fertilization is not available or affordable.

(A) INTRACYTOPLASMIC SPERM INJECTION (ICSI)

In intracytoplasmic sperm injection (ICSI), a single sperm is injected directly into an egg using a tiny glass needle to create an embryo prior to *in-vitro* fertilization. ICSI therapy can be used when sperm are scarce, have poor motility, or are otherwise unable to fertilize an egg. Because the procedure has only been in effect since the early 1990s, the side effects of ICSI are not well known but may include genetic or chromosomal abnormalities, major birth defects, and infertility particularly in males.

A scientific approach will require efficient and complete evaluation of the infertile couples. Many couples have more than one contributory causes which should be identified early. Detailed history and physical examination followed by investigations for specific diseases like diabetes mellitus, sickle cell anemia and sexually transmitted diseases (STDs) should be performed routinely besides blood counts, semen analysis and karyotyping whenever indicated.

Diagnostic evaluation of uterus to detect disorders is limited to organic rather than functional abnormalities.[1] Ultrasonography is helpful in detecting intrauterine adhesions, septa, polyps and uterine myoma. Normal and abnormal endometrial growth can also be evaluated.[2] Combinations of hysterosalpingography, hysteroscopy and laparoscopy provide the clinicians excellent information regarding and suspected uterine condition and help to plan the therapeutic approach.

(a) Direct Intraperitoneal Insemination (DIPI)

A prepared sample of semen is placed in the pouch of Douglas under ultrasound guidance at the time of ovulation.

The patient is placed in a "sitting lithotomy position" to ensure that the peritoneal fluid gravitates to the pouch of

1. Randolph, J.R., Ying, Y.K., Maier, D.B. *et al.*: Comparison of real time ultrasonography, hysterosalpingography, laparoscopy/hysteroscopy in the evaluation of uterine abnormalities, *Fertile Sterile*, 46:828, 1986.
2. Valdos, E., Malini, S., Malinak, R. Ultrasound Evaluation of Female Genital Anomalies. *Am J. Obstet Gynaecology*, 149:285, 1984.

Douglas. After cleaning the vagina with an antiseptic solution a transvaginal ultrasound scan is performed to identify the fluid. Once the site is determined, a 19 G disposable needle is passed through the ultrasound biopsy guide into the peritoneal fluid with a single rapid movement.

The patient should be warned that she would feel a sharp pain. Once the needle tip is identified within the fluid a small amount of peritoneal fluid is aspirated to confirm correct placement. The prepared semen sample is then injected into the pouch of Douglas. If the patient is apprehensive a mild analgesic or sedative may be given.

In theory the procedure is very simple but in practice it can be quite cumbersome. Identification of a good pocket of fluid may be difficult at times because only a small quantity of fluid is present and it is hidden between loops of bowel. Excessive bowel movement further adds to the problem.

(b) Direct Intrafollicular Insemination (DIFI)

A prepared sample of semen is injected directly into the pre-ovulatory follicles under ultrasound guidance. With the patient in lithotomy position a transvaginal scan is done to identify the pre-ovulatory follicles. After cleaning the vagina a 16 C needle is introduced into the follicle and the prepared semen sample is injected into it. Generally, the procedure is well tolerated and does not require anesthesia or analgesia. However if there are more than one or two follicles the patient may be given light sedatives.

The first successful pregnancy was reported by Lucena *et. al.* in 1991.[3] Since then many centers have tried the procedure. Success rates vary from 2 to 20 percent.

The logic of this procedure defies understanding. In addition, there remains a theoretical risk of an ovarian ectopic pregnancy in case the fertilized oocyte fails to extrude. No recommendations can be made for the use of this technique.

(c) Intrafallopian Insemination (IFI)

Success of transcervical tubal cannulation prompted the

3. Lucena, E., Ruiz, J.A., Mendoza, J.C. *et al:* Direct Intrafollicular Insemination—a case report. *J. Reprod Med,* 36(7): 525-26, 1991.

use of tubal cannulation for intrafallopian insemination. Jansen and Anderson in 1987 reported the first procedure.[4] Tubal cannulation is carried out under ultrasound guidance, hysteroscopic control or using a tactile technique.

A coaxial catheter system (Cook OB/GYN) is used to enter the tube. The outer catheter is guided toward the tubal ostia, the inner catheter loaded with the prepared sperm in 0.3 ml of medium is moved through the outer catheter into the tube and the sperm is delivered 2 to 4 cm distal to the tubal ostium. Insemination can be done on the side with the greater number of mature ovarian follicles or bilaterally.

The procedure never gained acceptance. The potential for increased risk from complications and no improvement in pregnancy rates does not justify its use.

(d) Fallopian Tube Sperm Perfusion (FTSP)

Fallopian tube sperm perfusion (FTSP) is being dealt with in detail elsewhere in the book. In short and to complete the overall picture, Kahn *et. al.* introduced FSP in 1992.[5] The procedure involves the perfusion of the fallopian tube with a prepared sample of semen diluted in 4 ml of medium. Sperm reflux is prevented by obstructing the internal so with an Allis forceps, a pediatric Foley's catheter[6] or specially designed systems. Apart from ensuring sperm delivery, it helps to overcome partial obstruction of the tube.

Initial reports of the procedure were very encouraging[7] but as more studies were carried out it was realized that PR's were no better than with IUI. It was Trout and Kemmann in

4. Oei, L.M., Surrey, E.S., McCaleb B. *et al:* A Prospective Randomized Study of Pregnancy Rates after Transuterotubal and Intrauterine Insemination. *Fertile Sterile,* 58: 167-71, 1992.
5. Kahn, J.A., Von, Durin V., Sunde, A. *et al:* Fallopian Tube Sperm Perfusion: First Clinical Experience, *Hum Reprod* 7, (Suppl 1): 19-24, 1992.
6. Li, T.C.: A Simple, Non-invasive Method of Fallopian Tube Sperm Perfusion, *Hum Reprod* 8: 1848-50, 1993.
7. Fanchin, R., Olivennes, F., Righini, C. *et al:* A New System for Fallopian Tube Perfusion Leads to Pregnancy Rates Twice as high as Standard Intrauterine Insemination, *Fertile Sterile,* 64: 505-10, 1995.

1999,[8] who revived the interest in this procedure. In a randomized controlled trial and a meta-analysis of literature, they reported that FSP did indeed increase the pregnancy rate significantly in patients with unexplained infertility.

However, pregnancy rates did not differ between the two procedures for all other etiologies of infertility.

(B) ALTERNATIVES TO IVF

These procedures can be used in women with bilateral tubal block.

(a) Peritoneal Oocyte Sperm Transfer (POST)

Peritoneal oocyte sperm transfer (POST) was described by Çoulam *et. al.* in 1989.[9] In this process ovum is picked-up, the pouch of Douglas is repeatedly rinsed with culture medium until the aspirate is clear. The aspiration needle is left in position and a maximum of 4 oocytes and 4 million motile spermatozoa in 1 mL Earl's medium are drawn into a long embryo transfer catheter. The catheter is passed through the aspiration needle and the oocyte-sperm mixture injected into the pouch of Douglas. The catheter and needle are then withdrawn simultaneously. The procedure is carried out on an outpatient basis.

This procedure has limited application. It can be used to reduce the risk of high order multiple pregnancy in patients stimulated for IUl who exhibit multi-folliculogenesis, when facilities for IVF are not available.

(b) Follicular Aspiration Sperm Injection and Assisted Rupture (FASIAR)

Follicular aspiration sperm injection and assisted rupture combines the concept of COH, IUI and POST. The pre-

8. Trout, S.W. and Kemmann, E.: Fallopian Sperm Perfusion *versus* Intrauterine Insemination: A Randomized Controlled Trial and Metaanalysis of the Literature, *Fertile Sterile, 7(5):* 881-85, 1999.
9. Coulam, C.B., Peters, A.J., Genting, M. *et at:* Pregnancy Rates after Peritoneal Ovum-sperm Transfer. *Am J. Obstet Gynaecology!* 164 (6 Pt 1): 1447-49, 1991.

ovulatory follicle(s) is punctured under ultrasound guidance. Two mL of follicular fluid is aspirated into a syringe containing 2 mL of sperm suspension. The sperm concentration used is 10 million motile sperms. This fluid is then injected around the ovary ensuring that the needle has been withdrawn from the follicle.[10] In the original technique as described by Paulson and Thornton an IUI was performed in addition.[11]

(c) Direct Oocyte Transfer (DOT)

Oocyte with sperm is transferred directly into the uterine cavity. This technique was first described by Craft *et. al.* in 1982 and later modified by Bucktt and Tan.[12]

After oocyte recovery, the oocytes are incubated for 6 hours in culture medium prior to: insemination and then incubated for a further hour. Four to six oocytes and about 1 20,000 sperm are then transferred into the uterine cavity in 20 mL culture medium with a normal embryo transfer catheter, 7 hours after pick-up. In the modified technique the cumulus cells are mechanically stripped off the oocytes. Insemination is done 3 hours after retrieval. A maximum of four oocytes with tightly bound sperm are then transferred into the uterine cavity, 5 hours after pick-up. Further simplification of the procedure entailed transfer of the gametes into the uterine cavity without preincubation.[13]

---

10. Lin, C.P., D'Amico, J.F., Nakajima, S.T.: Initial Experience with a Modification of the Follicle Aspiration, Sperm Injection, and Assisted Rupture Technique. *Fertile Sterile,* 73: 855-58, 2000.
11. Paulson, R.J., Thornton, M.H.: Follicle Aspiration, Sperm Injection, and Assisted Rupture (FASIAR): A Simple New Assisted Reproductive Technique. *Fertile Sterile,* 68: 1148-51, 1997.
12. Bucktt, W.M. and Tan, S.L.: Alternative Assisted Conception Techniques. In Brinsden, P.R. (Ed): *A Textbook of In-vitro Fertilization and Assisted Reproduction* (2nd edn) 243-55, 1999.
13. Ransom, M.X., Garcia, A.J., Doherty, K. *et al.*: Direct Gamete Uterine Transfer in Patients with Tubal Absence or Occlusion. *J Assist Reprod Genet,* 14(1): 35-38, 1997.

(d) Intravaginal Culture (IVC)

Ranoux *et. al.*[14] came up with the novel idea of using the vagina as an incubator.

A small 3 mL polypropylene tube is filled with culture medium. One to four oocytes and 10 to 20,000 motile sperm are added to the tube. The tube is hermetically sealed making sure that no air is trapped inside and placed in the posterior vaginal fornix. Usually a tampon or contraceptive diaphragm is used to keep the tube(s) in place.

After 48 to 50 hours, the tube is removed and transferred to the laboratory. The resultant embryos are then identified and transferred using standard embryo transfer techniques. Spare embryos may be cryopreserved.

A fertilization rate of 60 percent and PR of 15 to 22 percent have been achieved. Initial results claimed this technique to be comparable to IVF. However, conventional IVF results are superior.

(e) Gamete Intrafallopian Transfer (GIFT)

Since the procedure is being dealt with in another chapter only a brief mention of this very important alternative technique will be made here of all the alternatives developed to overcome the limitations of IVF, GIFT is perhaps the one most widely used. Numerous trials have been carried out to assess its efficacy and various modifications introduced to improve the technique and make it less invasive. GIFT was introduced[15] in an era when oocyte recovery was done laparoscopically and therefore delivering gametes into the fallopian tube did not involve any extra surgical procedure.

Transvaginal GIFT was introduced to combine the advantage of in-vivo fertilization and transvaginal ultrasound-guided follicular puncture.

Gamete intrafallopian transfer (GIFT) is similar to IVF except that eggs and sperm are mixed and placed immediately

14. Ranoux, C., Aubriot, F.X., Dubuisson, J.B. *et. al.* : A New *in vitro* Fertilization Technique: Intravaginal Culture. *Fertile Sterile,* 49: 654-57, 1988.
15. Asch, R.H., Ellsworth, L.R., Balmaceda, J.P. *et. al.* : Pregnancies after Translaparoscopic Gamete Intrafallopian Transfer. *Lancet II*: 1034-103, 1984.

into the woman's fallopian tubes using laparoscopic surgery. In zygote intra fallopian transfer (ZIFT), eggs and sperm are fertilized in the laboratory, but the resulting zygotes are not incubated and are placed in the woman's fallopian tubes rather than her uterus. Although more complicated, GIFT and ZIFT are thought to more closely simulate natural events and have a higher (5 to 10 percent higher) success rate than IVF. Unfortunately, women with severely diseased fallopian tubes cannot use them.

The success rate of GIFT equals that of IVF. An average pregnancy rate of 25 percent has been reported. SART (Science for Assisted Reproduction Technology) results for 1996,[16] in an assessment of 44,647 cycles of IVF and 2,879 of GIFT showed that for IVF the pregnancy rate per transfer was 33.3 percent and delivery rate per transfer 27.9 percent. For GIFT the pregnancy rate per transfer was 35.1 percent and delivery rate per transfer was 29.3 percent.

Transcervical GIFT did not enhance the pregnancy rate when compared to IVFET.[17]

Efforts to simplify GIFT by developing transcervical methods of transfer have not translated into higher pregnancy rates than those of 1VF-ET. Tubal cannulation, either laparoscopic or transvaginal, is more difficult to learn than simple intrauterine embryo transfer. However, compared to IVF this method requires less laboratory equipment and renders in-vivo fertilization possible.

Since pregnancy rates are similar, it is logical that one would opt for a simpler and less invasive method of gamete delivery. The use of this procedure is justified in cases where the possibility for IVF does not exist, or for patients who refuse IVF.

---

16. Assisted Reproductive Technology in the United States: 1996 Results Generated from the American Society for Reproductive Medicine/ Science for Assisted Reproductive Technology Registry. *Fertile Sterile* 71: 798-807, 1999.
17. Hurst, B.S., Tucker, K.E., Guadagnoli, S. *et. al.*: Transcervical Gamete and Zygote Intrafallopian Transfer. Does it Enhance Pregnancy Rates in an Asisted Reproduction Program? J. *Reprod Med,* 41(11): 867-70, 1996.

Transvaginal GIFT offers an acceptable pregnancy rate for patients who cannot be treated with laparoscopic GIFT. Results of transvaginal GIFT are lower than laparoscopic GIFT[18] therefore recommendations for its routine use become questionable.

The large numbers of alternative techniques that have cropped up over the years are testimony to the fact that we have not yet optimized ART.

A number of these techniques have been validated and may be applied where indicated. Others need to be relegated to history. They came up in an era when there were a lot of limitations in culture media, culture techniques and our very understanding of reproduction.

While using these procedures, one has to weigh the cost of ITF against the lower success rates achieved with many of these techniques. Wasting time, money and effort not to mention the emotional stress associated with failure to achieve pregnancy is not justified. Referral to an ART center is definitely a better option. New developments are an important facet of science, however, there is the need to evaluate each technique and compare it to the existing well-established reproductive technologies through well-controlled prospective randomized controlled trials.

---

18. Strowtzki, T., Korell, M., Seehaus, D. *et. al.*: 'Bland' Transvaginal Gamete Intra-fallopian Transfer in Distal Tubal and Peritubal Pathology—An Evaluation in Respect to the Laparoscopic Approach. *Hum Reprod*, 8(10): 1703-07, 1993.

Challenges of Reproductive Technology and Human Rights

Major breakthroughs in medical science and technology affect everyone. The life span has been dramatically extended. The role of medical science is to compress morbidity—to push illness further and further to the end of the life span so that people will enjoy many more years in good health than ever before.[1]

Although the impact of medical science is widely felt across the life span, those technologies that have changed the nature and process of reproduction may be of greatest consequence to women. To take only a few examples, infertile couples now have many more ways to have natural children, genetic testing provides opportunities for families to make decisions about what type of child they will have, and new ways of monitoring fetal development bring more precision to child bearing than ever before. Despite these dramatic

1. Fries, Issue and Challenges of NPT, 1980.

opportunities, however, the new reproductive technologies are not without problems.

There are many points, which explore the complex array of benefits and problems presented by the new reproductive technologies as a result of medical science's invention. The issues are complex, and the debate often acrimonious. More significant than the question of whether the technologies are good or bad, however, are the questions related to for whom they are good, in what instances, and for whom they should be made accessible.

These thorny issues can be debated at multiple levels, from the ethical implications, to the social and psychological consequences for society and for the individual, to the legal and the medical outcomes. All viewpoints are represented in this chapter, which highlights a different array of problems and opportunities.

The right to make decision about reproduction is essentially a very personal decision either on the part of the man or woman. Necessarily, such a right includes the right not to reproduce. The intrusion of the state into such a decision-making process of the individual is scrutinized by the constitutional courts with great care.[2]

Now physicians have made available a technique called PGD (Pre-implantation Genetic Diagnosis), which allows physicians to screen embryos for a wide range of possible diseases as well as for gender. Suitable embryos can then be implanted, while the future parents may decide not to implant other embryos. These other embryos, depending on the reasons why they were rejected, may be destroyed or given to other infertile couples, where they will be implanted in the woman and (hopefully) brought to term.

In our modern world, sex is no longer the exclusive method for humans to reproduce. A new group of medical options, known as "assisted reproductive technologies," are challenging our understanding of parenthood and biological relationships.

---

2. Skinner *v.* Oklahoma (1941) 316 US 535. The U.S. Supreme Court has Characterized the Right to Reproduced as "One of the basic Civil Rights of Man".

Louise Brown, the world's first "test tube baby", as cited above was born in 1978. Since then, the field of assisted reproduction has taken off, bringing increasingly new and innovative ways to create children—as well as increasingly more complex family relationships and ethically fraught medical practices. The right to reproduction now becomes established universally.[3]

Assisted reproductive technologies bring to the fore important questions about who we are as individuals and families and whom society deems entitled to reproduce and parent. And these questions are not going to go away. While some might like to stop the clock so they can hash out the ground rules, others keep right on playing. The latest case in point: In January 2007, a team of doctors announced plans to undertake the first uterine transplant in the United States. Nearly every day, a story comes out about new technologies and their impact on the families who have used them.

It is clear that balancing of these competing interests is a difficult matter that requires a full debate, discussing the merit of each case. However, in future it might well be the choice to be made between a reduced, non-anonymous programme that respects the child's right to know and a much wider anonymous programme that seeks to benefit a greater number of childless couples.

The disputes described above reveal the painful and emotionally fraught controversies that can arise when assisted reproductive arrangements do not go as planned. But as a political issue, assisted reproductive technologies provide our society with the opportunity to have thoughtful, respectful debates about a whole host of critical questions, from how we define family to when we think human life begins—deeply felt beliefs that in other contexts have proven to be quite volatile and polarizing.

Given the novelty of assisted reproductive technologies and the absence of entrenched positions on what services should be permitted or prohibited and under what circumstances, there is reason to hope that the discussion in

3. Eisenstadt *v.* Baird, (1972) 405 U.S. 438.

this context can be civil and productive, perhaps even changing the way we think about our more settled positions and helping us better understand others' perspectives on more familiar socio-legal topics.

The questions about assisted reproduction come at a time when various groups within the progressive movement are making a concerted effort to work together on issues of common concern and speak with a more unified voice on the pressing topics of the day.

All members of the progressive movement have a stake in what types of assisted reproductive technologies are available, to whom they are available, and how they are used—especially the reproductive rights, health, and justice community; the LGBT (lesbian, gay, bisexual, transgender) community; the disability rights community; the environmental community; and the economic, racial, and social justice communities. It is critical that the groups who focus on these issues begin to address assisted reproduction in their work.

Ultimately, human values from all viewpoints will be challenged by the questions raised by assisted reproductive technologies. To that end, the Center for American Progress has prepared this report so that people can become familiar with some of these technologies, understand how the law has developed in this area thus far, and ask how we want to proceed in the future. It is hoped that "Future Choices" will lay the groundwork for the progressive movement to make hard but essential decisions about how to move forward in this complicated field.

The progressive movement can lead the way in forging just policies regarding these new ways of creating families. As we seek to answer the numerous questions raised by the few laws governing assisted reproduction, it may be useful to keep in mind the following progressive values:

- The right to privacy
- Procreative liberty
- Social justice
- The health and well-being of women and children
- Equality of the sexes

- Equal opportunity for parenting by people of all backgrounds
- Equitable access to health care
- Respect for moral and autonomous personal decisions
- Cautious optimism with regard to scientific progress
- Regard for biological and genetic diversity
- Evidence-based policy-making

The policy decisions we must make are difficult and may reveal tensions among our sometimes competing interests, but the process of developing our positions ultimately should help us clarify our values and priorities, make the progressive movement stronger overall, and, most importantly, improve people's lives.

In this process, the doctors first provided a basic overview of assisted reproduction then, we address three primary areas in which legislators and courts have already spoken to some degree—health insurance coverage, embryo disposition, and parentage determinations—and examine the policy implications that their decisions create.

Traditional reproduction is an unambiguous three dimensional phenomenon involving natural mother, natural father and natural child sharing amongst them the entire natural biological process, allowing no intervention from any other external agencies except for minimal medical expertise. In contrast, artificial reproduction though not truly artificial, adds extra dimensions to the traditional biological process through intervention of external agencies and intensive medical involvement.

The impact of advances in reproductive technology is more on women for the obvious reason that it is the woman who has to undergo a major share in the biological process of pregnancy. Thus, the new medical advancements existent and anticipated bring about ethos of moral, social and legal dilemmas with special reference to women.

Assisted reproductive technologies such as artificial insemination, in-vitro fertilization, surrogate motherhood have been proved to be a blessing for many infertile couples. The new reproductive technologies have given hope too many women and helped many women to have children that they would not have had otherwise.[4]

But along with potential benefits, modern reproductive technologies have posed various complex legal problems relating to family law and basic human rights. Assisted reproductive technologies have raised a number of human rights issues, including right of dignity, individual autonomy, right to know, procreative liberty, etc.

Those who seek to use these technologies include those who are infertile for both medical and social or situational reasons. Medical infertility affects about 10 percent of the reproductive age population—approximately 7.3 million people—and strikes people of all socio-economic backgrounds.

Infertility affects men and women equally: men and women each account for 35 percent of infertility cases, 20 percent of cases result from combined problems in the woman and the man, and in 10 percent of cases the cause of infertility cannot be identified. Although age can be a factor in infertility, sexually transmitted infections, exposure to certain chemical agents, tobacco and alcohol use, and excessive weight gain or loss are all risk factors for infertility as well.

In addition to those who experience physiological obstacles to conceiving or maintaining a pregnancy, those who are physically capable of reproducing but do not have a partner of the opposite sex with whom to reproduce are increasingly taking advantage of assisted reproductive services. They include lesbian, gay, and transgender couples as well as single individuals of any sexual orientation or gender identity.

---

4. Bennett, Belinda, "Reproductive Technology, Public Policy and Single Motherhood", 22, *Sydney Law Review*, 631 (2000).

Constitution of India and Reproductive Technology

The relationship between technology and the law in this context is symbiotic. If we think of the new technologies as plants, growing toward the sky and leading us into new medical, scientific, and ethical realms, then the legal terrain is the soil, dictating which practices can develop and thrive and which must wither away. Every decision to regulate or not creates unique incentives and disincentives for the fertility industry and those it serves.[1]

For now, the fertility industry remains largely unregulated in the Western world and Asian Countries. Where regulation of these technologies has occurred, however, it has had real-life consequences for thousands of people and ripple effects on multiple areas of the law, from adoption to abortion, from health insurance to inheritance.

While some nations have passed laws that indirectly affect the practices of fertility clinics, legislatures and courts have

1. Griswold *v.* Connecticut, (1965) 381 US 479.

focused more on the ramifications of these procedures. Who are the legal parents of a child who was created by the efforts of five people—two genetic donors, one gestational mother, and two "intended" parents who set it all in motion? In a custody dispute over a frozen embryo, what principles of law should apply—property, contract, family, constitutional, or some combination thereof?

The Indian government has not fully committed to the reproductive rights approach. In other words, it has not explicitly created a legally enforceable reproductive rights regime through either legislative or judicial acts. There are, however, a number of legislations relating to children and women in India. There has been an articulation for the general rights to health and for specific aspects of reproductive health within Constitutional law

The Constitution of India provides Fundamental Rights under Chapter III. These rights are guaranteed by the constitution. One of these rights is provided under Article 21 which reads as follows:

(A) PROTECTION OF LIFE AND PERSONAL LIBERTY

Article 21 of the constitution of India provides that no person shall be deprived of his life or personal liberty except according to procedure established by law.[2] Though the phraseology of Article 21 starts with negative word but the word No has been used in relation to the word deprived. The object of the fundamental right under Article 21 is to prevent encroachment upon personal liberty and deprivation of life except according to procedure established by law.

It clearly means that this fundamental right has been provided against state only. If an act of private individual amounts to encroachment upon the personal liberty or deprivation of life of other person such violation would not fall under the parameters set for the Article 21.

In such a case the remedy for aggrieved person would be either under Article 226 of the constitution or under general law. But, where an act of private individual supported by the

2. Article 21, Constitution of India, 1950.

state infringes the personal liberty or life of another person, the act will certainly come under the ambit of Article 21. Article 21 of the Constitution deals with prevention of encroachment upon personal liberty or deprivation of life of a person.

The state cannot be defined in a restricted sense. It includes Government Departments, Legislature, Administration, Local Authorities exercising statutory powers and so on so forth, but it does not include non-statutory or private bodies having no statutory powers. For example: company, autonomous body and others. Therefore, the fundamental right guaranteed under Article 21 relates only to the acts of State or acts under the authority of the State which is not according to procedure established by law.

The main object of Article 21 is that before a person is deprived of his life or personal liberty by the State, the procedure established by law must be strictly followed. Right to Life means the right to lead meaningful, complete and dignified life. It does not have restricted meaning. It is something more than surviving or animal existence. The meaning of the word life cannot be narrowed down and it will be available not only to every citizen of the country.

As far as Personal Liberty is concerned, it means freedom from physical restraint of the person by personal incarceration or otherwise and it includes all the varieties of rights.[3] Procedure established by Law means the law enacted by the State.

Deprived has also wide range of meaning under the Constitution. These ingredients are the soul of this provision. The fundamental right under Article 21 is one of the most important rights provided under the Constitution which has been described as heart of fundamental rights by the Apex Court.

The meaning of the word life includes the right to live in fair and reasonable conditions The expanded scope of Article 21 has been explained by the Apex Court in the case of *Unni Krishnan* v. *State of A.P.*[4] provided the list of some of the rights

3. Article 19, Constitution of India, 1950.
4. Unni Krishnan *v.* State of Andhra Pradesh, AIR 1993 SC 2178, 2230.

covered under Article 21 on the basis of earlier pronouncements and some of them are listed below:

(1) The right to go abroad.
(2) The right to privacy.
(3) The right against solitary confinement.
(4) The right against hand cuffing.
(5) The right against delayed execution.
(6) The right to shelter.
(7) The right against custodial death.
(8) The right against public hanging.
(9) Doctor's assistance.

It was observed in *Unni Krishnan's case* that Article 21 is the heart of Fundamental Rights and it has extended the Scope of Article 21. Through various judgments the Apex Court also included many of the non-justifiable Directive Principles embodied under Part IV of the Constitution and some of the examples are as under :

(a) Right to pollution free water and air.
(b) Protection of under-trial.
(c) Right of every child to a full development.
(d) Protection of cultural heritage.

While dealing with the provision of Article 21 in respect of personal liberty, Hon'ble Supreme Court put some restrictions in a case of *Javed and others v. State of Haryana*[5] as follows: at the very outset we are constrained to observe that the law laid down by this court in the decisions relied on either being misread or read divorced of the context. The test of reasonableness is not a wholly subjective test and its contours are fairly indicated by the Constitution.

The requirement of reasonableness runs like a golden thread through the entire fabric of fundamental rights. The lofty ideals of social and economic justice, the advancement of the nation as a whole and the philosophy of distributive

5. Javed and others *v.* State of Haryana, AIR 2003 SC 3057.

justice—economic, social and political—cannot be given a go-by in the name of undue stress on fundamental rights and individual liberty.

Reasonableness and rationality, legally as well as philosophically, provide colour to the meaning of fundamental rights and these principles are deducible from those very decisions which have been relied on by the learned counsel for the petitioners.

The Apex Court led a great importance on reasonableness and rationality of the provision and it is pointed out that in the name of undue stress on Fundamental Rights and Individual Liberty, the ideals of social and economic justice cannot be given a go-by. Thus, it is clear that the provision of Article 21 was constructed narrowly at the initial stage but the law in respect of life and personal liberty of a person was developed gradually and a liberal interpretation was given to these words.

New dimensions have been added to the scope of Article 21 from time to time. It imposed a limitation upon a procedure which prescribed for depriving a person of life and personal liberty by saying that the procedure which prescribed for depriving a person of life and personal liberty by saying that the procedure must be reasonable, fair and such law should not be arbitrary, whimsical and fanciful. The interpretation which has been given to the words life and personal liberty in various decisions of the Apex Court, it can be said that the protection of life and personal liberty has got multi-dimensional meaning and any arbitrary, whimsical and fanciful act of the State which deprived the life or personal liberty of a person would be against the provision of Article 21 of the Constitution.

(B) RIGHT OF EQUALITY

According to natural rights theory all humans are equal and every human being should get equal opportunity for his/her development. The Constitution of India clearly and fairly provisions the equality under Article 14-18. The right to equality is the faith and creed of our democratic republic. It forms the foundation of socio-economic justice. Article 14 embodies the idea of equality as expressed in the preamble.

The succeeding Articles 15, 16, 17 and 18 lay down specific application of general rule laid down in Article 14 of the Constitution. Article 14 provides:

> "The State shall not deny to any person equality before the law or equal protection of the laws within the territory of India".

This provision is like the provisions of Article 1 and 7 of the universal declaration of human Rights, 1948. Articles 2(2) and 3 of the International Covenant on Economic, Social and Cultural Rights, 1966 also talk about equality among men and women. Articles 3 and 26 of the International Covenant on Civil and Political Rights also mention about the equal rights of men and women and equality before law and equal protection of laws respectively.

The reference to the principles of equality and non-discrimination is also found in the Charter of United Nations. Other basic instruments adopted by the United Nations and specialized agencies which expressly provide for equality and the prevention of discrimination are, International Covenant on the Elimination of All forms of Racial Discrimination; the International Covenant on the Suppression and Punishment of the Crime of Apartheid; the Discrimination (Employment and Occupation) Convention, 1958 (No. III) of ILO; the Convention against Discrimination in Education of UNESCO, the Equal Remuneration Convention, 1951 (No. 100) of ILO and the Declaration on the Elimination of Discrimination against women.

The principle of equality as enshrined in the Constitution of India is not merely guideline or recommendation but a strict and fundamental provision which imposes on the judiciary the obligation to find out if the legislative, executive and administrative authorities have respected the equality of all individuals. If the Court finds that this principle has been violated then it may issue order that such laws, acts, ministerial decisions or administrative regulations involved should not be imposed.

However, equal protection of the laws guaranteed under Article 14 of the Constitution does not mean that all the laws must be general in character. In certain cases the States are obliged to adopt laws or take administrative measures which differentiate between individuals and they cannot be said to be discriminatory, for example, national tax legislation, which must necessarily differentiate between taxpayers according to their capital or income.

Here, Article 14 permits reasonable classification but prohibits class legislation. It must always be remembered that the classification must not be arbitrary, artificial or evasive but must be based on some real and substantial distinction having rational relation with the object to be achieved.

Applying the general principle of equality, Article 15 of the Indian Constitution specifically prohibits discrimination on grounds of religion, race, caste, sex or place of birth. It provides:

(C) PROHIBITION OF DISCRIMINATION

(a) The State shall not discriminate against any citizen on grounds only of religion, race, caste, sex, and place of birth or any of them.

(b) Nothing in this article shall prevent the State from making any special provision for women and children.

The above fundamental right is available to all the citizens of India. The corresponding provision to Article 15(1) of the Indian Constitution can be found in Article 2 of the Universal Declaration of Human Rights, 1948; Article 2(1) of the International Covenant on Civil and Political Rights, 1966 and Article 2(2) of the International Covenant on Economic, Social and Cultural Rights, 1966.

Once the principle of equality is accepted, it becomes impossible to discriminate against any person or group of persons. The principle of non-discrimination is based on equality and dignity. Discrimination can be said to be the denial of the fundamental and universally accepted rights of all human beings to persons or group of persons who are excluded.

Right to life and personal liberty—is most fundamental of all fundamental rights. Article 21 of the Constitution secures this right to all persons. It provides:

> "No person shall be deprived of his life or personal liberty except according to procedure established by law".

This Article advances the object of Article 3 of the universal Declaration of Human Rights. Similar provision is also found in Article 6 of the International Covenant on Civil and Political Rights.

The right guaranteed under Article 21 is available to both—the citizens of India as well as to non citizens. To begin with, the Indian Supreme Court interpreted the words "personal liberty" narrowly to mean nothing more than the liberty of the physical body, i.e. freedom from arrest and detention, from false imprisonment or wrongful confinement.[6] But in the later years the Supreme Court gave the widest possible meaning to the expression "personal liberty" so as to include within itself all the varieties of rights which go to make up the personal liberty of man other than those dealt with in Article 19(1) of the Constitution. In other words, while Article 19(1) deals with particular species or attributes of the freedom, "personal liberty" in particular species or attributes of that freedom, "personal liberty" in Article 21 takes in and comprises the residue.[7]

In *Maneka Gandhi* v. *Union of India*,[8] Bhagwati, J. (as he then was) while expanding the scope and ambit of Article 21 observed:

> "The expression 'personal liberty' in Article 21 is of the widest amplitude and it covers a variety of rights which go to constitute the personal liberty of men and some of them have been raised to be status of distinct fundamental rights and given additional protection under Art. 19."

6. A.K. Gopalan *v.* State of Madras, A.I.R 1950 S.C. 27.
7. Kharak Singh *v.* State of U.P., A.I.R 1963 S.C 1295.
8. A.I.R 1978 S.C 597.

He was further of the opinion that the attempt of the Court should be to expand the reach and ambit of the fundamental rights rather than attenuate their meaning and content by a process of judicial construction.[9]

The Supreme Court has also given very wide interpretation to the expression "life" in Article 21 of the Constitution of India. The right to "livelihood" has been held to be implicit in the expression "life" in Article 21 of the Constitution. In *Olga Tellis* v *Bombay Municipal Corporation,*[10] the Supreme Court Observed:

The sweep of the right to life conferred by Article 21 is wide and far reaching. It does not mean merely that life cannot be extinguished or taken away as, for example, by the imposition and execution of death sentence, except according to procedure established by law.

An equally important facet of that right is the right to livelihood because; no person can live without the means of living, which is the means of livelihood. If the right to livelihood is not treated as a part of Constitutional right to life, the easiest way of depriving a person of his right to life would be to deprive him of his means of livelihood to the point of abrogation. Such deprivation would not only denude the life of its effective concept and meaningfulness but it would make life impossible to life.[11]

Thus, we find that the Constitution of India is an Umbrella over the Human Rights of the citizens of the India. It is in fact the protector of the rights of the people. The Preamble, fundamental Rights and Directive Principles of State Policy provided in the Indian Constitution aim at protecting and promoting the human rights.

The philosophical background of the Constitution is based in totality on the humanitarian law. Most of the provisions of the various international declarations of Human Rights are incorporated under various articles of the Constitution of India. It is the Supreme legal document of the India who safeguards

9. Pathuma *v.* State of Kerala, (1978) 2 SCC1.
10. AIR 1986 SC 180; (1985) 3 SCC 545.
11. Delhi Development Horticulture Employee's Union *v.* Delhi Administration, Delhi (1992) 4 SCC 99 at 110.

and protects the rights of the people making any discrimination. Hence, there is no doubt about the statement that the Constitution of India is an umbrella under which the rights of the people get protection.

(D) THE ASSISTED REPRODUCTIVE TECHNOLOGY (REGULATION) BILL, 2008

The Indian Council of Medical Research (ICMR) has enacted the Assisted Reproductive Technology (Regulation) Bill, 2008 ("Bill"), which, in all likelihood, will become a law in the parliament.

However, there are certain confusing definitions in the bill which need further explanation and clarifications. Section 32(1) of the Bill, which is the enabling provision, states: "That subject to the provisions of this Act and the rules and regulations made thereunder, Assisted Reproductive Technology (ART) shall be available to all persons including single persons, married couples and unmarried couples".

Therefore, it becomes pertinent to understand that how a couple is defined here. Under Section 2(e) of the Bill, a couple means: "The persons living together and having a sexual relationship that is legal in the country/countries of which they are citizens or they are living in".

This definition is inclusive in nature and covers all kinds of couples, whether they are homosexuals or not. Furthermore, the definition does not prevent the citizens of a country (where homosexual marriage is legal), from having a surrogate child. So, if section 377 of IPC is amended so as to be in consonance with the scheme of the Bill (as and when it is passed by both the houses to give it a legal effect), there will be no impediment in including same-sex couples within the definition of 'couple' as defined under Section 2(e) of the Bill. The effect of the definition appears to do away with the legal limitation imposed by Section 377 of IPC, and is not just a mere co-incidence of legal drafting.

As we ponder upon some other definitions in the Bill, an "unmarried couple" is defined under Section 2(w) to mean: "A man and a woman, both of marriageable age, living together with mutual consent but without getting married".

So when these two definitions are read simultaneously, it clearly delineates that for an unmarried couple to get a surrogate child, they have to be heterosexual; but on the other hand, no such condition is applicable to married couples, i.e. they might be homosexual or heterosexual.

This leaves us in sheer confusion as Section 32(1) is not restricted, but extended to include 'single persons', 'married couples' and 'unmarried couples' as well. There is perhaps a window left open for a foreign married homosexual couple who, according to the two definitions under the Bill, are a 'couple' having a valid married status under their jurisdiction. The non-exhaustive language used herein should allow the courts to fill in the gap.

Discrimination

Since a homosexual relationship or marriage is not legal in India, this Bill by ICMR seems discriminatory in nature towards Indian homosexuals as homosexuality is legally prohibited in the country. On the other hand, homosexuals from the countries (where homosexual marriages are legal) can freely come to India and get a surrogate child. Moreover, an Indian homosexual couple cannot have a surrogate child; an Indian homosexual person can do so only by invoking his status as a 'single person' under the Bill, and not as a homosexual. Marital status of a homosexual individual, therefore, does not matter either for having a surrogate child.

In addition, Section 34(10) of the Bill states that "The birth certificate issued in respect of a baby born through surrogacy shall bear the name(s) of the genetic parents/parent of the baby." This implies that the child belongs to them (him) who contribute(s) to the genetic make-up of the child (excludes anonymous donors). Only one of the two partners in a homosexual couple can make such a contribution; under Section 33(3) of the Bill states that: "A donor shall relinquish all parental rights over the child who may be conceived from his or her gamete." For this purpose and therefore, the child will bear only the name of the contributing partner of the homosexual couple. The question now is: 'is marital status going to be a restrictive factor preventing Indian unmarried homosexual couples from having a surrogate child?'

In the light of above stated, the answer for this question would certainly be no, but still there is a discriminating factor against Indian homosexual couples and in favour of foreign homosexual couples (who can legally get a surrogate child as per ICMR).

This kind of problem can be conveniently solved by passing the bill only when the status of the Indian homosexual couples is brought at par with the foreign homosexual couples; either legalize homosexual relationships/marriages in India or else, put such restrictions on a foreign married couple as are faced by Indian homosexuals (where the issue of getting a surrogate child is concerned).

(E) ASSISTED REPRODUCTIVE TECHNOLOGY (REGULATION) BILL, 2010

It is estimated that 15 percent of couples around the world are infertile. This implies that infertility is one of the most highly prevalent medical problems. The magnitude of the infertility problem also has enormous social implications. Besides the fact that every couple has the right to have a child, in India infertility widely carries with it a social stigma.

With the enormous advances in medicine and medical technologies, today 85 percent of the cases of infertility can be taken care of through medicines, surgery and the new medical technologies like Reproductive Technology. These technologies not only require expertise but also open up many avenues for unethical practices which can affect adversely the recipient of the treatment, medically, socially and legally.

In view of the above, in public interest, it has become important to regulate the functioning of such clinics to ensure that the services provided are ethical and that the medical, social and legal rights of all those concerned are protected.

The bill details procedures for accreditation and supervision of infertility clinics (and related organizations such as semen banks) handling spermatozoa or oocytes outside of the body, or dealing with gamete donors and surrogacy, ensuring that the legitimate rights of all concerned are protected, with maximum benefit to the infertile couples/

individuals within a recognized framework of ethics and good medical practice.

India Promise and the Price

Bioethics in India is almost non-existent. There is need for a broad public education system in heath literacy and individual health and responsibility. Such education programmes should be introduced into the curriculum at school level and included at the college/universities level also. A center for ethics in sciences in general and genetic and medical ethics in particular needs to be established, because of the pluralistic nature of the Indian society which is multicultural, multi-religious and multi-ethnic.

Man must master the benefits and risks of genetic knowledge as well as the power of manipulation to strengthen the ethos and ethics of responsibility in support of individual self-determination, cultural diversity and political stability. The UNESCO Declaration also covers the application of the principles embodied in the Indian ICMR Guidelines, calling for professionalism, honesty, integrity and transparency in decision-making as well as the creation of independent, multidisciplinary and pluralist ethics committees.

Referring to transnational practices, it specifies: When research is undertaken or otherwise pursued in one or more States the host State(s) and funded by a source in another State, such research should be the object of an appropriate level of ethical review in the host State(s) and the State in which the founder of the research is located. This is similar to a lot of the ideals the 2000 Guidelines speak about in the Indian context, but the qualitative difference comes, as usual, in the chasm between policy and implementation.

The Consumer Education and Research Society (CERS), Ahmedabad, has petitioned the National Human Rights Commission (NHRC) for a probe into testing of sex on unsuspecting patients in violation of ethical and medical norms. The CERS petition follows reports of more than 20 clinical evaluations of sex determination being conducted in India, on human subjects.

Many of these studies were unauthorised and not properly monitored by competent regulatory medical or ethics bodies, it added. In fact, the women on whom the tests were being conducted were not made aware of the risks involved. "It is highly unethical to carry out clinical trials on humans without explaining to them the risks involved in a language they understand and their consent taken in writing before witnesses," CERS said.

In this connection, it referred to the tests conducted on the 'helpless patients' at the Regional Cancer Centre (RCC) at Thiruvananthapuram in Kerala and the Metro Hospital in New Delhi. CERS also referred to New Delhi's Metro Hospital where Dr Purushottama Lal injected vascular endothelial growth factor into 11 heart patients without informing them of the risks involved.

CERS pointed out that the Indian Council of Medical Research (ICMR) has adopted elaborate ethical guidelines for biomedical research including clinical trials on humans and said these tests have to be undertaken with the prior permission of the DGCI. Further, the clinical tests are to be monitored at the site of the test by an appropriately constituted institutional ethics committee (IEC).

CERS is concerned about the alleged human rights violation of the patients who have received these experimental drugs without their written consent, without their knowledge and without following the established guidelines for these tests and of course, prior permission of the DGCI. It is possible that "the IEC did not perform its expected duty by strictly monitoring these clinical studies on patients", the petition said.

Though the Kerala state government has constituted an enquiry under Dr. Purvesh Parikh to look into the RCC experiments, the NHRC will have to investigate the issue in its entirety, CERS said. It called upon the NHRC to see that the DGCI submits a list of all the clinical trials being conducted on humans and the names of the clinical centers where these are conducted in the country.

Ethical and Legal Issues of Reproductive Technology and Judicial Response

Today, the family has come to be defined by individuality and choice. Pre-nuptial agreements, non-marital cohabitation, gay and lesbian marriages have all profoundly altered our ideas about marriage and family. In the last few years, reproductive technology has accelerated this process of change at a breathtaking rate.

Due to reproductive technology some simple questions have taken on a dizzying complexity; who are the "real" parents of a child? What are the relationships and responsibilities between a child, the woman who carried it to term, and the egg donor?, Between the child and the sperm donor?

The courts and the law have been wildly inconsistent and indecisive when grappling with these questions. Should these cases be decided in light of laws governing contracts and property? Or is it more appropriate to act in the best interests of the child, even if that "child" is unborn, or even not conceived? No longer merely settling disputes between family members, the law is now seeing its own role expand, to the point where it is asked to regulate situations unprecedented in human history.

The human genome is the common heritage of humankind and humankind's link to other forms of life. Traditional moral principles such as autonomy, privacy, justice, equity, literacy, and responsibility have to be redefined in the light of benefits, risks and uncertainty of applying genetic knowledge. Moral and cultural traditions play an important role in shaping individual and society's competence to deal with new challenges. Traditions may not be used in an individual way, as traditions also contain antiquated customs, which have to be cut-off.

(A) REPRODUCTIVE TECHNOLOGY AND HUMAN DIGNITY

Nevertheless, a commitment to human dignity is a widely accepted value and the foundation for our understanding of human rights. The preamble to the Universal Declaration of Human Rights, adopted by the United Nations General Assembly in 1948, states that "recognition of the inherent dignity and of the equal and inalienable rights of all members of the human family is the foundation of freedom, justice, and peace in the world".

For an example, the report of the *President's Council on Bioethics 2002* is titled *"Human Cloning and Human Dignity: An Ethical Inquiry"*, but it fails to conceptualize human dignity or address the specific ways in which human cloning may impinge on human dignity.[1] This lack of clarity has the potential to hurt policy-making and, in the long-run, degrade the possible substantive value of the principle of human dignity. The dilemma is that human dignity is a poorly conceptualized and vague concept.

1. James Childress, Human Cloning and Human Dignity: The Report of the President's Council on Bioethics. Hasting Cent Rep., 2003.

Further complicating matters, in a pluralistic society various groups and communities bring a diversity of views, religious values, and cultural understandings that inform and shape their use of the concept of human dignity.

There are numerous examples of policies that cite human dignity as a standard for dealing with controversial science issues. The UN Educational, Scientific, and Cultural Organization's "Universal Declaration on the Human Rights" recommends a ban on "practices which are contrary to human dignity, such as reproductive cloning".[2] A World Health Organization Report, 2003 suggests that genetic databases create the need to balance "human dignity and human rights as against public health, scientific progress and commercial interests in a free market".[3]

The Japan Stem Cell Research Guidelines, 2001 and recent Legislation of Canada's pertaining to research, involving human reproductive material, claim the protection of human dignity as a primary objective of the regulatory regimes.[4] The concept of human dignity also permeates research ethics policy.

Canada's primary research ethics document, the "Tri-Council Policy Statement", declares that the "cardinal principle of modern research ethics, is respect for human dignity".[5] In these documents, the concept of human dignity is often used in the conventional, legal and ethical manner to emphasize the right of individuals to make autonomous choices. This is most

2. United Nations Educational, Scientific and Cultural Organization. Universal Declaration on the Human Genome and Human Rights, 1979 November.
3. WHO, European Partnership on Patients' Rights and Citizens' Empowerment, Genetic Databases: Assessing the Benefits and the Impact on Human and Patient Rights, 2003.
4. Assisted Human Reproduction Act R.S.C., 2004, Ministry of Education, Culture, Sports, Science, and Technology (Japan). The Guidelines for Derivation and Utilization of Human Embryonic Stem Cells, 2001.
5. Medical Research Council of Canada, Natural Sciences and Engineering Research Council of Canada, Social Sciences and Humanities Research Council of Canada. Tri-Council policy statement: Ethical conduct for research involving humans, 2003 June.

apparent in the context of research ethics documents and informed-consent policies. This conception treats human dignity as a means of empowerment.

Some scholars suggest that this is the only appropriate normative use of the idea of dignity. Human dignity is a good yardstick in the realm of science policy. Thus no science policy is usually allowed that encroach upon human dignity.

Costa Rica's recent proposal to the UN for an international treaty for banning cloning stands as a good example of this trend. The Costa Rican Draft convention sought to ensure respect for the dignity and basic rights of the human being in the face of the threat posed by experiments in the cloning of human beings.[6] Likewise, in the area of stem cell research, opponents refer to the dignity implications as a rationale for limiting research on human embryos.

In Europe, it is an underpinning of the "order public" (public policy) to restrict patent law, which has been used to deny patents on cloning technologies and human embryonic stem cells.[7] Some policy-makers argue that human cloning would infringe dignity, but they rarely explain how to judge such infringement. Indeed, dignity is meant to reflect a broad social or moral position that a particular type of activity is contrary to public morality or the collective good.

Thus, Human Dignity is not used as a source of individual rights, but as a justification for a policy response. Though human dignity is closely tied to the idea of the inherent worth of humans yet policy documents and legal instruments rarely provide an explicit definition of dignity as failed to explain how human worth might be degraded by a given technology or scientific activity.

---

6. United Nations General Assembly, Annex I to the letter dated 2 April 2003 from the Permanent Representative of Costa Rica to the United Nations addressed to the Secretary-General: Draft international convention on the prohibition of all forms of human cloning. UN Doc. A/58/73, 2003 April.
7. European Group on Ethics in Science and New Technologies Opinion of the European Group on Ethics and Science and New Technologies to the European Commission: Ethical aspects on patenting invention involving human stem cells, 2002 May.

Indeed the meaning of dignity has been left to intuitive understanding on cultural factors. As such, its meaning will be very different depending on the values and background that an individual or community brings to the deliberations.

Now the question is what is Human Dignity? Moreover, without a clearer conception of human dignity and its requirements, it is not possible to evaluate technological innovation or scientific developments in protecting human dignity. In addition, because human dignity is viewed as a foundational concept, its use may imply a degree of social consensus that rarely exists. If something is AIH to infringe human dignity, one would expect a degree of agreement that this is inevitable to some extent.

However, modern societies are often pluralistic, and in pluralistic societies, consensus is often difficult to obtain, whether about human dignity or other complex social and ethical issues introduced by scientific innovations. There is not even agreement about the foundation of human dignity, whether it is faith-based or secular alone, what human dignity entails.

In the debate on stem cell research, most of the people not agree on the moral status of the embryo and, as such, they cannot reach agreement on the degree to which embryonic stem cell research challenges human dignity. As a result, the use of dignity will not necessarily represent a broadly accepted social value, but, instead, it may express a particular view; a view that may not even reflect the majority opinion.

In the context of legal instruments and policy documents, the use and contents of human dignity may amount to a "political compromise reached by cultural, political, constitutional and other conditions. In more extreme circumstances, it could involve voices expressing negative attitudes about certain practices, which are often translated into restrictions ostensibly in the interest of respect for human dignity.[8]

8. Wright, Karen, "Human in the Age of Mechanical Reproduction". *Discover,* 19, No. 5 (1998): 74-81.

Conclusion and Suggestions

There are many areas of reproductive technology viz. Artificial Insemination, In-Vitro Fertilization, Surrogate Motherhood, Cloning, Intra Cytoplasmic Sperm Injection, Direct Intra-peritoneal Insemination, Direct Intra-follicular Insemination, Intra-fallopian Insemination, Fallopian Tube Sperm Perfusion, Peritoneal Oocyte Sperm Transfer, Follicular Aspiration Sperm Injection and Assisted Rupture, Direct Oocyte Transfer, Intra-vaginal Culture, Gamete Intra-fallopian Transfer, etc. but first four technologies are popular and posed a number of challenges in legal, ethical and religious realm.

Modern reproductive technology, while offering vistas of hopes to infertile couple to satisfy their biological urge to have a child, is subject to considerable moral, social and legal considerations. Such a close focus on women's reproductive capacity magnifies the stereotypical gender notions of women as child bearers. It also overemphasizes the genetic links and overlooks the necessity of treating parenthood more as a societal relationship.

Each reproductive technology by itself is capable of raising social, ethical, psychological and legal questions of its own kind that one perhaps might have to ask "is it the right thing to do so?" The touchstone for evaluation of any reproductive technology should be public policy with reference to the interests of the society in general, because technology should serve rather than dictate the social needs. It should be realized that there cannot be an absolute individual choice in a social structure. The real choice is where the exercise of choice meets the expectations to the society.

In the Western Countries, procreation of children by Artificial Insemination is gaining popularity because the adoption takes lots of time and creates problems of adjustability. The governments are keen to permit the Artificial Insemination but only under the close control of law. The law thus permits it only in exceptional cases so that there cannot be deceptive use of it. Still some legal problems related to Artificial Insemination are unresolved and exercise is on to make a perfect law.

In India the practice of Artificial Insemination has started, but it cannot gain popularity, because of poverty and high fertility rate. Children are available in plenty for adoption, and also the procedure for it is simple. One of the reasons for unpopularity is the religious sanctions against it also.

Now, there is need to have a comprehensive legislation, with prime object to allow Artificial Insemination to a married woman only on written consent of the husband, and to allow Artificial Insemination donation only when Artificial Insemination of husband is not possible. The process of Artificial Insemination must be closely regulated by law and confidentiality, to the extent mentioned, should be maintained. Indeed, in India, in view of the fact that artificial insemination will further increase the population, we cannot have a liberal view in favour of it.

Artificial Insemination donation is not an ethically acceptable alternative to childlessness in the case of male infertility. The donor remains anonymously hidden from the mother and the child for defusing his responsibility as father. His function remains that of a sperms salesman, failing to take full responsibility for his biological offspring.

We need to be concerned not only about right ends, but also about correct means, and in this case the means violate the fundamental meaning of sexual intercourse within the covenant of marriage. Even when the husband consents, Artificial Insemination donation signifies less than an unreserved commitment to share another's life for better or worse, in sickness and in health.

When spouses find themselves childless because of male infertility are advised either to come to terms with their childlessness or to seek children through Artificial Insemination. The procedure has become widely used in animal breeding and for the impregnation of women whose husbands are sterile or impotent.

In a well-coordinated artificial insemination donor program, a success rate of 70 to 80 percent can be expected, with approximately 75 percent of those pregnancies occurring in the first four to five cycles. A couple must accept the fact that there is only a 25 percent chance of getting pregnant in any given cycle and therefore, not be discouraged, if several unsuccessful cycles occur.

It is interesting to note that in the 225 pregnancies established to date at Pennsylvania Hospital, our most successful cycle has been the first, followed by the second and third. Because of the anxieties evident at the start of an artificial insemination donor program and the frequent irregularities of ovulation as a consequence of that, it would be reasonable to expect the bulk of the pregnancies to occur after the first couple of cycles; that does not happen. Very few pregnancies occur after a year of insemination and a couple should be told that at the outset. It is inappropriate to continue artificial insemination donor indefinitely.

In Artificial Insemination there is controversy on the issue that who is real mother of the child conceived by the process of Artificial Insemination. The Australian State of Victoria there is a presumption that the woman who actually gives birth to the child is the mother of the child and that the egg donor is not the mother.

Though not absolutely determinative from an ethical viewpoint, the psychological dangers weigh heavily against a decision to employ artificial insemination donor. The radical asymmetry of the parent's relationship to the artificial insemination donor child opens the door to a host of psychological difficulties. It should be acknowledged that in theory, of course, these psychological difficulties are not insurmountable, but they appear sufficiently grave to compel extreme caution.

More serious from an ethical standpoint is the moral assessment of the role played by the donor. Even though it may be argued that, he does what he does as an act of love to provide a child for a childless couple; nevertheless love can never oblige one to perform an action which by its nature violates the fundamental unity of the personal and biological dimensions of sexual intercourse within the covenant of marriage.

It is the natural of marital covenant and the meaning of parenthood that provide the critical norm for judging the fundamental ethical stance towards artificial insemination donation. It is submitted that marriage is a commitment of person in which husband and wife mutually confer exclusively fidelity to one another, including the mutual commitment of procreative powers. Artificial insemination donation separates procreation from marriage and thereby violates the marriage covenant.

Those who offer contrary arguments in favour of artificial insemination donation explicitly or implicitly adversely affect the marital faith of the spouses. Western culture, whereby the personal or spiritual is understood as the specifically human, and the physical or bodily is frequently depreciated. The personal is too readily understood as a disembodied spiritual reality.

It is submitted that we cannot separate the meaning of "personal" and "human" from physical, bodily processes. The "one-flesh unity" of marriage holds together in a unity the love-making and life-giving dimensions of sexual intercourse. Only when this unity is maintained can children be understood in the full sense as the visible fruit and extension of conjugal love.

Artificial insemination donation cannot be ethically accepted merely because it gives a child to a childless couple. The legal community is yet to resolve the problems raised by the use of artificial insemination for procreation. The existing system is not fully equipped to deal with the controversial issues which have arisen from bio-technological developments. Though issues like artificial insemination amounting to adultery have been put at rest by the judiciary, answering in the negative, many issues still need to be resolved.

In spite of legislative intervention, issues like legitimacy of the child conceived and born by artificial insemination donation is a sore point in the legal system. It is suggested that there should be thorough debate on this issue and the issue should be resolved according to the need of the society and parliament has to intervene and provide a legislative solution.

Thus, we find there is a haze of confusion and uncertainty surrounding the concept of artificial insemination donation. In view of its far-reaching consequences, an immediate legislative action is required. Artificial insemination donation should not constitute a criminal act of adultery because of the absence of physical act of union of flesh and flesh.

Besides, there is no guilty intent of the wife resorting to Artificial Insemination donation. Also, if it were to be treated as adultery, it would give rise to a number of absurdities and complications, e.g., the donor would be an adulterer, the carrier of the semen and the doctor who performs the operation would be participants in an offence. Suppose sperm is used after the donor's death, would the woman be guilty of committing adultery with a dead man? In case, the doctor performing the operation is female doctor, what would be the consequences? A very queer situation would arise in a case, where the husband himself transmits by natural act a third person's sperm to his wife.

Nevertheless, it cannot be denied that the practice of Artificial Insemination donation is very likely to affect family peace and harmony. The presence of another man's child is bound to create emotional conflicts and tensions in the family and therefore, it would be reasonable, necessary, to provide matrimonial relief to the husband, if the wife resorts to AI donation without his consent. It is submitted that only childless couples where the husband's sterility has been medically established should resort to AI donation.

It is suggested that the written consent of the husband should be taken and if he consents or ratifies the act the child should be deemed to be his legitimate child. Only licensed doctors of high repute should be authorized to perform the operation. The doctor should carefully select the donor also maintain a strict secrecy. In other words, to needs of a progressive society should be reconciled with the demands of propriety and legal precedent while dealing with such cases.

Donation of gametes is essential for the smooth practice of treatment of infertility. But it should not turn out to be a profession by the 'donor' done on a commercial basis. Hence, some kind of legal control is necessary.

It is suggested that a statutory duty should be imposed on the donor to disclose his medical history and any congenital or other diseases that his ancestors and lineal descendants might have suffered. Further, the statute has to prescribe the number of times, say three, over which a donor should not be allowed to donate throughout his life, the violation of which should be made punishable.

It is submitted that the Consent form to be obtained from the donor should specifically contain all the declarations made by him and his spouse, if married, and this should be kept in safe custody by the Authority.

In-vitro fertilization (IVF) is another new reproductive technique. In-vitro, as the name implies, involves fertilization of an egg, or oocyte with sperm in a petri dish supplies with nutrients. The result is a pre-embryo, called that because it is not yet implanted. Once it becomes implanted in the woman's uterus, it becomes an embryo.

Many are familiar with in-vitro fertilization techniques. The woman is stimulated with hormones to produce multiple follicles, containing oocytes, or eggs. This is done to increase the chances for pregnancy. In a typical IVF cycle, a woman may receive anywhere from two to as many as six embryos in her uterus. However, frequently there are a number of oocytes, or eggs that remain after the initial IVF cycle.

These oocytes are fertilized and stored in suspended animation through cryo-preservation. The embryos are kept frozen theoretically for the future use of the couple who created them. However, recently, there have been a number of legal cases that have brought ethical and moral issues regarding the disposition of these embryos into the forefront.

In-vitro fertilization is one of several possible methods to increase the chances for an infertile couple to become pregnant. Its use depends on the reason for infertility. In-vitro fertilization may be an option, if there is a blockage in the fallopian tube or endometriosis in the woman or low sperm count or poor quality sperm in the man and In-vitro fertilization will not work for a woman who is incapable of ovulating or with a man who is not able to produce at least a few healthy sperm.

In-vitro fertilization is a procedure in which the joining of egg and sperm takes place outside of a woman's body. A woman may be given fertility drugs before this procedure so that several eggs mature in the ovaries at the same time. The mature eggs (ova) are removed from the woman's ovaries using a long thin needle. They are mixed with sperm in a laboratory dish or test tube. (This is the origin of the term "test tube baby"). The eggs are monitored for several days. Once there is evidence that fertilization has occurred and the cells have begun to divide, they are then returned to the woman's uterus.

In-vitro fertilization, hormones are administered to the patient, and then eggs are harvested from her ovaries. The eggs are fertilized by sperm donated by the father. Once the cells begin to divide, one or more embryos are placed into the woman's uterus to develop and the pregnancy carries the same risks as any pregnancy achieved without assisted technology.

Also called test tube conception medical procedure in which mature egg cells are removed from a woman, fertilized with male sperm outside the body, and inserted into the uterus of the same or another woman for normal gestation and if the procedure is successful, the embryo implants itself in the uterine wall and pregnancy begins.

However, this does not speak to the many dilemmas regarding extra embryos which are now stored all over the world. In Great Britain, embryos are stored for five years and then destroyed. In most South American countries, the laws prohibit the storing of frozen embryos. This is because in most South American countries, the laws are impacted by the state religion. Only in Bolivia, law permits the storage of frozen embryos.

The existence of thousands upon thousands of pre-embryos in cryo-preservation raises a number of potential dilemmas. Some of these potential problems have been litigated in the courts. For example, what happens to the embryo when the couple divorces? Does the husband or wife have a greater interest in the embryo? Do they own the embryo jointly, or does the embryo belong to the one who would give it life? These issues were addressed in the case of Davis v. Davis (824 S.W.2d 588(1992).

In the David case, a Tennessee couple used the high tech procedure to produce a number of fertilized ova, which were cryo-preserved for future implantation. The couple then divorced, and the husband did not want to have children with his former spouse. The wife then petitioned the court for custody of the pre-embryos, because she believed that these frozen embryos were her last chance for having children.

The trial court awarded custody of the embryos to the wife, relying on the best interest of the children theory. The court reasoned that the individual who would give life or the potential for life to the embryos was acting in the embryos best interest. The judge's ruling was reversed by the Appellate Court and later affirmed by the Supreme Court.

This verdict seems to be reasonable and most appropriate in modern perspective and suitable legislation should be made throughout the globe so as to resolve this critical and controversial issue.

Doctors at many clinics perform what they term embryo adoption. This is the transfer of an embryo to an infertile couple. The embryos are either from a couple that has donated the embryo or from an anonymous egg donor and anonymous sperm donor. The doctors who take part in these procedures believe that apart from the fact that embryo adoption occurs far earlier than baby adoption, there is otherwise little difference between the two processes.

The practice to create embryos and store them via cryopreservation has been going on since at least 1986. As a result, thousands of embryos remain in storage long after a couple as created them. A couple that has gone through In-vitro fertilization and were successful in achieving a pregnancy and birth are usually busy raising the child, and not preoccupied with the embryos frozen in a tank.

Ethically, having an abundance of frozen embryos and a shortage of donors presents a temptation to some people in the field to misappropriate and profit from these microscopic beginnings of life. Legally, we are faced with the reality that there are no laws nation wide to regulate the fertility clinics, or to provide criminal penalties for those professionals who do cross the line.

Therefore, it is submitted that the parliament should take note of it and start the process to pass appropriate legislation in this regard with any further delay.

The need in the field of reproductive medicine is not only ethics and morality, but laws. Certainly morality and ethics cannot be legislated. However, this area of medicine and high tech fertility procedures has outpaced the laws, which reflect only traditional ways of "making babies".

Another area of debate in reproductive technology is the surrogacy of motherhood. Surrogate Motherhood involves the artificial insemination of a women with a man's sperm is his wife is infertile or does not want to carry a pregnancy. The surrogate mother conceives a child and relinquishes the child to the contracting couple immediately after birth.

In most cases the surrogate mother agrees to do this only for a fee but there are also agreements without financial implications. Surrogacy agreements intend that the genetic mother (who produced the egg) will also be the nurturing mother after the child's birth, and that the surrogate mother will only function as carrying mother and surrender the child immediately after birth to the nurturing mother.

Surrogate Motherhood however, in the best interests of the society and the new born child there is a strong need to restrict the application of the new technique to help only childless couples on considerations of love and affection including payment of expenses.

In addition, its commercial application, brokerage, and advertisements through media, for protecting the "figure" and for the luxury of avoiding conception and delivery pains for avoiding the "wastage" of time (nine months in pregnancy and then years for rearing the child) should be formulated to process and permit the application of childless couples and those coming forward to surrogate.

The medical and legal records regarding the surrogacy contracts must be kept confidential, with the provision for access to children born out of such arrangement. All agreements and arrangements beyond this authority must be treated as null, void and unenforceable.

Surrogate mothers, in permitted cases, should be given visiting rights and the right to share affection for the child she gave birth to. Medical problems, if an, shall be dealt by the commissioning parents in consultation with the regulating authority and other medical experts. For all legal social, economic and practical purposes the genetic parents should be treated as the "real parents" of the child.

Thus in surrogacy, there are three types of mother, the genetic mother (who donates the eggs and contributes to half the genetic code, i.e. 23 chromosomes), the gestational mother (who carries the foetus in her womb) and the social mother (who provides for the care and upbringing of the child). Each is important for the care and well-being of the child.

It is submitted that the surrogacy is not a simple arrangement; it is extremely complex. The situation can be stressful, overwhelming and intense. It is suggested that both, the surrogate and the infertile couple should engage a legal counsel before entering into and signing a contract. It is in their best interest to know how the law addresses to certain aspects of surrogacy as it pertains to their own interests.

Disclosure of the surrogate relationship should be limited so as to avoid unwarranted scrutiny. In all the future legislation, the paramount welfare of the unborn child must be kept in mind. Certain measures must also be taken in order to keep this child at par with the other children born out of wedlock.

As several legislative enactments and moral codes oppose commercial surrogacy, love and affection are necessary for replacing the "fee" element to generously help a childless couple to get a child. Altruistic surrogacy is permitted by several legislative measures based on the moral fabric of human society. But in a mechanical and a need based world, such a human gesture is either very rare or impossible.

Though ostensibly the arrangements are altruistic, several indirect favour, gifts, monetary returns or properties will be worked out, as the carrying mother feels entitled to some reciprocation, while commissioning couple continue to live under the obligation to repay the debt. In the absence of real or genuine altruistic surrogacy arrangement, there will be no difference between altruistic or commercial surrogacy with a fixed price.

Sometimes altruistic surrogacy is more exploitative than commercial surrogacy, as it makes it impossible for surrogate mother to keep the child if she so desires, the loss of her family as a retribution may be too much for her to give up, whereas, it may be easy for a commercial surrogate mother to cancel the contract.

It is submitted that allowing one's womb to accommodate others child for money, cannot be claimed as a matter of right to body because using other woman's womb for her child will be a violation of that right belonging to the 'surrogate mother by commissioning couple. In the name of exercising a right, one cannot permit mothers to violate it for a price.

It is submitted that violation of right to person, right to bear a child, right to motherhood are undoubtedly the natural rights available to every person as long as the process is natural. There is no right to have unnatural usage of one's own body. As such, right to one's own person is limited by the laws of obscenity, unnatural sexual offences like sodomy, etc. and immoral trafficking. If scientific advancement and technological innovations are permitted to split motherhood into genetic mother and social mother, society would further split the family ties and umbilical bonds creating several problems.

If childlessness and a strong desire to have a child is the genuine purpose, adoption is the only right course available. Even the western laws suggested adoption as a measure to end the legal conflicts. At the same time it is not advisable to totally disuse the scientifically evolved techniques of continuing the progeny of the clan through surrogacy and IVF methods.

The cloning of human beings is a subject fraught with ethical and moral controversy. If cloning can ensure the infinite replication of specific genetic traits, a judgment would need to be made as to which traits are desirable and therefore worthy of perpetuation. The persons empowered to exercise such judgment would be in a position to change the course of human development.

Cloning is fundamental to most living things, since the body cells of plants and animals are clones ultimately derived from the mitosis of a single fertilized egg. More narrowly, a clone can be defined as an individual organism that was grown from a single body cell of its parent and that is genetically identical to it. Also spelled clone population of genetically identical cells or organisms that are derived originally from a single original cell or organism by a sexual methods.

Cloning means production of identical daughter cells from a parental cell. The process of cloning can be used to derive either multiple cell types or an entire individual being. This process can start from either an egg cell or from stem cells. Stem cells are cells derived from 1-14 day old embryos.

Cloning as: human asexual reproduction, accomplished by introducing nuclear material from one or more human somatic cells into a fertilized or unfertilized oocyte [an egg] whose nuclear material has been removed or inactivated so as to produce a living organism (at any stage of development) that is genetically virtually identical to an existing or previously existing human organism.

Cloning in itself refers to the production of a biological entity which is genetically identical or very similar to the one from which it originated. Human cloning is the scientific technique by which a human being is generated. The early but unavoidable result of both embryo splitting and nuclear transfer cloning is the reproduction of a human being at its embryonic stage of development. Thus, human cloning and human embryo are identical with one another.

It is difficult to gauge the extent to which 'repugnance' toward cloning generally rests on a belief in genetic determinism. Hoping to account for the fact that people 'instinctively recoil' from the prospect of cloning.

There is a natural sentiment that is offended by the mental picture of identical babies being produced in some biological factory. Which raises the question: once people learn that this picture is mere science fiction, does the offense that cloning presents to 'natural sentiment' attenuate, or even disappear.

Until recently, there were few ethical, social, or legal discussions about human cloning via reproductive technology, since the scientific consensus was that such a procedure was not biologically possible. With the appearance of Dolly, the situation has changed. But although it now seems more likely that human cloning will become feasible, we may doubt that the practice will come into widespread use.

Since cloning, a new promising technique is full of controversial effects, therefore, it is suggested that the law suffering from inertia, should be reformed only when social circumstances necessitate it.

Few countries have enacted half-hearted laws to regulate cloning. It will be wise to enact a comprehensive law, keeping a balanced view after thoroughly examining the positive and negative aspects of this technique so that we can reap the benefits of this modern technology and avoid a legal vacuum in case of some negative outcome in future.

In relation to human cloning, it is suggested that the permission should be granted only in rarest of rare circumstances, when all other methods of human reproduction have failed. If there is a total ban on human reproductive cloning, if it becomes, possible would be tantamount to attempting to resist the advancement of evolution itself.

Every process involving human cloning is in itself a reproductive process in that it generates a human being at the very beginning of his or her development, i.e., a human embryo. The Holy See regards the distinction between "reproductive" and "therapeutic" (or "experimental") cloning as unacceptable by principle since it is devoid of any ethical and legal ground.

This false distinction masks the reality of the creation of a human being for the purpose of destroying him or her to produce embryonic stem cell lines or to conduct other experimentation. Therefore, human cloning should be prohibited in all cases regardless of the aims that are pursued. The Holy See support research on stem cells of post-natal origin since this approach is a sound, promising, and ethical way to achieve tissue transplantation and cell therapy.

One goal of human cloning focuses on the creation of an embryo that will not be allowed to come to term. It will be used for medical research and other objectives that have been labeled as "therapeutic". Another purpose associated with human cloning is "reproductive", i.e., the creation of a human embryo that will come to term and replicate the person from whom his or her genetic material came.

The ethical problems surrounding clone research, at present receiving such publicity due to the birth of a cloned sheep, were understood at an early stage and argued about worldwide, especially in Christian countries. We must honestly admit, however, that in Japan the problem was not widely discussed or investigated for its implication in the field of ethics and the theology of human life.

It is our hope that the problems that cloning research gives rise to will be argued and sifted thoroughly and moral guidelines clearly established. However, we wish to emphasize once more that no matter what way the argument develops, the act of creating a human being endowed with absolute worth and dignity is the province of God alone and can never be entrusted to human enterprise.

The unique prospect, vividly raised by Dolly, is the creation of a new individual genetically identical to an existing (or previously existing) person—a "delayed" genetic twin. This prospect has been the source of the overwhelming public concern about such cloning. While the creation of embryos for research purposes alone always raises serious ethical questions, the use of somatic cell nuclear transfer to create embryos raised no new issues in this respect.

The unique and distinctive ethical issues raised by the use of somatic cell nuclear transfer to create children relate to, for example, serious safety concerns, individuality, family integrity, and treating children. Consequently, the Commission focused its attention on the use of such techniques for the purpose of creating an embryo which would then be implanted in a woman's uterus and brought to term. It also expanded its analysis of this particular issue to encompass activation in both the public and private sector.

Careful assessment of that response revealed fears about harms to the children who may be created in this manner, particularly psychological harms associated with a possibly diminished sense of individuality and personal autonomy. Others expressed concern about degradation in the quality of parenting and family life.

In addition to concerns about specific harms to children, people have frequently expressed fears that the widespread practice of somatic cell nuclear transfer cloning would undermine important social values by opening the door to a form of eugenics or by tempting some to manipulate other as if they were objects instead of persons.

Arrayed against these concerns are other important social values, such as protecting to procreation and child rearing, maintaining privacy and the freedom of scientific inquiry, and encouraging the possible development of new biomedical breakthroughs.

It is submitted that this technique is not safe to use in humans at this point, indeed, I believe it would violate important ethical obligations were clinicians or researchers to attempt to create a child using these particular technologies, which are likely to involve unacceptable risks to the fetus and/ or potential child. Moreover, in addition to safety concerns, many other serious ethical concerns have been identified, which require much more widespread and careful public deliberation before this technology may be used.

The use of any other technique to create a child genetically identical to an existing (or previously existing) individual would raise many, if not all, of the same non safety related ethical concerns raised by the creation of a child by somatic cell nuclear transfer. Therefore, human cloning should be prohibited in all cases regardless of the aims that are pursued.

The law that is suffering from inertia, being reformed only when social circumstances absolutely necessitate it. Nowhere is this more salient than in laws governing specialized areas of science and medicine, due to its highly specialized nature and vocabulary, research is often conducted in a coterie, intrinsically inaccessible to the public, and thus unsurprisingly fails to command media attention until a breakthrough such as 'Dolly' Occurs. Consequently, the law is condemned to be phlegmatic compared to scientific innovation.

It is submitted that legal prohibition is not the way forward. Regardless of the obvious ethical, moral and practical dangers of human cloning, couples and individuals desperate to have children will inevitably succumb to the fundamental biological drive to reproduce. Individually, people will accept collateral risks such as castigation, imperfect clones (Stern, 1994) or irreversible changes to society in order to fulfil their primordial need to reproduce by whatever means available. Such manifest desperation will be readily exploited by entrepreneurs driven by the prospect of economic reward.

It would be expedient to accept a pragmatic approach to human cloning and commence an informed debate about how trade might be regulated (Kelleher, 1998) and economically influenced in the future.

A total ban on human reproductive cloning, if it becomes possible, would tantamount to attempting to resist the advancement of evolution itself. Common sense, supported by the 'selfish gene theory' (Dawkins, 1976) suggests such a response would be both naïve and arrogant. Any attempt to hinder the progress of evolution is useless, particularly utilizing an instrument as blunt as legal prohibition. The birth of 'Dolly' will surely be regarded as an epoch. The technology to allow cloning is now available. Realistically, it is likely to be the market more than the law that will dictate how this knowledge is used in the future.

Essentially, through this present work on reproductive technology, the hope is being expressed that, by a systematic breakdown of arguments against genetic adventurism, largely a First World imposition on the Third World, it can be shown that there is nothing inherently evil, wrong or unnatural about genetic adventurism; in this slippery slope of human existence that are teetering on today, it is the thinking community of the world alone that makes any judgments, decisions or steps and it is time India took that step ahead.

The system of forcing individuals to make out-of-pocket payments for health care denies basic care to the poorest members of the society. It is evident that majority of doctors in India have no training in medical ethics. Teaching, training, following and practising ethics among doctors in our country is the only solution for the unethical medical problems flourishing in our country amidst poverty. We have to uplift the four big values in bioethics: autonomy, beneficence, non-malfeasance and distributive justice.

It is submitted that in formulating an Indian law on Reproductive Technology such as Artificial Insemination and In Vitro Fertilization, Organ Transplantation etc the following fundamental issues will need to be necessarily tackled by policy makers:

- The ethical and moral consequences of AI and IVF.
- The primacy to be accorded to the biological need to bear a child.

Pending legislation doctors who perform AI donation on childless couples should observe certain precautions. Before performing the operation, the doctor should insist upon the knowledge and full consent of both the adoptive parents. To avoid the chances of any inconsistent claim the identity of the donor of the seed to the recipient-couple and *vice-versa* should not be disclosed nor should the donor know the result of AID.

To avoid the possibility of transmission of any genetic defect on to a child, the donor and the surrogate parent should be, free from all physical and mental defects. To avoid any kind of legal dispute, the consent in writing of the spouse of the donor or surrogate parent, for donation of seed or surrogacy as the case may be, should also be obtained by the doctor. To avoid the chances of prosecution of the doctor for any sexual or other offences, the presence of a nurse or a medical assistant should be compulsory when AI is performed embryo is transferred or seed is procured by the donor.

Proper sanction for all such propositions and to deal effectively with many other aspects of the medical practice of artificial insemination and in-vitro fertilization, an independent and comprehensive legislation on the subject is required.

A video of the consent of an individual could be made, in addition to the written statement, during donation to avoid further legal complications. Medical professionals must set ethical guidelines and take action against violators.

However, there are some concrete suggestions pertaining to reproductive technology, which are as under :

- Artificial Insemination should always be allowed to unmarried woman.
- It should be allowed to married woman only on the written consent of her husband.
- The child in all circumstances should be declared legitimate under the provisions of law and for that present provision of law should be amended accordingly.
- The doctor should maintain records, pertaining to artificial insemination so that in case of any need the genetic origin of the child can be traced out. Before, starting the process of insemination, the doctor should examine the sperms of the donor for health point of view of child and mother.
- A female nurse should always remain present at the time of insemination procedure is carried out.
- There should be some penal provisions to deal with the violation of such norms.
- In-vitro fertilization should be undertaken only after an exhaustive evaluation of infertility is made.
- In no case inhuman or degrading treatment should be allowed.
- Surrogate motherhood should be allowed on comprehensive agreement between genetic mother, father and surrogate mother.
- Looking to all probable consequences of surrogacy, the rights and duties of genetic mother, father and surrogate mother should be determined in agreement and appropriate law should be made to give effect to such agreement.
- The legal position of the husband of surrogate mother, if married, should also be made clear in law. It is suggested that as far as possible, surrogate mother should be unmarried woman.
- There must be some social security provisions of law regarding surrogate child.
- Surrogacy should not be for the purpose of human trafficking or other illegal purposes.
- Payment of money, if any, to surrogate mother should be made with the prior permission of the court.

- Counseling should be made mandatory for donors, as well as for infertile couples.
- Family history of genetic defects should be known by the parties because that might adversely affect the baby.
- There should be complete examination of the donor who donates oocyte or embryo for health point of view of mother and child.
- The wife of the artificial insemination donor must agree for donating semen and the semen should be obtained from an act of masturbation.
- Cloning should not be totally banned and it should be allowed only for treatment purposes.
- There should be debate on various issues of reproductive technology and careful consideration should be given to the medical, emotional, ethical, legal and social issues.
- There should be amendments in the area of family law, contract law, and other fields of law that directly or indirectly related to reproductive technology.
- A campaign should be launched to impart education relating to reproductive technology.

In order to deal with the vices of Reproductive Technology, the Parliament, after thorough discussion and debate, may pass an appropriate Act that may be known as the Reproduction Technology (Regulation and Control) Act.

ANNEXURE A

THE ASSISTED REPRODUCTIVE TECHNOLOGY (REGULATION) BILL, 2010

STATEMENT OF OBJECTS AND REASONS

An act to provide for a national framework for the accreditations, regulation and supervision of assisted reproductive technology clinics, for prevention of misuse of assisted reproductive technology, for safe and ethical practice of assisted reproductive technology services and for matters connected therewith or incidental thereto.

BE IT ENACTED by the Parliament in the 60th year of the Republic of India as follows:

PRELIMINARY

1. Short title, extent and commencement—(1) This Act may be called the Assisted Reproductive Technology (Regulation) Act, 2010.

(2) It applies, in the first instance, to the whole States of .... and.. and the Union Territories; and it shall apply to such other States which adopt this Act by resolution passed in that behalf under Clause (1) of Article 252 of the Constitution.

(3) It shall come into force at once in the States of .... and .... and the Union Territories, on such dates as the Central Government may, by notification appoint, and in any other States which adopt this Act under Clause (1) of Article 252 of the Constitution, on the date of such adoption; and any reference in this Act to the commencement of this Act shall, in relation

to any State or Union Territory, mean the date on which this Act comes into force in such a State or Union Territory.

2. Definitions—In this Act, and in any rules and regulations framed hereunder, unless the context otherwise requires—

(a) "ART bank", means an organisation that is set-up to supply sperm/semen, oocytes/oocyte donors and surrogate mothers to assisted reproductive technology clinics or their patients;

(b) "artificial insemination", means the procedure of artificially transferring semen into the reproductive system of a woman and includes insemination with the husband's semen or with donor semen;

(c) "assisted reproductive technology" (ART), with its grammatical variations and cognate expressions, means all techniques that attempt to obtain a pregnancy by handling or manipulating the sperm or the 3 oocyte outside the human body, and transferring the gamete or the embryo into the reproductive tract;

(d) "assisted reproductive technology clinic", means any premises used for procedures related to assisted reproductive technology;

(e) "biological parent(s)", means genetic parent(s);

(f) "child", means any individual born through the use of assisted reproductive technology;

(g) "Commissioning parents/couples/individuals", means parents, couples or individuals, respectively, who approach an ART clinics or ART bank for providing a service that the ART Clinic or the ART bank is authorized to provide.

(h) "couple", means two persons living together and having a sexual relationship that is legal in India;

(i) "cryo-preservation", means the freezing and storing of gametes, zygotes and embryos;

(j) "Department of Health Research", means Department of Health Research, Ministry of Health and Family Welfare, Government of India;

(k) "donor", means the donor of a gamete or gametes but does not include the husband who provides the sperm or the wife who provides the oocyte to be used in the process of assisted reproduction for their own use;

(l) "egg", means the female gamete (that is, oocyte);

(m) "embryo", means the fertilized ovum that has begun cellular division and continued development up to eight weeks;

(n) "fertilization", means the penetration of the ovum by the spermatozoon and fusion of genetic materials resulting in the development of a zygote;

(o) "foetal reduction", means reduction in the number of foetuses in the case of multiple pregnancies;

(p) "foetus", means the product of conception, starting from completion of embryonic development until birth or abortion;

(q) "gamete", means sperm and oocyte (that is egg);

(r) "gamete donor", means a person who provides sperm or oocyte with the objective of enabling an infertile couple or individual to have a child;

(s) "Indian Council of Medical Research", means the Indian Council of Medical Research (ICMR) as registered under the Societies Registration Act, 1860;

(t) "implantation", means the attachment and subsequent penetration by the zona-free blastocyst, which starts five to seven days following fertilization;

(u) "infertility", means the inability to conceive after at least one year of unprotected coitus; or an anatomical/physiological condition that would prevent an individual from having a child;

(v) "married couple", means two persons whose marriage is legal in the country/countries of which they are citizens;

(w) "oocyte" and "ovum", mean, respectively, the female gamete (that is, egg) present in the ovary, and an ovulated oocyte in which the first polar body has been released;

(x) "patient(s)", means an individual/couple who comes to an infertility clinic and is under treatment for infertility;

(y) "Pre-implantation Genetic Diagnosis", includes the technique in which an embryo formed through in-vitro fertilisation is tested for specific disorders prior to the transfer;

(z) "sperm", means the male gametes produced in the testicles and contained in semen;

(aa) "surrogacy", means an arrangement in which a woman agrees to a pregnancy, achieved through assisted reproductive technology, in which neither of the gametes belong to her or her husband, with the intention to carry it and hand over the child to the person or persons for whom she is acting as a surrogate;

(bb) "surrogate mother", means a woman who is a citizen of India and is resident in India, who agrees to have an embryo generated from the sperm of a man who is not her husband and the oocyte of another woman, implanted in her to carry the pregnancy to viability and deliver the child to the couple/individual that had asked for surrogacy;

(cc) "surrogacy agreement", means a contract between the person(s) availing of assisted reproductive technology and the surrogate mother;

(dd) "unmarried couple", means two persons, both of marriageable age, living together with mutual consent but without getting married, in a relationship that is legal in the country/countries of which they are citizens; and

(ee) "zygote", means the fertilized oocyte prior to the first cell division.

CONSTITUTION OF AUTHORITIES TO REGULATE ASSISTED REPRODUCTIVE TECHNOLOGY

3. Establishment of National Advisory Board—(1) With effect from such date as the Central Government may, by notification, appoint, there shall be established a Board to be known as the National Advisory Board for Assisted Reproductive Technology, hereafter referred to as the National Board, to exercise the jurisdiction and powers and discharge the functions and duties conferred or imposed on the Board by or under this Act.

(2) The National Board shall consist of such number of members, not exceeding twenty-one, as may be prescribed by the Central Government and, unless the rules otherwise provide, the National Board shall consist of the following—

(a) Secretary, Department of Health Research, Government of India, who shall be the Chairman of the Board;
(b) A senior scientist having knowledge of assisted reproductive technology, from the Department of Health Research or the Indian Council of Medical Research, who shall be the Member Secretary of the Board;
(c) A representative, not below the rank of Joint Secretary, from the Ministry of Health and Family Welfare;
(d) The nominee of an Indian professional society concerned primarily with assisted reproduction; and
(e) Up to sixteen other experts—of whom one each shall be a nominee of the Ministry of Health and Family Welfare and Indian Council of Medical Research, and at least six of whom shall be women—in the fields of assisted reproduction, gynaecology, embryology, andrology, bioethics, mammalian reproduction, medical genetics, social science, law, or human rights, to be nominated by the Central Government.

(3) The Chairman of National Board shall nominate a Vice-Chairman from among its members.

4. Meetings of National Advisory Board—(1) The National Board shall meet as and when necessary, not less than two times a year, and at such time and place in the country as the Chairperson of the National Board may think fit.

(2) The Chairperson of the National Board shall preside over the meetings of the National Board.

(3) If, for any reason, the Chairperson of the National Board is unable to attend any meeting of the National Board, the Vice-Chairperson of the National Board shall preside over the meeting.

5. Functions of National Advisory Board—(1) The National Board may recommend modification from time to time in the attached rules and schedules where relevant in regard to the following, and perform any other functions and tasks assigned to it by the Central Government:

(a) minimum requirements related to staff and physical infrastructure for the various categories of assisted reproductive technology clinics;
(b) regulations in respect of permissible assisted reproductive technology procedures;
(c) regulations in respect of selection of patients for assisted reproductive technology procedures;
(d) encouragement and promotion of training and research in the field of assisted reproduction;
(e) encouragement of the establishment and maintenance of a national database in respect of infertility;
(f) guidelines for counselling and providing patients with all necessary information and advice on various aspects of assisted reproductive technology procedures;
(g) ways and means of disseminating information related to infertility and assisted reproductive technologies to various sections of the society;
(h) regulations in respect of research on human embryos;
(i) proformae for obtaining information from donors of gametes and surrogate mothers, consent forms for various procedures, and contracts and/or agreements between the various parties involved, in all of the languages listed in the Eighth Schedule of the Constitution; and
(j) policies from time to time on assisted reproduction;

6. Establishment of State Boards—(1) Every State Government shall, within 180 days of the issue of the notification under sub-section (1) of section 3, by notification in the Official Gazette, establish a State Board for Assisted Reproductive Technology to exercise the jurisdiction and powers and discharge the functions and duties conferred or imposed on the State Boards by or under this Act.

(2) The State Boards shall consist of such number of members, not exceeding twelve, as may be prescribed by the State Government and, unless the rules otherwise provide, the State Boards shall consist of the following members, namely—

(a) The Secretary of the Department of Health and Family Welfare, who shall be Chairperson, ex-officio;
(b) The nominee of an Indian professional society concerned primarily with assisted reproduction who shall be the Vice-Chairperson, ex-officio;
(c) An officer not below the rank of a Joint Secretary, who shall be the Member-Secretary of the Board; and
(d) Up to nine other members—of whom at least four shall be women—who shall be experts in the fields of assisted reproduction, gynaecology, embryology, andrology, bioethics, mammalian reproduction, medical genetics, social science, law, or human rights, to be nominated by the State Government.

(3) The Chairman of the State Board shall nominate a Vice-Chairman from among its members.

7. Meetings of State Boards—(1) The State Board shall meet as and when necessary, but not less than three times a year, and at such time and place as the Chairperson of the State Board may think fit.

(2) The Chairperson of the State Board shall preside over the meetings of the State Board.

(3) If for any reason the Chairperson of the State Board is unable to attend any meeting of the State Board, the Vice-Chairperson of the State Board shall preside over the meeting.

8. Powers and Functions of State Boards—(1) Subject to the provisions of this Act and the rules and regulations adopted thereunder, the State Board shall have the responsibility for laying down the policies and plans for assisted reproduction in the State.

(2) Without prejudice to the generality of the provisions contained in sub-section (1) of this section, the State Board, taking into account the recommendations, policies and regulations of the National Board, may—

(a) advise the State Government to constitute a Registration Authority or Authorities as required, at least of six experts in assisted reproduction technology or a related field, for the use of assisted reproductive technology in the State;
(b) monitor the functioning of the Registration Authority subject, in particular, to the guidelines laid down by the National Advisory Board;
(c) coordinate the enforcement and implementation of the policies and guidelines for assisted reproduction;
(d) constitute advisory committees consisting of experts in the field of assisted reproduction and related fields at the State or district level, to make recommendations on different aspects of assisted reproduction; and
(e) perform such other functions prescribed under this Act.

(3) Notwithstanding anything contained in section 12 of this Act, the State Board may, *suo moto*, whether on the basis of a complaint or otherwise, examine and review any decision of the Registration Authority.

(4) In the exercise of its functions under this Act, the State Board shall give such directions or pass such orders as are necessary, with reasons to be recorded in writing.

9. Term of office, conditions of service, etc., of Chairperson and other members of State Boards—(1) Before appointing any person as the Chairperson or other member, the appropriate Government shall satisfy itself that the person's integrity is such that his/her professional interest shall not affect prejudicially his functions as such member.

(2) The Chairperson and every other member shall hold office for such period, not exceeding five years, as may be specified by the appropriate government in the order of his appointment, but shall be eligible for re-appointment.

(3) Notwithstanding anything contained in sub-section (1) of this section, a member may by writing under his/her hand and addressed to the appropriate Government resign his/her office at any time;

(4) A vacancy caused by the resignation or removal of the Chairperson or any other member shall be filled by fresh appointment.

(5) In the event of the occurrence of a vacancy in the office of the Chairperson by reason of his/her death, resignation or otherwise, such one of the members as the appropriate Government may, by notification, authorise in this behalf, shall act as the Chairperson till the date on which a new Chairperson, appointed in accordance with the provisions of this Act to fill such vacancy, takes charge of the office.

(6) When the Chairperson is unable to discharge his/her functions owing to absence, illness or any other cause, the Vice-Chairperson shall discharge the function of the Chairpersons, till the date on which the Chairperson resumes his duties.

(7) The salaries and allowances payable to and the other terms and conditions of service of the Chairperson and other members shall be such as may be prescribed: provided that neither the salary and allowances nor the other terms and conditions of service of the Chairperson or any other member shall be varied to his disadvantage after his appointment.

(8) The Chairperson and every other member shall, before entering upon his/her office make a declaration of fidelity and secrecy in the form set out in the Schedule.

(9) The Chairperson ceasing to hold office as such shall not hold any appointment or be connected with the management or administration in any company, hospital, clinic, society, trust or other undertaking in relation to which any matter has been the subject matter of consideration before the State Board, for a period of three years from the date on which he ceases to hold such office.

10. Procedure of State Boards—(1) Subject to the provisions of this Act, the State Board shall have powers to—

(a) regulate the procedure and conduct of the business; and

(b) delegate its powers or functions to such persons or

authorities as prescribed in the rules or regulations made under this Act.

(2) The State Boards shall, for the purposes of any inquiry or for any other purpose under this Act, have the powers to—

(a) summon and enforce the attendance of any witness and examine him/her on oath;
(b) order the discovery and production of document or other material objects producible as evidence;
(c) receive evidence on affidavit;
(d) requisition any public record from any court or office;
(e) issue any order for the examination of witnesses; and
(f) any other matter which may be prescribed.

11. Constitution and functions of the Registration Authority—(1) The State Government shall constitute the Registration Authority as per the advise of the State Board, within a period of three months of the advise.

(2) The Registration Authority shall have a full-time Chairman of the level of a Secretary to the State Government, who shall be a recognised expert in assisted reproductive technology or a related field.

(3) The other members of the Registration Authority shall be part-time members, and shall be adequately compensated for their services.

(4) Before appointing any member of the Registration Authority, the Government shall satisfy itself that his/her integrity is such that his/her professional interest shall not affect prejudicially his/her functions as a member.

(5) The Registration Authority shall be provided by the State Government with adequate supporting staff and secretarial assistance, and suitable accommodation.

(6) The Registration Authority shall issue an appropriate letter granting or rejecting registration to an assisted reproductive technology clinic.

12. Proceedings before State Boards to be judicial proceedings—(1) Every State Board shall be deemed to be a civil court and when any offence as is described in this Act is committed in the view or presence of the State Board, the State

Board may, after recording the facts constituting the offence and the statement of the accused as provided for in the Code of Criminal Procedure, 1973, forward the case to a Magistrate having jurisdiction to try the same, and the Magistrate to whom any such case is forwarded shall proceed to hear the complaint against the accused as if the case has been forwarded to him under section 346 of the Code of Criminal Procedure, 1973.

(2) Every proceeding before a State Board shall be deemed to be a judicial proceeding within the meaning of sections 193 and 228, and for the purposes of section 196 of the Indian Penal Code, and the Board shall be deemed to be a civil court for all the purposes of section 195 and Chapter XXVI of the Code of Criminal Procedure, 1973.

PROCEDURES FOR REGISTRATIONS AND COMPLAINTS

13. Registration and accreditation of clinics—(1) All assisted reproductive technology clinics shall, within such period and in such form and manner as may be prescribed, register themselves with the Registration Authority.

(2) An application for registration by an assisted reproductive technology clinic under sub-section (1) of this section shall contain the particulars of the applicant including all details of techniques and procedures of assisted reproductive technology practiced at such clinic.

(3) The State Board may, subject to such terms and conditions as may be prescribed, register any assisted reproductive technology clinic on the basis of the techniques and procedures of assisted reproductive technology practiced at such clinic, such as—

(a) infertility treatment, including Intra-Uterine Insemination (IUI), Artificial Insemination with Husband's semen (AIH), and Artificial Insemination using Donor Semen (AID), involving the use of donated or collected gametes;

(b) infertility treatment involving the use and creation of embryos outside the human body;

(c) processing or storage of embryos; and
(d) research.

(4) Notwithstanding anything contained in this Act or any of the Rules made thereunder, no assisted reproductive technology clinic performing any of the functions under sub-section (3) of this section, or any other advanced diagnostic, therapeutic or research functions, shall practice any aspect of such diagnosis, therapy or research without a certificate of accreditation issued by the State Board.

(5) The practice of any aspect of assisted reproductive technology in contravention of the provisions of this section shall constitute an offence under this Act.

(6) Assisted reproductive technology clinics registered under this Act shall be deemed to have satisfied the provisions of the PC & PNDT Act, 1994 [amended in 2002], and shall not be required to seek a separate registration under the said Act.

14. Who may apply for registration—(1) Assisted reproductive technology clinics, ART banks and research organizations using human embryos, operative on the date of notification of this Act, shall obtain a temporary registration within six months of the notification of the State Registration Authority by the State Board, and regular registration within 18 months of the above notification. If an assisted reproductive technology clinic that has applied for temporary registration under this clause to the State Registration Authority does not receive the registration or hear from the above Authority within 60 days of the receipt of the application by the Authority, the clinic would be deemed to have received the temporary registration.

(2) No assisted reproductive technology clinic, ART bank or research organisation using human embryos, other than the ones specified above, shall practice any aspect of assisted reproductive technology, or carry out any research on or using human embryos, or use any premises for such purposes, without a registration under this Act.

(3) Any assisted reproductive technology clinic or ART bank or research organisation using human embryos, by whatsoever name called, may apply to the Registration

Authority for registration to operate the clinic, ART bank or research organisation in accordance with the procedure and criteria laid down in this Act.

(4) Every application under sub-section (2) of this section shall be in such form and shall be accompanied by such fee and such documents as may be prescribed by the State Government.

15. Grant of registration—(1) The Registration Authority may, if it is satisfied that the criteria specified in the Rules have been met, grant registration to the applicant for a term of three years under such terms and conditions as it thinks fit.

(2) The Registration Authority shall, within one month of a registration being granted under this section, report such registration to the State Board.

(3) The State Board shall maintain a record of all registrations applied for and granted under this section.

(4) No registration shall be granted unless the Registration Authority, or such authorised person or persons acting on its behalf, have inspected the premises of the applicant.

16. Renewal, suspension or revocation of registration—(1) The Registration Authority may, on an application made to it in such form and manner as may be prescribed, renew a registration granted under the provisions of this Act with effect from the date of its expiry if it is satisfied that the criteria prescribed in the Schedule continue to be met.

(2) The Registration Authority may at any time suspend the operation of a registration and call upon the holder of the registration to produce such documents or furnish such evidence as may be required if it has reasonable grounds to believe that the terms and conditions of the registration have not been met.

(3) When acting under sub-section (2) of this section, the Registration Authority shall either revoke the registration or continue the registration, as the case may be, after giving the holder of the registration adequate opportunity to be heard.

(4) The Registration Authority shall inform the concerned State Board of every assisted reproductive technology clinic in respect of which it has granted, renewed, revoked or denied a registration under this Act within one month of such an action being taken.

(5) The Registration Authority shall be deemed to have granted renewal for three years to the applicant if the applicant does not receive a definitive communication from the Registration Authority regarding the renewal application within sixty days of the receipt of the application in the office of the Registration Authority.

17. Registration Authority to inspect premises—In the exercise of its powers under this Act, the Registration Authority shall have the power to inspect, with or without prior notice on a working day during working hours, any premises or call for any document or material in the discharge of its powers and functions.

18. Applicability to ART banks and research organisations—The provisions of sections 13 to 16, as relevant, shall apply also to ART banks and research organisations using human embryos.

19. Appeal to the State Board—(1) Any person aggrieved by the decision of the Registration Authority made under this Act may, within such period and in such manner and form as may be prescribed, prefer an appeal to the State Board.

(2) On receipt of an appeal under sub-section (1) of this section, the State Board may, after giving an opportunity to the appellant to be heard, and after making such further inquiry as it thinks fit, confirm, modify or set aside the decision of the Registration Authority, within three months of the receipt of the appeal.

DUTIES OF AN ASSISTED REPRODUCTIVE TECHNOLOGY CLINIC

20. General duties of assisted reproductive technology clinics—(1) Assisted reproductive technology clinics shall ensure that patients, donors of gametes and surrogate mothers are eligible to avail of assisted reproductive technology procedures under the criteria prescribed by the rules under this Act and that they have been medically tested for such diseases, sexually transmitted or otherwise, as may be prescribed and all other communicable diseases which may endanger the health of the parents, or any one of them, surrogate or child.

(2) It shall be the responsibility of an assisted reproductive technology clinic to obtain, from ART bank(s), all relevant information, other than the name, personal identity and address, of possible gamete donors, and assist the couple or individual desirous of the donation, to choose the donor.

(3) When an ART bank receives a request from an assisted reproductive technology clinic for a donor oocyte, a responsible member of the staff of the ART bank will accompany the particular donor to the assisted reproductive technology clinic, and obtain a written agreement from the authority designated for this purpose by the clinic, that the clinic shall, under no circumstances (except when asked by a court of law), reveal the identity of the donor to the recipient couple or individual or to anyone else; the clinic shall also ensure that all its staff is made aware of the fact that any step leading to disclosure of the identify (i.e., name and address) to the recipient couple or individual or to anyone else, shall amount to an offence punishable under this Act.

(4) Either of the parties seeking assisted reproductive technology treatment or procedures shall be entitled to specific information in respect of donor of gametes including, but not restricted to, height, weight, ethnicity, skin colour, educational qualifications, medical history of the donor, provided that the identity, name and address of the donor is not made known.

(5) Assisted reproductive technology clinics shall obtain donor gametes from ART banks that have ensured that the donor has been medically tested for such diseases, sexually transmitted or otherwise, as may be prescribed and all other communicable diseases which may endanger the health of the parents, or any one of them, surrogate or child.

(6) Assisted reproductive technology clinics shall provide professional counselling to patients or individuals about all the implications and chances of success of assisted reproductive technology procedures in the clinic and in India and internationally, and shall also inform patients and individuals of the advantages, disadvantages and cost of the procedures, their medical side effects, risks including the risk of multiple pregnancy, the possibility of adoption, and any such other matter as may help the couple or individual arrive at a decision

that would be most likely to be the best for the couple or individual.

(7) Assisted reproductive technology clinics shall make couples or individuals, as the case may be, aware of the rights of a child born through the use of assisted reproductive technology.

(8) Assisted reproductive technology clinics shall explain to couples or individuals, as the case may be, the choice or choices of treatment available to them and the reason or reasons of the clinic for recommending a particular treatment, and shall clearly explain the advantages, disadvantages, limitations and cost of any recommended or explained treatment or procedure.

(9) Assisted reproductive technology clinics shall ensure that information about clients, donors and surrogate mothers is kept confidential and that information about assisted reproductive technology treatment shall not be disclosed to anyone other than a central database to be maintained by the Department of Health Research, except with the consent of the person or persons to whom the information relates, or in a medical emergency at the request of the person or persons or the closest available relative of such person or persons to whom the information relates, or by an order of a court of competent jurisdiction.

(10) No assisted reproductive technology clinic shall consider conception by surrogacy for patients for whom it would normally be possible to carry a baby to term. Provided that where it is determined that unsafe or undesirable medical implications of such conception may arise, the use of surrogacy may be permitted.

(11) Assisted reproductive technology clinics shall provide to couples or individuals, as the case may be, a pre-stamped self-addressed envelop to inform the clinic of the results of the assisted reproductive technology procedure performed for the couple or the individual.

(12) No assisted reproductive technology clinic shall obtain or use sperm or oocyte donated by a relative or known friend of either of the parties seeking assisted reproductive technology treatment or procedures.

(13) Every assisted reproductive technology clinic shall establish a mechanism to look into complaints in such manner as may be prescribed.

(14) No assisted reproductive technology procedure shall be performed on a woman below 21 years of age, and any contravention of this stipulation shall amount to an offence punishable under this Act.

(15) All assisted reproductive technology clinics shall issue to the infertile couple/individual a discharge certificate stating details of the assisted reproductive technology procedure(s) performed on the couple/individual.

(16) Only a registered ART bank (and no other organization) shall be authorised to advertise for, procure or provide semen, oocyte donor or surrogate mother.

21. Duty of the assisted reproductive technology clinic to obtain written consent—(1) No assisted reproductive technology clinic shall perform any treatment or procedure of assisted reproductive technology without the consent in writing of all the parties seeking assisted reproductive technology to all possible stages of such treatment or procedures including the freezing of embryos.

(2) No assisted reproductive technology clinic shall freeze any human embryos without specific instructions and consent in writing from all the parties seeking assisted reproductive technology in respect of what should be done with the gametes or embryos in case of death or incapacity of any of the parties.

(3) No assisted reproductive technology clinic shall use any human reproductive material to create an embryo or use an in-vitro embryo for any purpose without the specific consent in writing of all the parties to whom the assisted reproductive technology relates.

(4) The consent of any of the parties obtained under this section may be withdrawn at any time before the embryos or the gametes are transferred to the concerned woman's uterus.

22. Duty of the assisted reproductive technology clinic to keep accurate records—(1) All assisted reproductive technology clinics shall maintain detailed records, in such manner as may be prescribed, of all donor oocytes, sperm or embryos used, the manner and technique of their use, and the individual or couple or surrogate mother, in respect of whom it was used.

(2) All assisted reproductive technology clinics will, as and when such central facilities are established, put on line all information available to them in regard to progress of the patient (such as biochemical and clinical pregnancy) within seven days of the information being available, withholding the identity of the patient.

(3) Records maintained under sub-section (1) of this section shall be maintained for at least a period of ten years, upon the expiry of which 18th assisted reproductive technology clinic shall transfer the records to a central database of a national ART registry to be set-up by the Department of Health Research at the Hqrs of the ICMR.

(4) In the event of the closure of any assisted reproductive technology before the expiry of the period of ten years under sub-section (2) of this section, the assisted reproductive technology clinic or ART bank shall immediately transfer the records to a central database of a national ART registry to be set up by the Department of Health Research at the Hqrs of the ICMR

23. Duties of assisted reproductive technology clinics using gametes and embryos—(1) Assisted reproductive technology clinics shall harvest oocytes in accordance with such regulations of the National Board or concerned State Board or any rule as may be prescribed under this Act.

(2) The number of oocytes or embryos that may be placed in a woman in any one cycle shall be according to the rules and regulations provided under this Act.

(3) No woman should be treated with gametes or embryos derived from the gametes of more than one man or woman during any one treatment cycle.

(4) An assisted reproductive technology clinic shall never mix semen from two individuals before use.

(5) Where a multiple pregnancy occurs as a result of assisted reproductive technology, the concerned assisted reproductive technology clinic shall inform the patient immediately of the multiple pregnancy and its medical implications and may carry out foetal reduction after appropriate counselling.

(6) The collection of gametes from a person whose death is imminent shall only be permissible if such person's spouse intends to avail assisted reproductive technology to have a child.

(7) No assisted reproductive technology clinic shall use ova that are derived from a foetus, in any process of in-vitro fertilisation.

(8) No assisted reproductive technology clinic shall utilise any semen, whether from an ART bank or otherwise, for any aspect of assisted reproductive technology unless such semen is medically analysed in such manner as may be prescribed.

(9) Any contravention of stipulation under sub-sections 3, 4, 7 and 8 of this section shall amount to an offence under this Act.

24. Pre-implantation Genetic Diagnosis—(1) Pre-implantation Genetic Diagnosis shall be used only to screen the embryo for known, pre-existing, heritable or genetic diseases or as specified by the Registration Authority.

(2) Destruction or donation (with the approval of the patient) to an approved research laboratory for research purposes, of an embryo after Pre-implantation Genetic Diagnosis, shall be done only when the embryo suffers from pre-existing, heritable, life-threatening or genetic diseases.

(3) The State Board may lay down such other conditions as it deems fit in the interests of Pre-implantation Genetic Diagnosis.

25. Sex selection—(1) No assisted reproductive technology clinic shall offer to provide a couple with a child of a pre-determined sex.

(2) It shall be a criminal offence and it is prohibited for anyone to do any act, at any stage, to determine the sex of the child to be born through the process of assisted reproductive technology.

(3) No person shall knowingly provide, prescribe or administer any thing that would ensure or increase the probability that an embryo shall be of a particular sex, or that would identify the sex of an in-vitro embryo, except to diagnose, prevent or treat a sex-linked disorder or disease.

(4) No assisted reproductive technology clinic will carry out any assisted reproductive technology procedure to

separate, or yield fractions enriched in sperm of X or Y variations.

(5) Any contravention of stipulation under sub-sections 1, 2, 3 and 4 of this section shall amount to an offence under this Act.

SOURCING, STORAGE, HANDLING AND RECORD KEEPING FOR GAMETES, EMBRYOS AND SURROGATES

26. Sourcing of gametes—(1) The screening of gamete donors and surrogates; the collection, screening and storage of semen; and provision of oocyte donor and surrogates, shall be done by an ART bank registered as an independent entity under the provisions of this Act.

(2) An ART bank shall operate independently of any assisted reproductive technology clinic.

(3) ART banks shall obtain semen from males between twenty-one years of age and forty five years of age, both inclusive, and arrange to obtain oocytes from females between twenty one years of age and thirty-five years of age, both inclusive, and examine the donors for such diseases, sexually transmitted or otherwise, as may be prescribed, and all other communicable diseases which may endanger the health of the parents, or any one of them, surrogate or child.

(4) All ART banks shall have standard, scientifically established facilities and defined standard operating procedures for all its scientific and technical activities.

(5) All ART banks shall cryo-preserve sperm donations for a quarantine period of at least six months before being used and, at the expiry of such period, the ART bank shall not supply the sperm to any assisted reproductive technology clinic unless the sperm donor is tested for such diseases, sexually transmitted or otherwise, as may be prescribed.

(6) An ART bank may advertise for gamete donors and surrogates, who may be compensated financially by the bank.

(7) An ART bank shall not supply the sperm of a single donor for use more than seventy-five times.

(8) No woman shall donate oocytes more than six times in her life, with not less than a three-month interval between the oocyte pick-ups.

(9) Eggs from one donor can be shared between two recipients only, provided that at least seven oocytes are available for each recipient.

(10) All unused oocytes would be either appropriately preserved by the assisted reproductive technology clinic for use on the same recipient(s), or given for research to a bonafide organisation.

(11) One sample of semen supplied by an ART bank shall be used by the assisted reproductive technology clinic only once on only one recipient.

(12) An ART bank shall obtain all necessary information in respect of a sperm or oocyte donor or a surrogate, including the name, identity and address of such donor or surrogate, in such manner as may be prescribed, and shall undertake in writing to the donor to keep such information confidential.

(13) No ART bank shall divulge the name, identity or address of any sperm or oocyte donor to any person or assisted reproductive technology clinic except in pursuance of an order or decree of a court of competent jurisdiction.

(14) Any person or ART bank who divulges the name, identity or address of a sperm donor in contravention of sub-sections 11 and 12 of this section shall be guilty of an offence under this Act.

(15) An ART bank may, for such appropriate fee as may be prescribed, store any semen obtained from a donor for the exclusive use of the wife or partner of the donor.

27. Storage and handling of gametes and embryos— (1) The highest possible standards should be followed in the storage and handling of gametes and embryos in respect of their security, and with regard to their recording and identification.

(2) No donor gamete shall be stored for a period of more than five years.

(3) An embryo may, for such appropriate fee as may be prescribed, be stored for a maximum period of five years and at the end of such period such embryo shall be allowed to perish or donated to an approved research organization for research purposes with the consent of the patients. If during the period of five years, one of the commissioning partners

dies, the surviving partner can use the embryo for herself or for her partner, provided an appropriate consent was taken earlier.

Provided that where the persons to whom such embryo relates fails to pay the fee, or both the commissioning persons die, the assisted reproductive technology clinic may, subject to such regulations as may be prescribed, destroy the embryo or transfer the embryo to any accredited research organisation under section 18 of this Act.

28. Records to be maintained by the ART bank—(1) The ART bank shall keep a record of all the gametes received, stored and supplied, and details of the use of the gametes of each donor.

(2) The records shall be maintained for at least ten years, after which the records shall be transferred to a central database of the Department of Health Research, Government of India.

(3) Where an ART bank closes before the expiry of the ten year period, the records shall be immediately transferred to the central database of the Department of Health Research, Government of India.

(4) If not otherwise ordered by a court of competent jurisdiction, all ART banks shall ensure that all information about clients and donors is kept confidential and that information about gamete donation shall not be disclosed to anyone other than the central database of the Department of Health Research.

29. Restriction on sale of gametes, zygotes and embryos—(1) The sale, transfer or use of gametes, zygotes and embryos, or any part thereof or information related thereto, directly or indirectly to any party outside India is prohibited and shall be deemed to be an offence under this Act except in the case of transfer of own gametes and embryos for personal use with the permission of the National Board.

(2) The sale of gametes, except for use by an assisted reproductive technology clinic for treating infertility, and the sale of zygotes and embryos, or of any information related to gametes, zygotes or embryos, within India, is prohibited and shall be deemed to be an offence under this Act.

REGULATION OF RESEARCH ON EMBRYOS

30. Permission of the Department of Health Research for research—(1) The sale of any gametes and embryos or their transfer to any country outside India, for research is absolutely prohibited and shall constitute a criminal offence under this Act.

(2) Research shall only be conducted on such gametes and embryos that have been donated for such purpose.

(3) No research shall be conducted using embryos except with the permission of the Department of Health Research.

(4) Any person or organisation, by whatsoever name called, may apply to the Department of Health Research for registration as a research institution permitted to conduct research on embryos.

(5) While granting permission on an application for registration made under sub-section 4 of this section, the Department of Health Research may prescribe, and the applicant shall be bound by such terms and conditions as it thinks fit.

(6) The Department of Health Research may, if it has reasonable grounds to believe that any of the terms and conditions prescribed under sub-section 5 of this section have not been met,—

(a) call for the production of such documents or the furnishing of such evidence as may be required;

(b) inspect, or order any officer authorised in this behalf to inspect, any premises related to the grant of registration; and

(c) suspend the registration of the research institution, after giving all concerned parties adequate opportunity to be heard.

(7) The Department of Health Research may make such regulations as it thinks fit to provide for research on embryos.

(8) Any act or thing done or omitted to be done in contravention of the provisions of this Chapter shall be deemed to be an offence under this Act.

31. Regulation of research—(1) In exercising its powers under this Chapter, the Department of Health Research shall ensure that—

(a) no research is conducted on any human embryo unless such research is necessary in public interest;
(b) no research is conducted on any human embryo created in-vitro unless such research is necessary in public interest to acquire further scientific knowledge;
(c) no research is conducted on any human embryo, other than embryos given for storage to an ART bank under sub-section (3) of section 27, unless full and informed consent in writing is obtained from the persons from whom such embryo was created;
(d) no advertisement is issued, and no purchase, sale or transfer is made, of any human embryo created in-vitro or any part thereof, except in accordance with this Act;
(e) no human embryo created in-vitro is maintained for a period exceeding fourteen days or such other period as recommended by the National Advisory Board;
(f) no work is done leading to human reproductive cloning; and
(g) such other terms and conditions that may be prescribed by the ICMR are adhered to.

(2) Any assisted reproductive technology clinic or other research institution or person conducting any research in contravention of the provisions of this Act or any rules or regulations prescribed hereunder shall be an offence under this Act.

RIGHTS AND DUTIES OF PATIENTS, DONORS, SURROGATES AND CHILDREN

32. Rights and duties of patients—(1) Subject to the provisions of this Act and the rules and regulations made thereunder, assisted reproductive technology shall be available to all persons including single persons, married couples and unmarried couples.

(2) In case assisted reproductive technology is used by a married or unmarried couple, there must be informed consent from both the parties.

(3) The parents of a minor child have the right to access information about the donor, other than the name, identity or address of the donor, or the surrogate mother, when and to the extent necessary for the welfare of the child.

(4) All information about the patients shall be kept confidential and information about assisted reproductive technology procedures done on them shall not be disclosed to anyone other than the central depository of the Department of Health Research, except with the consent of the person or persons to whom the information relates, or by a court order.

33. Rights and duties of donors—(1) Subject to the other provisions of this Act, all information about the donors shall be kept confidential and information about gamete donation shall not be disclosed to anyone other than the central database of the Department of Health Research, except with the consent of the person or persons to whom the information relates, or by an order of a court of competent jurisdiction.

(2) Subject to the other provisions of this Act, the donor shall have the right to decide what information may be passed on and to whom, except in the case of an order of a court of competent jurisdiction.

(3) A donor shall relinquish all parental rights over the child which may be conceived from his or her gamete.

(4) No assisted reproductive technology procedure shall be conducted on or in relation to any gamete of a donor under this Act unless such donor has obtained the consent in writing of his or her spouse, if there, to such procedure.

(5) The identity of the recipient shall not be made known to the donor.

34. Rights and duties in relation to surrogacy—(1) Both the couple or individual seeking surrogacy through the use of assisted reproductive technology, and the surrogate mother, shall enter into a surrogacy agreement which shall be legally enforceable.

(2) All expenses, including those related to insurance if available, of the surrogate related to a pregnancy achieved in furtherance of assisted reproductive technology shall, during the period of pregnancy and after delivery as per medical advice, and till the child is ready to be delivered as per medical advice, to the biological parent or parents, shall be borne by the couple or individual seeking surrogacy.

(3) Notwithstanding anything contained in sub-section (2) of this section and subject to the surrogacy agreement, the surrogate mother may also receive monetary compensation from the couple or individual, as the case may be, for agreeing to act as such surrogate.

(4) A surrogate mother shall relinquish all parental rights over the child.

(5) No woman less than twenty-one years of age and over thirty-five years of age shall be eligible to act as a surrogate mother under this Act. Provided that no woman shall act as a surrogate for more than five successful live births in her life, including her own children.

(6) Any woman seeking or agreeing to act as a surrogate mother shall be medically tested for such diseases, sexually transmitted or otherwise, as may be prescribed, and all other communicable diseases which may endanger the health of the child, and must declare in writing that she has not received a blood transfusion or a blood product in the last six months.

(7) Individuals or couples may obtain the service of a surrogate through an ART bank, which may advertise to seek surrogacy provided that no such advertisement shall contain any details relating to the caste, ethnic identity or descent of any of the parties involved in such surrogacy. No assisted reproductive technology clinic shall advertise to seek surrogacy for its clients.

(8) A surrogate mother shall, in respect of all medical treatments or procedures in relation to the concerned child, register at the hospital or such medical facility in her own name, clearly declare herself to be a surrogate mother, and provide the name or names and addresses of the person or persons, as the case may be, for whom she is acting as a surrogate, along with a copy of the certificate mentioned in clause 17 below.

(9) If the first embryo transfer has failed in a surrogate mother, she may, if she wishes, decide to accept on mutually agreed financial terms, at most two more successful embryo transfers for the same couple that had engaged her services in the first instance. No surrogate mother shall undergo embryo transfer more than three times for the same couple.

(10) The birth certificate issued in respect of a baby born through surrogacy shall bear the name(s) of individual/ individuals who commissioned the surrogacy, as parents.

(11) The person or persons who have availed of the services of a surrogate mother shall be legally bound to accept the custody of the child/children irrespective of any abnormality that the child/children may have, and the refusal to do so shall constitute an offence under this Act.

(12) Subject to the provisions of this Act, all information about the surrogate shall be kept confidential and information about the surrogacy shall not be disclosed to anyone other than the central database of the Department of Health Research, except by an order of a court of competent jurisdiction.

(13) A surrogate mother shall not act as an oocyte donor for the couple or individual, as the case may be, seeking surrogacy.

(14) No assisted reproductive technology clinic shall provide information on or about surrogate mothers or potential surrogate mothers to any person.

(15) Any assisted reproductive technology clinic acting in contravention of sub-section 14 of this section shall be deemed to have committed an offence under this Act.

(16) In the event that the woman intending to be a surrogate is married, the consent of her spouse shall be required before she may act as such surrogate.

(17) A surrogate mother shall be given a certificate by the person or persons who have availed of her services, stating unambiguously that she has acted as a surrogate for them.

(18) A relative, a known person, as well as a person unknown to the couple may act as a surrogate mother for the couple/individual. In the case of a relative acting as a surrogate, the relative should belong to the same generation as the women desiring the surrogate.

(19) A foreigner or foreign couple not resident in India, or a non-resident Indian individual or couple, seeking surrogacy in India shall appoint a local guardian who will be legally responsible for taking care of the surrogate during and after the pregnancy as per clause 34.2, till the child/children are delivered to the foreigner or foreign couple or the local guardian. Further, the party seeking the surrogacy must ensure and establish to the assisted reproductive technology clinic through proper documentation (a letter from either the embassy of the Country in India or from the foreign ministry of the Country, clearly and unambiguously stating that (a) the country permits surrogacy, and (b) the child born through surrogacy in India, will be permitted entry in the Country as a biological child of the commissioning couple/individual) that the party would be able to take the child/children born through surrogacy, including where the embryo was a consequence of donation of an oocyte or sperm, outside of India to the country of the party's origin or residence as the case may be. If the foreign party seeking surrogacy fails to take delivery of the child born to the surrogate mother commissioned by the foreign party, the local guardian shall be legally obliged to take delivery of the child and be free to hand the child over to an adoption agency, if the commissioned party or their legal representative fails to claim the child within one month of the birth of the child. During the transition period, the local guardian shall be responsible for the well-being of the child. In case of adoption or the legal guardian having to bring up the child, the child will be given Indian citizenship.

(20) A couple or an individual shall not have the service of more than one surrogate at any given time.

(21) A couple shall not have simultaneous transfer of embryos in the woman and in a surrogate.

(22) Only Indian citizens shall have a right to act as a surrogate, and no ART bank/ART clinics shall receive or send an Indian for surrogacy abroad.

(23) Any woman agreeing to act as a surrogate shall be duty-bound not to engage in any act that would harm the foetus during pregnancy and the child after birth, until the time the child is handed over to the designated person(s).

(24) The commissioning parent(s) shall ensure that the surrogate mother and the child she deliver are appropriately insured until the time the child is handed over to the commissioning parent(s) or any other person as per the agreement and till the surrogate mother is free of all health complications arising out of surrogacy.

35. Determination of status of the child—(1) A child born to a married couple through the use of assisted reproductive technology shall be presumed to be the legitimate child of the couple, having been born in wedlock and with the consent of both spouses, and shall have identical legal rights as a legitimate child born through sexual intercourse.

(2) A child born to an unmarried couple through the use of assisted reproductive technology, with the consent of both the parties, shall be the legitimate child of both parties.

(3) In the case of a single woman the child will be the legitimate child of the woman, and in the case of a single man the child will be the legitimate child of the man.

(4) In case a married or unmarried couple separates or gets divorced, as the case may be, after both parties consented to the assisted reproductive technology treatment but before the child is born, the child shall be the legitimate child of the couple.

(5) A child born to a woman artificially inseminated with the stored sperm of her dead husband shall be considered as the legitimate child of the couple.

(6) If a donated ovum contains ooplasm from another donor ovum, both the donors shall be medically tested for such diseases, sexually transmitted or otherwise, as may be prescribed, and all other communicable diseases which may endanger the health of the child, and the donor of both the ooplasm and the ovum shall relinquish all parental rights in relation to such child.

(7) The birth certificate of a child born through the use of assisted reproductive technology shall contain the name or names of the parent or parents, as the case may be, who sought such use.

(8) If a foreigner or a foreign couple seeks sperm or egg donation, or surrogacy, in India, and a child is born as a

consequence, the child, even though born in India, shall not be an Indian citizen.

36. Right of the child to information about donors or surrogates—(1) A child may, upon reaching the age of 18, ask for any information, excluding personal identification, relating to the donor or surrogate mother.

(2) The legal guardian of a minor child may apply for any information, excluding personal identification, about his/her genetic parent or parents or surrogate mother when required, and to the extent necessary, for the welfare of the child.

(3) Personal identification of the genetic parent or parents or surrogate mother may be released only in cases of life threatening medical conditions which require physical testing or samples of the genetic parent or parents or surrogate mother.

Provided that such personal identification will not be released without the prior informed consent of the genetic parent or parents or surrogate mother.

OFFENCES AND PENALTIES

37. Prohibition of advertisement relating to pre-natal determination of sex and punishment for contravention—(1) No assisted reproductive technology clinic shall issue or cause to be issued any advertisement in any manner regarding facilities of prenatal determination of sex.

(2) No assisted reproductive technology clinic, or agent thereof, shall publish or distribute or cause to be published or distributed any advertisement in any manner regarding facilities of pre-natal determination of sex.

(3) Any person who contravenes the provisions of this section shall be punishable with imprisonment for a term which may extend to five years and with fine which may be specified.

Explanation—For the purposes of this section, "advertisement" includes any notice, circular, label wrapper or other document and also includes any visible representation made by means of any light, sound, smoke or gas.

38. Offences and penalties—(1) Any medical geneticist, gynaecologist, registered medical practitioner or any person who owns or operates any assisted reproductive technology clinic, or is employed in such a facility and renders his professional or technical services to such facility, whether on an honorary basis or otherwise, and who contravenes any of the provisions of this Act or rules made there under, shall be punishable with imprisonment for a term which may extend to three years and/or with fine which may be specified, and on any subsequent conviction, with imprisonment which may extend to five years and/or fine which may be specified.

(2) The name of the registered medical practitioner who has been convicted by the court under sub-section 1 of this section shall be reported by the State Board to the respective State Medical Council for taking necessary action including the removal of his name from the register or the Council for a period of two years for the first offence and permanently for any subsequent offence.

(3) Any person who seeks the aid of assisted reproductive technology or of a medical geneticist, gynaecologist or registered medical practitioner for conducting pre-natal diagnostic techniques on any pregnant woman for purposes other than those specified in clause (2) of section 4 of the Pre-natal Diagnostic Techniques (Regulation and Prevention of Misuse) Act, 1994 [Act 57 of 1994], shall be punishable with imprisonment for a term which may extend to three years and with fine which may be specified, and on any subsequent conviction with imprisonment which may extend to five years and with fine which may be specified.

(4) The transfer of a human embryo into a male person or into an animal that is not of the human species shall be an offence under this Act and shall be punishable with imprisonment for a term which may extend to three years and with fine which may be specified.

(5) The sale of any embryo for research is absolutely prohibited and shall be an offence under this Act punishable by imprisonment for a term which may extend to three years and with fine which may be specified.

(6) Use of individual brokers or paid intermediaries to obtain gamete donors or surrogates shall be an offence under this Act, punishable by imprisonment for a term which may extend to three years and fine which may be specified.

39. Presumption in the case of conduct of pre-natal diagnostic techniques—Notwithstanding anything in the Indian Evidence Act, 1872, the court shall presume, unless the contrary is proved, that the pregnant woman has been compelled by her husband or the relative to undergo pre-natal diagnostic technique.

40. Penalty for contravention of the provisions of the Act or rules for which no specific punishment is provided—Whoever contravenes any of the provisions of this Act or any rules made thereunder, for which no penalty has been elsewhere provided in this Act, shall be punishable with imprisonment for a term which may extend to three years, or with fine which may be specified, or with both, and in the case of continuing contravention, with an additional fine which may be specified.

41. Offences by companies—(1) Where any offence, punishable under this Act has been proven to be committed by a company, every person who at the time the offence was committed was in charge of, and was responsible to, the company for the conduct of the business of the company, as well as the company, shall be deemed to be guilty of the offence and shall be liable to be proceeded against and punished accordingly:

Provided that nothing contained in this sub-section shall render any such person liable to any punishment, if he proves that the offence was committed without his knowledge or that he had exercised all due diligence to prevent the commission of such offence.

(2) Notwithstanding anything contained in sub-section (1) of this section, where any offence punishable under this Act has been committed by a company and it is proved that the offence has been committed with the consent or connivance of, or is attributable to any neglect on the part of, any director, manager, secretary or other officer of the company, such director, manager, secretary or other officer shall also be deemed to be guilty of that offence and shall be liable to be proceeded against and punished accordingly.

Explanation—For the purposes of this section,

(a) "company" means any body corporate and includes a firm or other association of individuals, and
(b) "director", in relation to a firm, means a partner in the firm.

42. Offence to be cognizable—Every offence under this Act shall be cognizable.

MISCELLANEOUS

43. Maintenance of records—(1) All records, charts, forms, reports, consent letters and all other documents required to be maintained under this Act and the rules shall be preserved for a period of ten years or for such period as may be prescribed :

Provided that, if any criminal or other proceedings are instituted against any facility using assisted reproductive technology, the records and all other documents of such facility shall be preserved till the final disposal of such proceedings.

(2) All such records shall, at all reasonable times, be made available for inspection to the concerned State Board or to any other person authorised by the concerned State Board in this behalf.

44. Power to search and seize records, etc.—(1) If the State Board has reason to believe that an offence under this Act has been or is being committed at any facility using assisted reproductive technology, such Board or any officer authorised thereof in this behalf may, subject to such rules as may be prescribed, enter and search at all reasonable times with such assistance, if any, as such authority or officer considers necessary, such facility, and examine any record, register, document, book, pamphlet, advertisement or any other material object found therein and seize the same if the State Board or officer has reason to believe that it may furnish evidence of the commission of an offence punishable under this Act.

(2) The provisions of the Code of Criminal Procedure, 1973, relating to searches and seizures shall, so far as may be, apply to every search or seizure made under this Act.

45. Power to remove difficulties—(1) If any difficulty arises in giving effect to the provisions of this Act, the Central Government may, by order published in the Official Gazette, make such provisions not inconsistent with the provisions of this Act as may appear to be necessary for removing the difficulty:

Provided that no order shall be made under this section after the expiry of three years from the commencement of this Act.

(2) Every order made under this section shall be laid, as soon as may be after it is made, before each House of Parliament.

46. Protection of action taken in good faith—No suit, prosecution or other legal proceeding shall lie against the Central or the State Government or the National Board or State Boards or Registration Authority or any officer authorised by any of them, for anything which is in good faith done or intended to be done in pursuance of the provisions of this Act.

47. Power to make regulations—The National Advisory Board may, with the previous sanction of the Central Government, by notification in the Official Gazette, make regulations not inconsistent with the provisions of this Act and the rules made thereunder, to provide for—

(a) the time and place of the meetings of the Board and the procedure to be followed for the transaction of business at such meetings, and the number of members which shall form the quorum;
(b) the conditions for the transfer of embryos and gametes to research institutions;
(c) regulation of Pre-implantation Genetic Diagnosis;
(d) research on embryos;
(e) the efficient conduct of the affairs of the Board; and
(f) any other purpose that may be prescribed.

48. Power of the Central Government to make rules—(1) The Central Government may make rules for carrying out the provisions of this Act.

(2) In particular, and without prejudice to the generality of the foregoing power, such rules may provide for—

(a) categories of assisted reproductive technology clinics;
(b) the minimum requirements regarding staff in assisted reproductive technology clinics;
(c) the minimum physical infrastructure requirements for an assisted reproductive technology clinic;
(d) the various assisted reproductive technology procedures to be adopted by an assisted reproductive technology clinic;
(e) the criteria for selecting patients for an assisted reproductive technology procedure;
(f) the criteria for selecting an assisted reproductive technology procedure for a patient;
(g) information and advise to, and counselling of patient;
(h) the eligibility of couples and individuals to use assisted reproductive technology;
(i) the eligibility of donors;
(j) the eligibility of surrogate mothers;
(k) the number of embryos that can be implanted in a woman;
(l) the number of times that a patient can be given a procedure;
(m) the maintenance of records;
(n) procedure to search and seize;
(o) the criteria to be fulfilled for a license; and
(p) the effective implementation of the Act.

(3) Every rule made by the Central Government under sub-section (1) of this section shall be laid, as soon as may be after it is made, before each House of Parliament, while it is in session, for a total period of thirty days which may be comprised in one session or in two or more successive sessions, and if, before the expiry of the session immediately following the session or the successive sessions aforesaid, both Houses agree in making any modification in the rule or regulation or both Houses agree that the rule or regulation should not be made, the rule or regulation shall thereafter have effect only in such modified form or be of no effect, as the case may be; so, however, that any such modification or annulment shall be without prejudice to the validity of anything previously done under that rule or regulation.

49. Power of State Government to make rules—Subject to the provisions of this Act and the rules and regulations made thereunder, the State Government may make rules to carry out the purposes of this Act.

50. Act to have effect in addition to other Acts—The provisions of this Act shall be in addition to, and not in derogation of, the provisions of any other law, for the time being in force, except for the following:

(a) Provision made in Section 13(6) of this Act; and
(b) Inapplicability of the provision of the Right to Information Act in regard to provision made in Section 20(9) and 26(13) of this Act.

List of Cases

Doornbos *v.* Doornbos, No. 54 S., 1495 (Superior Court Cook Co. December 13, 1954). 62, 77
Delhi Development Horticulture Employee's Union *v.* Delhi Administration, Delhi (1992) 4 SCC 99 at 110. 243
Eisenstadt *v.* Baiord, 405 U.S. 438 (1972). 231
Francis Coralie *v.* Union Territory of Delhi, AIR 1978 SC 597.
Griswold *v.* Connecticut, 381 U.S. 479 (1965). 143, 235
Gitabai *v.* Fattoo, A.I.R. 1966 M.P. 130.
Gursky *v.* Gursky, 39 Misc., 2d 1983, 242 N.S.S., 2d 406 (sup. Ct. 1963). 62, 79, 176
Haryana *v.* Smt. Santara, AIR 2000 SC 1888.
Inre Anthony, A.I.R. 1960 Mad. 308.
Inre Baby M., 217 N.J. Super 313, 525 A, 2d 1128 (N.J. 1987). 146
Jhordan *v.* Mary, 224 Cal. Reporter 530 (1986). 81, 107
Javed and others *v.* State of Haryana, AIR 2003 SC 3057. 238
Johnson *v.* Calvert 5 Cal,1993. 4th 84,851 P.2d 776.
Kharak Singh *v.* State of U.P, A.I.R 1963 S.C 1295. 242
Kirloskar Brothers Ltd. *v.* Employees' State Insurance Corporation (1996) 2 SCC 682.
Lamaritata *v.* Lucas (823 So. 2d 316 (2002). 175
Litcher *v.* Hartigan, 735 F. Supp. 1361 (No. III 1990).
Maclennan *v.* Maclennan, Klayman E.I., (1958) Sess. Cas. 105. 75
Maneka Gandhi *v.* Union of India, A.I.R 1978 S.C 597. 242
Mr. 'X' *v.* Hospital 'Z', AIR 1995 SC 495.
Murari Mohan Koley *v.* The State and Anr. (2004)3 CAL LT 609(HC).
Ms X *v.* Mr. Z and Anr. 96 (2002) DLT 354.
Margaret, S. *v.* Treen, 597 F. Supp. 636 (E.D. La. 1984).
Maher *v.* Roe, 432 U.S. 438 (1977).
Natason *v.* Kline, 186 Kan. 393, 350 P.2d 1093 (1960).
Orford *v.* Orford. 58 D.L.R. 251 (1921); 49 Ontario L.R. 15. 54, 74, 93
Olga Tellis *v.* Bombay Municipal Corporation, AIR 1986 SC 180; (1985) 3 SCC 545. 243
Planned Parenthood *v.* Casey, 505 US 833 (1992) at 852, 857, 896. 195

Smedes *v.* Wayne State University, (E.D. Mich. Field, July 16, 1980).

Smith *v.* Jones No. 8553201402 (Michigan Cir. Ct) 1986.

Thiebaud *v.* Kaiser Foundation Health Plan, (Cal Super Ct., May 1985).

Unni Krishnan *v.* State of Andhra Pradesh, AIR 1993 SC 2178, 2230. Wayne Co., March 14, 1986). 237

W.J. Phillips *v.* Emperor, A.I.R. 1939 Oudh 506. 54

Witcraft *v.* Sundstrand Health and Disability Group Benefit Plan, 420 N.W. 2d 785 (Iowa, 1988).

Bibliography

Agarwal, H.O., Human Rights (2005), Central Law Publications.

Awasthi, S.K and Kataria R.P., Law Relating to Protection of Human Rights (2000), Orient Publishing Company, Allahabad.

Ardatti Rita, Kleen Renate Duells and Minden Shelly, Test-Tube Women. What Future for Motherhood (1989), Pawora Press.

Alcorn, P., Social Issues in Technology—A Format for Investigation (1986), Prentice-Hall, Englewood-Ciffs, N.J.

Basu, D.D., Human Rights in Constitutional Law (2003), 2nd Edition, Wadhwa and Company Nagpur.

Basu, Dr. (Justice), D.D., Human Rights in Constitutional Laws (1994), Prentice Hall of India Pvt. Ltd., New Delhi.

Bach, Julie S., "Should Limits Be Placed on Reproductive Technology?" In Biomedical Ethics: Opposing Viewpoints. (1998), San Francisco, CA: Green Haven Press.

Ben Emerson and Andrew Ashworth, Human Rights and Criminal Justice (2001), Sweet and Maxwell Publications.

Bakshi, P.M. and Singh Jaswant, The Constitution of India (1991), Vol. I, *Madras Law Journal Office*, Madras.

Baruch Adamo and Seager Johi, Embryos, Ethics and Women's Rights (1988), Haworth Press.

Baxi Upendra, Future of Human Rights (2002), Oxford University Press, New Delhi.

Chandra, U., Human Rights (1999), Allahabad Law Agency Publications.

Cook Rebecca J. and Dickens Bernard H., Considerations for formulating reproductive health laws (1998), Discussion Paper of W.H.O., Geneva.

Corillon, C., Science and Human Rights (1988), National Academy Press, Washington.

Donnelly Jack, Universal Human Rights in Theory and Practice (2003), 2nd Ed., Cornell University Press.

Dooley Dolores, Ethics of New Reproductive Technologies (2003), Berghahn Books.

Ellul, J., The Technological Society (1965), Alfred A. Knopf, New York.

Forsythe David P., Human Rights in International Relations (2000), Cambridge University Press.

Francis and Grootings P., New Technologies and Work-Capitalist and Socialist Perspectives (1989), Rutledge, London/New York.

Gaur, K.D., The Indian Penal Code (2004), Universal Law Publishing Co., Delhi.

Goonesekere Savitri, Children Law and Justice (2000), Allahabad Law Agency.

Greyear Regina and Morgan Deeny, The Hidden Gender of Law (1990), The Federation Press.

Haarscher, G., Philosophie des droits de l'homme (1987), Editions de l'Université de Bruxelles.

Hawrylyszyn, B., Road Maps to the Future Human Rights of Disadvantaged Groups (1980), Oxford Printing Press.

Hudson Carl, Human Rights : A Compilation of International Instruments (1988), New York Press.

Holmes, Helen B., Issue in Reproductive Technology (1994), NYU Press.

Hull Richard T., Ethical Issues in the New Reproductive Technologies (2005), Wadsworth.

Havilland William A., Anthropology: The Human Challenge (2005), 10th edition, Thomson Wadsworth Printing Press London.

Jaswal, Paramjit S. and Jaswal, Nishtha, Human Rights and the Law (1996), APH Publishing Corporation, Delhi.

Johnston and Sasson A., New Technologies and Development: Science and Technology as Factors of Change: Impact of Recent and Foreseeable Scientific and Technological Progress on the Evolution of Societies, Especially in the Developing Countries (1986), UNESCO, Paris.

Jones Richard Evan and Lopez Kristin H., Human Reproductive Biology (2006), Elsevier.

Jain, M.P., Indian Constitutional Law (2005), 5th Edition Wadhwa and Company, Nagpur.

Kamat, Vikas, India's Arranged Marriages (2003), Penguin Printing Press, New Delhi.

Khosla, Justice G.D., Our Judicial System (1992), The University Book Agency, Allahabad.

Klitou Demetrius, The Friends and Foes of Human Rights (1989), Manchester University Press.

Kochler Hans, The Principles of International Law and Human Rights (2006), A. Mukherji and Co., Calcutta.

Lasker, Judith N. and Susan Borg, In Search of Parenthood (1994), Philadelphia, PA, Temple University Press.

Latour, B., Science in Action (1987), Open University Press.

Littman David, Universal Human Rights (1999), St. Martin's Press, Oxford Printing Press, 1980.

Murphy, J.W. and Pardeck, T., Introduction to J.W. Murphy End D. Pardeck, eds., Technology and Human Productivity—Challenges for the Future (1986), Quorum Books, New York.

Medical Ethics and Human Rights: The Guiding Principles (1993), Commonwealth Medical Assoc. London.

M.P. Tandon, Public International Law (1996), 13th Edition, Allahabad Law Agency, Allahabad.

Mehta, P.L. and Verma, Neena, Human Rights under the Indian Constitution (1999), Deep and Deep Publications, New Delhi.

Nirmal, C.J., Human Rights in India (2000), Oxford University Press, USA.

Ogburn, W.F., On Culture and Social Change (1964), University of Chicago Press, Chicago/London.

Overall, Christine, Ethics and Human Reproduction: A Feminist Analysis (1987), Allen and Unwin Hyman Ltd., London.

Petchesky Rosalind Pollack, Abortion and Woman's Choice. The State, Sexually and Reproductive Freedom (1985), North-eastern University Press.

Robertson John Ancona, Children of choice: Freedom and the New Reproductive Technologies (1994), Princeton University Press.

Seervai, H.M., Constitutional Law of India—A Critical Commentary (1975), Vol. I, 2nd Edition, N.M. Tripathi Pvt. Ltd Company, Bombay.

Sen, Amartya, Human Rights and Asian Values (2004), Vikash Publications Pvt. Ltd.

Saxena, K.P., Human Rights : Perspective and Challenges (In 1900's and beyond), World Congress on Human Rights, 1995 Re-Print, Lancers Books, New Delhi.

Siemienski, F., Constitutional Law (1976), Warsaw.

Sadik, N., Right to Choose, Reproductive Rights and Reproductive Health (1997), U.N. Population Fund, New York.

The Pre-Conception and Pre Natal Diagnostic Techniques (Prohibition of Sex Selection) Act, 1994, (2005), Universal Law Publishing Co., Delhi.

The Indian Penal Code, 1860 (2005), Universal Law Publishing Co., Delhi.

T.K. Tope, Constitutional Law of India, 2nd Edition, Eastern Book Company, Lucknow.

Universal Declaration of Human Rights, The International Bill of Human Rights (United Nations, New York, 197X).

Wolicki, K. and Marx, Karl, The Emancipation of Humanity and Individual Freedom (1984), New York Review of Books No. 4.

Weeramantry, C.G., The Slumbering Sentinels; Law and Human Rights in the Wake of Technology (1983), Penguin Books Australia.

Weeramantry, C.G., Human Rights and Scientific and Technological Development (1990), United Nations University, Tokyo.

Acts

Artificial Conception Act, 1985.
Assisted Human Reproduction Act, R.S.C 2004.
Genetic Privacy Act, 1995.
Human Reproductive Cloning Act, 2001.
Hindu Marriage Act 1955.
Infertility (Medical Procedures) Act, 1984 (IMP Act).
In-Vitro Fertilization (Restriction) Act, 1987.
Parsi Marriage and Divorce Act, 1936.
Surrogate Parenthood Act 1988.
Substitute Parents Agreement Act, 1993.
Special Marriage Act, 1955.
The Indian Evidence Act, 1872.
The Human Tissue Act, 1961.
The Family Relationship Act, 1975.
The Adoption Act 1984.
The Status of Children (Amendment) Act, 1984.
The Federal Embryo Protection Act, 1990.
The Human Fertilization and Embryology Act, 1990 (HFE Act).
The Surrogacy Contract Act, 1993.
The Substitute Parent Agreements Act, 1994.
The Infertility Treatment Act, 1995.
The Human Cloning Prohibition Act, 2003.

Documents and Articles

All India Reporters, New Delhi.
International Covenant on Civil and Political Rights, 1966.
International Covenant on Economic, Social and Cultural Rights, 1966.
International and Comparative Law Quarterly.
Protection of Human Rights Act, 1993.
The Employment News, New Delhi.

The Hindu, Newspaper.
Universal Declaration of Human Rights, 1948.
World Health Organization Manual.

Journals

B. Joerges, "Technology in Everyday Life: Conceptual Queries," *Journal for the Theory of Social Behaviour*, Vol. 18, No. 2 (1988).

Baxi, "Gender and Reproductive Rights in India: Problems and Prospects for the New Millennium," A Report by UNFPA, New Delhi (2001).

Chatterje, "A Century of Social Reform for Women's Status", *Indian Journal of Social Work*, Vol. XLI, No. 3, October (1980).

Human Right Annual Journal.

Indian Journal of Legal Studies, JNVU, Jodhpur.

Journal of the Indian Law Institute, New Delhi.

Joshi, K.C., "Universalisation of Human Rights of Women", AIR 2001 Journal 59.

Kumari, "Fertility Revolution and Changing Concept of Family and Identify", *Delhi Law Review*, Col. XXV (2003).

Reddy, G.B., "Role of Judiciary in protection of Human Rights of Women", AIR 1999 Journal 148.

Internet Sources/Web Sites Visited

http://www.yale.edu/ynhti/curriculum/units

http://www.answers.com/topic/surrogate mother

http://www.bma.org.uk/ap.nsf/content/considering surrogacy

http://www.answers.com/topic/in-vitro-fertilization

http://www.savegirlchild.org.

http://www.savethechildren.net.

http://www.indianchild.com.

Murthy, Sex Selection: Getting Down to Business (2005), available at http://infochangeindia.org

Newman, July 24, 2008 Life Site News.Com

On the Internet

www bellonline.com/articles/art1203.asp
www.imapctpress.com/articles/febmarch 98/clone.htm
www.lawindia.com
www.unicef.org
www.findlaw.com
www.unesco.org
www.cehat.org
www.surrogacy.com
www.epw.org.in
www.un.org/womenwatch
www.girlsrights.org

Index